Building **ATLANTA'S FUTURE**

Building
ATLANTA'S
FUTURE

BY *John E. Ivey, Jr.*
Nicholas J. Demerath
Woodrow W. Breland

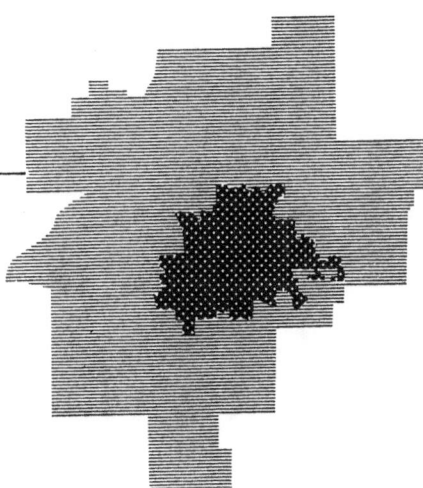

CHAPEL HILL

THE UNIVERSITY OF NORTH CAROLINA PRESS

COPYRIGHT, 1948, BY

THE UNIVERSITY OF NORTH CAROLINA PRESS

A SPECIAL PROJECT OF
DIVISION OF RESEARCH INTERPRETATION
INSTITUTE FOR RESEARCH IN SOCIAL SCIENCE
UNIVERSITY OF NORTH CAROLINA

*Maps, charts, and sketches
by Don White and Carolyn McCarthy Bolt*

PRINTED I THE UNITED STATES OF AMERICA

A. B.

Preface

THE Atlanta Board of Education, through the medium of *Building Atlanta's Future*, desires to make possible a constructive study of Atlanta as a growing city. The setting and approach used in the book are designed to associate intimately the youth of Atlanta with its historical, regional, economic, and sociological aspects. The Board realizes that it is the youth of today who will be responsible for the continuing growth of Atlanta. It hopes that this study will render obvious the mistakes of the past so that they will not be repeated and will not hinder progress.

Building Atlanta's Future should be vitalized by its teachers. Its information dealing with the past is to be interpreted in terms of current affairs and probable action. It should be activated by the students in terms of a challenge to know Atlanta's people, what they do, how they live together, and how they work together—how people cooperate to build a city. Hence the material in the book must constantly be in a state of adaptation so that its principles and applications will be utilized in Atlanta and potentially spread to other cities and countries—and to the world.

Ira Jarrell, Superintendent
Atlanta Public Schools

ADVISORY COMMITTEE

DR. ALLEN ALBERT	MR. OTIS M. JACKSON
MR. JARVIS BARNES	MISS IRA JARRELL
MR. GEORGE C. BIGGERS	MR. FRANK NEELY
MRS. WARREN H. BRADLEY	MR. C. F. PALMER
MRS. JOHN M. BREDFELD	MR. G. Y. SMITH
MR. ROY W. DAVIS	MISS MARGARET SOLOMON
MR. JAMES C. FAIN	MR. JAMES H. THERRELL

THE ATLANTA BOARD OF EDUCATION

MR. ED S. COOK, PRESIDENT

MR. DEVEREAUX F. McCLATCHEY, VICE PRESIDENT

MR. J. AUSTIN DILBECK   DR. CHARLES C. RIFE

MR. J. H. LANDERS   MR. D. M. THERRELL

Contents

Part One: Raw Materials of Cities

1. ATLANTA AND YOU   3

The Growth of Atlanta, Growth Brings New Problems, Tomorrow's Problems Will Be Yours, A City Is a Place to Live, Measuring a City, Planning a City for People, Atlanta and Your Future, Looking Toward a Better Atlanta

2. WHAT IS ATLANTA?   20

Where Is Atlanta? Metropolitan Atlanta, City or Country Environment, How Do City and Country Life Differ? City and Country Depend on Each Other

3. ATLANTA'S REGIONAL SETTING   35

Atlanta Is a Transportation Center, Atlanta As a Regional Center, Geography and the Region, Culture and the Region, Culture and History, Regions of the United States, The Region and Atlanta's Future, Your Part in Our Region's Future

4. ATLANTA'S RESOURCE BASE   51

Three Kinds of Resources, Using Resources in Living, What Are Atlanta's Resources? What Is Conservation? Resources in Everyday Living, Atlanta and Our Region's Resources

Part Two: Cities Serve People

5. ATLANTA'S PEOPLE   71

People Use Resources, Kinds of People, How Population Changes, Migration, What Is a Census? Men and Women Workers, Population Pyramids, A City for All the People

Contents

6. THE ECONOMY OF ATLANTA   90
Work and Money, Goods and Services, What Atlanta Workers Do, The Industries of Atlanta, What Atlanta Workers Produce, Income and Purchasing Power, Economy and Living, Democracy and Our Economy

7. OUR COMMON WEALTH   111
Fitting the Parts into a City, The Sections of Atlanta, Using the Land in a City, Controlling the Use of Land, Political Boundaries Block Sound Planning, Land Use Outside Atlanta, Orderly Development to Meet Our Needs

Part Three: Meeting Group Needs

8. COMMUNITIES IN ATLANTA   137
The Problem: A Paradox, The Suburban Push, Atlanta's Neighborhood Communities, The Garden City, The Neighborhood Approach

9. THE HOUSES WE LIVE IN   156
Houses, People, and Cities, Slums and Blight, Why We Have Slums and Blight, Housing in Atlanta, The Federal Housing Program, Why Is Public Housing Necessary? Private Enterprise and Public Housing

10. OUR STREETS AND SERVICES   180
Inventions and the Growth of Cities, Services Within Modern Cities, Transportation and the Map of Atlanta, Automobiles and Residential Sections, Street Plans and Business, Atlanta Traffic Problems, Water, Sewers, and Sanitation, Gas and Electricity, Communication Services

11. USING SOCIAL RESOURCES   206
Social Services, Health Services in Atlanta, Good Health Programs, Crime and Delinquency, Recreation, Education, Community Schools, Other Agencies of Education, Our Social Welfare

Part Four: Guiding City Growth

12. HOW PEOPLE BUILD CITIES   235
The Organization of a City, Atlanta's Municipal Government, Public Needs: Present and Future, Atlanta's City Planning Commission, How

Good Is Our Government? Government and Planning for Orderly Development, Planning for Our Metropolitan Community, Planning and Citizenship, Private Agencies

13. THE PROBLEMS ATLANTA MUST SOLVE 260

What Are Our Problems? Planning to Solve Our Problems, What Is Good Planning? Making a Master Plan, Planning the Outskirts, Replanning the Central City, The Citizen's Place in Planning

14. HOW TO MEET OUR CHALLENGE 279

Our Challenge as Individuals, Our Challenge as Groups, Planning a Community Program, Putting Ideas into Action, The Skills of Group Work, Our Future Together, Your Personal Challenge

Introduction

THIS BOOK has grown out of Atlanta. It is an attempt to picture the spirit and shape of your city. It attempts to help you find a new way of studying Atlanta and many ways of making Atlanta a better place to live.

A book can give you and your teachers only a starting place for digging into the real Atlanta. It can come to life only as you see and live in the situations it describes. In studying this book, Atlanta is your classroom. Newspapers, current reports of agencies, radio programs, today's happenings, community leaders, the people you know—all are sources of important information. Your own reports of what you learn can give valuable sources of material for you and your classmates. A book lives only through ideas.

It is through the vision of the Atlanta Board of Education that you have this book. They know that in your hands and minds rests the future of Atlanta. They wanted to help you become aware of the importance of your trust. They wanted you to have a book that would suggest ways by which you might better shape Atlanta's future.

The idea for such a book first came out of a talk between Mr. C. F. Palmer, a practical businessman who had for a long time devoted himself to improving Atlanta, and Mr. Devereaux McClatchey, an Atlanta lawyer and member of the Board of Education. Mr. Palmer explained what had been done in Chicago with the *Wacker Manual,* a textbook something like this written for students in Chicago schools nearly thirty years ago. He pointed out how it had helped those future citizens understand the problems they faced and how they had taken hold when the responsibility became theirs. Mr. Palmer urged a similar book for Atlanta. Miss Ira Jarrell, Superintendent of Schools, quickly joined in and the entire Board of Education became enthusiastic.

Miss Jarrell invited the authors to meet with Mr. Palmer, Mr. McClatchey, and Mr. Ed S. Cook, President of the Board of Education, to discuss how this book might be written. We also had a deep interest in writing books that can help young people learn about city resources and their development.

After several conferences with members of the Board of Education, the book was begun. An Advisory Committee was appointed to assist the authors. Their names are listed in the front of the book. They have given us

Introduction

much help and encouragement. As Chairman of this committee, Mr. C. F. Palmer has read the entire manuscript and made many inspiring contributions.

So many people have helped with this book that we cannot list them all here. Teachers and principals, especially those serving on curriculum committees, have met with us many times. Mr. James Fain, Miss Jessie Lowe, and members of the Social Studies Committee have given much time and effort and valuable suggestions. We have talked with many of Atlanta's civic leaders and with hundreds of pupils like yourself. From these young Atlantans who studied a preliminary version have come some of the most helpful suggestions for revising the book.

Mr. Jarvis Barnes has supplied us with a steady stream of facts and figures and other materials from the Board of Education offices in City Hall. From these offices also, Mr. Walter S. Bell, Director of the Department of Audio-Visual Education, has personally made, copied, and gathered from many sources most of the photographs in the book. The extent of their effort is not fully portrayed in the acknowledgments given at the back of the book. Mrs. Kie S. Fullerton, Miss Frances H. Osborne, and other members of the Division of Research Interpretation staff have assisted with the research and typing details.

Most of these people have volunteered their time and effort in the interest of you and of Atlanta. We are indeed grateful for their assistance. You can repay them in no better way than through learning and applying the information and skills herein made available to you.

J. E. I., Jr.
N. J. D.
W. W. B.

Part One

RAW MATERIALS OF CITIES

1. Atlanta and You

THIS is a book about your city, Atlanta. It is about places and people you know. It will call back events and people of Atlanta's past years and bring up visions of those yet to come. People have made Atlanta what it is and Atlanta has left a mark on many people. It will be a different city for your having lived in it. Because of it you have good times and you have troubles.

Has a trolley ever passed you by because it was already packed full—when you were in a big hurry to get somewhere? Have you ever wanted to roller-skate or play baseball, but there was no place near by which was suitable? Have you hunted for a spare-time job but there seemed to be none? These are important problems at the moment they happen. They make you angry or at least unhappy. The best thing to do is to look for a way around the problem.

Many of our problems are caused by the city.

Perhaps you can walk to where you are going, or play ball in the street, or do without the money you wanted to earn. But these are poor substitutes. Your problems are only partly solved. If you are late getting to your destination, or if you get hurt while playing in the street, the problems get worse.

Problems like these are part of life in a city. If you lived in a small town or in the open country you would have different problems. There are reasons for our problems just as there are reasons for cities. They don't just happen. In this book we shall examine some of these reasons and some ways by which we may solve many of our problems.

We are also going to study some of the things which make cities good places to live. Why do so many people live in cities? There are reasons for that too. Why do you live here? If there are no good reasons to stay in a city, people move away. This has happened in many places. All that is left are dreary "ghost towns"—empty buildings laced with cobwebs.

It is easy to see why old mining towns become ghost towns. If there is no more coal, or iron, or gold in the earth at such a place, the mines close. People can no longer make a living. They must move away to find work. This is not hard to understand. It is much more difficult to understand a large city than a small mining town. We must know

Atlanta and You

many things about city life to understand why some cities are better places to live than others.

You have already learned a great deal about Atlanta through everyday happenings. You will learn much more in the same way. But unless you make a special effort to study a city, there are many things you may never notice. Unless you know a great deal about several cities, you have nothing to compare with Atlanta. Cities are so large and complex they are hard to study as one unit.

While you study this book, you should also study Atlanta on the spot. You can learn much from talking to people. Ask them about their biggest problems and what they think are the solutions. Try to find out what they do for Atlanta and what Atlanta does for them. Look for the things which seem to be good or poor in terms of the city. Don't be afraid to ask questions of those who know nor to think for yourself.

We learn from asking questions and talking with others.

Building Atlanta's Future

It takes some study and some thinking to understand a city. You aren't in school long enough to go around and study everything in Atlanta in person. Neither can you learn everything from a book. Put them both together and you have a better system. This book and your teachers can help you to learn faster by bringing together some of the facts and ideas which other people have already figured out. You can profit from the work of many people over many years—and perhaps add something of your own making.

THE GROWTH OF ATLANTA

How did Atlanta become what it is today? In 1842 there were about six houses in a small clearing in the forest where Atlanta now stands. This point marked the end of the Western and Atlantic Railroad. The little village was called "Terminus" because the railroad "terminated" there. The "Old Sandtown" and "Peachtree" trails, which were then little more than footpaths, joined near by. Most of the people who lived in Terminus were railroad workers.

The Western and Atlantic Railroad was to connect the western country with the Atlantic Ocean. This part of the railroad connected the Chattahoochee River with the Tennessee River. It ended here because this was a good place to connect with other railroads to be built

Atlanta's first post office—Peachtree and Decatur streets, 1845.

to Athens, Madison, Milledgeville, Forsyth, and Columbus, all of which were old towns and cities even then. The rolling hills, ridges, and valleys around Terminus made it easy to build railroads in all directions.

In 1843 Terminus was renamed Marthasville and was chartered by the state government as a town. Marthasville had a five-man commission as a governing body. These commissioners asked the state to grant a new charter in 1845. About 300 people lived in Marthasville then. They wanted to change the name to Atlanta and to survey a street plan. A charter was granted and Marthasville became Atlanta. But some townspeople didn't want the new streets because they would mean more taxes. The streets stayed as they were.

Therefore, new houses and stores were built along the narrow crooked trails which were already there. These winding Indian trails, cowpaths, and wagon roads became the streets of Atlanta. Where the Old Sandtown trail joined the Peachtree Trail is now Five Points. The Indians who traveled these trails would be startled to see how much traffic follows these routes today.

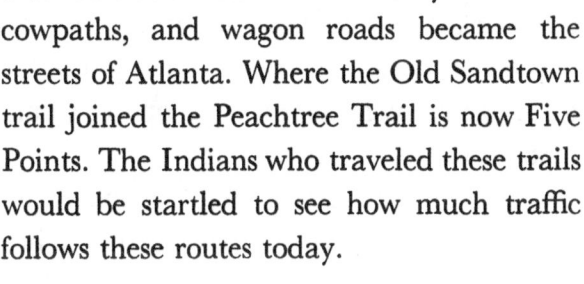

Railroads and highways followed the paths of Indian trails as Atlanta grew.

Building Atlanta's Future

New railroads came into Atlanta. The "Georgia Railroad" to Madison, connecting with the cities on the coast, and the "Macon and Western" to Macon attracted more people. In 1847 a new charter made it the "City of Atlanta" instead of the "Town of Atlanta." The population was then about 500. Three years later, in 1850, it was nearly 2,600—more than five times as large. The city spread out rapidly and with little regard for future needs.

GROWTH BRINGS NEW PROBLEMS

Of course some people realized that plans should be made for a beautiful, useful layout of streets and buildings. Others believed Atlanta would die after the railroad builders finished their job and left. People didn't want their houses torn down or moved in order to straighten streets. They didn't want to pay taxes for improvements which would bring them no profit at the time. Very few thought of the future. They didn't think about how much more their property would be worth later if they planned wisely for a growing city.

Atlanta was booming! The new railroads brought in meat and grain and supplies for the plantations. The planters raised cotton. They brought cotton to Atlanta to be shipped out by railroad to all parts of the world. More land was cleared so more cotton could be raised. More stores, hotels, factories, and workers came to Atlanta because of increased trade. Land prices and rents went up. Houses were jammed closer together to get more rent from land. The usual city problems grew faster than the city limits.

The people in Marthasville didn't have to worry about traffic jams. Narrow, crooked streets were not a great problem to people who walked or drove wagons. In 1850 early Atlantans were more concerned with mud and stumps in the streets than with traffic. However, as trade increased, wagon and buggy traffic needed more space and more speed. Streets were gradually straightened. New buildings were lined up and made more orderly. Pavement and sidewalks were added.

Wagons traveling north from the railroad on muddy Peachtree Street in early Atlanta.

Usually, however, they just built more and bigger buildings along the old streets.

In 1860 Atlanta had a population of almost 10,000 and was still growing rapidly. Goods flowed in and out in all directions over the railroads. During the Civil War, Atlanta was one of the principal centers of trade and transportation in the Confederacy. It was so important a city that when it was sacked by General Sherman in his "march to the sea," the Confederate armies were greatly weakened. Atlanta was rebuilt into an even greater city soon after this war. This shows that the reasons for needing a city here were very strong.

In rebuilding from the ashes of the Battle of Atlanta, the city fathers might have made a new and better street plan. In most cases whole new streets of houses had to be rebuilt. There were few old houses left to be saved. However, many buildings were put up along the same haphazard old streets which were already there.

Building Atlanta's Future

Some improvements were made during this rebuilding, to be sure. But everybody was too busy building his own house to think of how the whole city would look when it was finished. Think how much better the city would be now if a plan had been made for the whole city!

Of course you can never be sure what will happen in the future. People in 1870 had no idea there would be so many people and automobiles in Atlanta today. That is the reason we must often change our plans as newer needs come along. We must look into the future the best we can, at the same time making the best of solving today's problems.

TOMORROW'S PROBLEMS WILL BE YOURS

A great many people have helped Atlanta grow up in the years since Indians and traders followed their trails through the forest. Today your parents are the workers, the citizens, the officials—the men and women carrying on where an older generation left off. Tomorrow it will be up to you.

So if you are planning to be alive five, ten, fifteen years from today, you should be interested in this. What kind of city would you like to live in then? The kind of house, transportation, work and recreation, and the kind of neighborhood you wish are yours to decide.

Perhaps you didn't know that anybody cared what you, personally, would like for your future. In a way, you are right. Nobody *will* care—unless *you* do!

Cave men had their problems too.

Many problems in early Atlanta were not the same as they are today—but some of them were very similar.

Perhaps—like so many people—you hadn't even realized that there could possibly be anything different from what there is today. We can make Atlanta a better place to live. But it can't be done by waiting for others to do it. We must carry on the work of improvement. That will be harder than just letting well enough alone. Many people must cooperate in doing it. We always seem to accept new things slowly.

We humans are funny that way. Even back in the days of the cave men, most people accepted their caves as the "last word" in shelter.

Smoke from the fires did make the place filthy with soot, and it was hard to breathe sometimes. And the path that led to the cave lay directly under a landslide that killed one or two of the family every year. Maybe the cave was half an hour's march from the stream of drinking water and even farther from the woods where they killed the game and collected the berries needed for food. But—you know how it is—the folks had done things that way for so long—and—well—

It wasn't until a few of the wiser ones got together and started to think about better conditions (very much as you are doing right now) that their caves were replaced by simple huts which gave them somewhat better light, air, and warmth and could be built where they were convenient. Even those improvements took a lot of planning before anything was accomplished. Do you think we still look at our surroundings like this?

A CITY IS A PLACE TO LIVE

Now, while the cities, streets, and houses of *your* tomorrow will certainly be different, they may not be much *better* than you have now. In fact, the sad truth is that they probably will be worse—unless you want them better, unless you plan them better, unless you *order* them better!

In this case, *you* means a majority of the citizens in our democracy. And that is a great many people to persuade to do something.

For instance, after you get through reading this book, you may be the *only one* in your family who knows how much finer a community we can order for tomorrow. You will know something about how Atlanta got the way it is and how we can make it better. Perhaps you can explain it to other people, build a picture so that they, too, can understand. Perhaps not. It will be an interesting experiment, because you will always run into the lazy, pessimistic type that says, "It's no use. It will always be the same."

Until enough people want it better, it probably will be the same.

But it is your world, your future, your life. So if you *are* planning to be alive—five, ten, fifteen years from today—start thinking about the city you would like.

While the cave man's problems may have been simpler than ours, he also knew much less than we know. Unfortunately, we haven't always used this greater knowledge for our own good.

Many of us still think about our cities in cave man fashion. We often think that bigger cities are better cities. But more often they are not. More smokestacks and payrolls do not always make a better city.

If we look at cities as *places for living*, we find many problems other than jobs and money. Most of these problems are tied together in some way. Prosperous cities are usually healthy and happy cities. Or, to put it the other way, healthy, intelligent, and happy people make a prosperous city.

We will see that keeping people happy is a problem common to all cities in our part of the world. More and more government and business experts, more and more scholars are recognizing these problems. We will explore them in some detail as they are in Atlanta.

MEASURING A CITY

Atlanta is a good place to live, but it could be much better. Here in Atlanta you have schools, hospitals, transportation systems, working conditions, houses, stores, parks, and playgrounds that are better than those in some other places and in other times. On the other hand, they are not as good as they could be. Some are not even as good as those in other cities and towns.

Keep in mind that cities are not merely centers of manufacturing and commerce. Good stores and large factories help make good cities. But people must have decent homes, good churches, good schools, friendly neighbors, and places to relax if they are to be happy. A city wherein many people lack these things is not a good city.

How well does Atlanta meet these needs? Are there many people here who live in tumble-down shacks? Are there dirty, noisy neighborhoods where people do not like to live? Is there work enough all the year for everyone who wants to work? Do we have good schools for all the children? Are there doctors and hospitals for all the sick people? Are there convenient playgrounds and parks to which we can go to rest and play and get away from the hustle of crowds and streets once in a while? Do most people earn enough to be able to buy food, shelter, and clothing so that they can live comfortable lives?

To be sure, you can answer "no" to all these questions for some people in Atlanta and in most other cities. You can also answer "yes" to these questions for parts of Atlanta and other cities. We have to weigh the "no's" against the "yes's" to find how good a city is as a place to live.

PLANNING A CITY FOR PEOPLE

There were no automobiles in 1870. Atlanta did not then need four- or six-lane boulevards to handle the traffic during rush hours. The people of that day did not know how much traffic there would be today. Good city plans in this respect in 1870 are not good plans today. Many changes have had to be made because of automobile traffic. Building bridges over the railroads in the business section of Atlanta was very expensive. It would have been cheaper to have built railroad yards somewhere else at first. But the need was different at the time. It was better in some ways to leave the yards where they were handy.

However, some facts of city planning do not change much. Noise and dirt were as disagreeable in 1870 as in 1948. People faced many needs and problems similar to ours. As the city grew, "zones" or blocks were set aside for factories, for business districts, and for dwelling houses. As each of these zones expanded, it spilled over into the others and changes had to be made. Growing business sections crowded into residential zones. The people then moved out into suburban areas to live. This brought up a new problem of transportation. People could not walk that far to get to work. Streetcars or buses were needed.

In most cities you find blocks of crowded, cheaply-built, low-rental houses. Here live the people with low income who can't afford high rents. Usually these sections are in the less desirable parts of a city—along the railroad tracks or near factories and warehouses. As the houses get old and run-down, these sections become dirty and ugly. We call them "slums." Sanitation is usually poor and health conditions bad. Hoodlums and ne'er-do-wells often gather in such neighborhoods and crime rates are high. Such areas are an eye-sore and cause trouble for the whole city.

You may ask, "Why don't people move out of these surroundings?" Then comes the question, "Where would they go?" They don't make enough money to pay rent for good homes at the usual price. Often there is no place for them to go.

Atlanta and You

One solution is to build better homes for them. However, the people who own the land and build the houses can't afford to build expensive houses unless they can raise the rents. Good, permanent

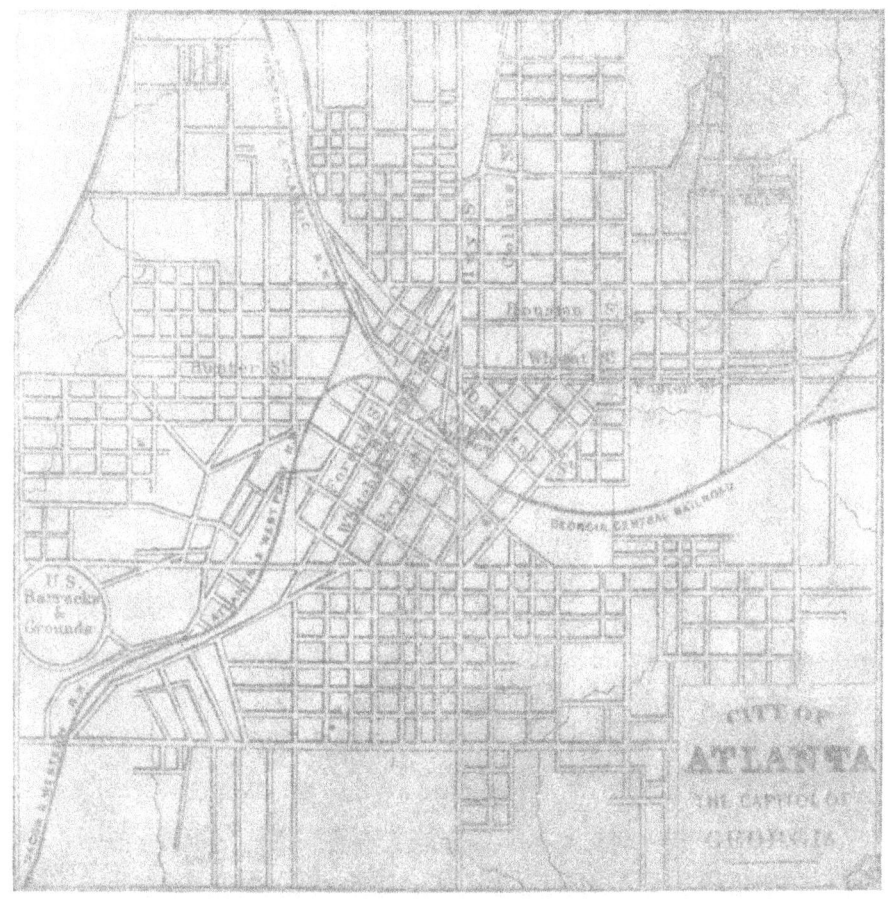

Today's street patterns show up in this old map of Atlanta as it was in 1873.

houses are expensive. Rents must be high enough to repay the cost of building before the houses are "worn out"; otherwise the builder loses money. He hasn't collected enough rent to build new houses and must go out of business.

You can see that slums are a great city problem. Atlanta, like most other cities, must face it. We can solve the problem by building good houses cheaper. Or we might raise the income of workers so that they

Factories are not good neighbors for pleasant homes. Many

can pay higher rent or buy more expensive houses. But we don't have enough good houses for them to buy, even if everyone had plenty of money. Much work and study has been done on "Slum Clearance" and "Housing Projects." We will study this problem in detail later.

We have mentioned only a few of the many things which help make a good or bad place in which to live. As you think of the kind of city you want, you will plan many improvements. Planning is more than just deciding what you want, though. Suppose you plan to have a playground for children in every block of residential area of your city. That would be a fine way to please the children. But playgrounds cost a great deal of money. If the city government is to build and maintain all those playgrounds, it must have more money. The money must come from taxes or other revenue sources. People who own property pay a large part of the taxes. To be able to pay the higher taxes, the property owners must charge higher rents. The people who live in

People prefer to live in the suburbs and ride farther to work.

your city, then, would have to pay very high rent or extra taxes or fees of some kind. If they didn't have enough money left to buy the right kind of food, their children wouldn't be healthy. They would need hospitals more than playgrounds.

So, you see, you must be content with fewer playgrounds or get money to pay for them some way. **Planning must take all things into consideration.**

ATLANTA AND YOUR FUTURE

In a few years you will finish school, get a job, and perhaps get married. Then you must pay rent, pay taxes, and help run the city. You will want to do a good job. Some of your classmates may live in small towns. Some may live in the country. Chances are that most of you will live in a city, Atlanta, or a city very much like it.

Building Atlanta's Future

Over half of the people in the United States live in cities—in places with more than 2,500 people. Here in the South there are fewer people living in cities than in other parts of the country. But southern cities are growing faster than those in other parts of the United States. During your lifetime you may see great changes in the cities of today. Even though you live in a little town or out in the country, you will want to know about cities. You will go to them to visit and play and to do business. Cities will always affect your everyday living.

LOOKING TOWARD A BETTER ATLANTA

The examples of traffic, street planning, zoning, playground, and slum problems should give you an idea of how complex a city is. To have a good city, we must make careful plans to improve every part of city life. Improvement will come because you vote for the best leadership and the best policies of city government. It will come as people learn to work together better. You can be sure you work and vote to best advantage only if you know the facts and problems.

City Hall represents the people's organization for working together.

Atlanta and You

You must think about the facts as they apply to Atlanta. You must also do something about your convictions once you know you are right. A really good city will not "just happen" unless you do your part to make it happen.

Atlanta citizens have done fine work in making a good place to live. There is still much to do and new problems will keep appearing. Keep in mind as you study this book that you will someday have to make decisions as to what is best for the city. The more you learn in school and in every day life the better you can make these decisions.

DISCUSSION QUESTIONS

1. What "city" problems have you had in the past few days?
2. Do some people still have the attitude of early Atlantans about new streets and other civic improvements?
3. Why can we not make exact plans for our city's future?
4. What have you seen in newspapers lately which voters should think about as means for making Atlanta a better city?
5. What programs and drives for civic improvement are now going on in Atlanta?

HAVE YOU READ?

1. *Atlanta, A City of the Modern South.* "History." American Guide Series. New York: Smith and Durrell, 1942.
2. *Atlanta Centennial Year Book, 1837–1937.* Atlanta, Georgia: Gregg Murphy, 1937.
3. Cooper, Walter G. *Official History of Fulton County.* Atlanta, Georgia: Walter W. Brown Publishing Company, 1934.
4. *The Story of Georgia, A School History of Our State.* Part I, "Georgia and Its Story." Atlanta, Georgia: Science Research Associates, 1942.

2. What is Atlanta?

HOW would you answer if someone said "Please define the word city"? Could you explain what makes Atlanta a city? A city includes so many things that we would need a very long definition to cover all of them.

Perhaps we cannot put it into a few easy words, but we can find answers to many questions about Atlanta's boundaries, people, and surrounding areas. Knowing these things is better than being able to memorize and repeat a definition in words. Perhaps when you know them you can make a definition of your own which you will remember longer than one you memorize now.

WHERE IS ATLANTA?

If you were in a foreign country, could you tell a native where Atlanta is in the United States? In the Southeast? In Georgia? Could you describe the location, the people, geography, climate, animals, and crops that are found near by? Let us review some of these.

What is Atlanta?

Atlanta is situated a little northwest of the center of the state of Georgia. It is the capital of Georgia and a very important city in the state. Much of its importance it owes to its location and to the country around it. The city's location and the geography of the area help determine the kind of city it is.

Atlanta is in the "Piedmont Plateau" section of Georgia. To the north are the Mountain and Valley sections. To the south and southeast lies the flat Coastal Plain section. The word "piedmont" means "at the foot of the mountains." "Plateau" means a high, flat tableland. Thus the "Piedmont Plateau" is a high, flat tableland at the foot of the mountains. This piedmont region extends through several states along the Atlantic coast, all the way from northern New Jersey to central Alabama. It forms about one-third of the area of Georgia. Where the piedmont meets the mountains it is about two thousand feet above sea level. From here it slopes gradually to about five hundred feet at its joining with the Coastal Plain.

The corporate city of Atlanta is located on a slight ridge which runs north and south. The west side slopes gently off to the northwest, and the east side slopes southeast. It has been said that rain which falls west of Peachtree Street drains into the Gulf of Mexico. The rain falling to the east of Peachtree drains into the Atlantic Ocean.

Being on this tableland at the foot of the mountains has meant much to Atlanta. The high plateau has a healthful climate and fairly good soil for raising food and other crops. The level or gently rolling land does not hinder travel. Roads do not have to be cut into or climb steep mountainsides. Mountains have always been barriers to land based travel and trade. Try climbing a steep mountain yourself and you see why. You get tired. So did the horses and mules of former years. For railroads and highways today it's a matter of expense.

The mountains in north Georgia are part of a long chain of mountains, known as the Appalachian Highlands, which run all the way from the Canadian border to central Alabama. These mountains are a barrier to east-west transportation. The early settlers found it easier

Building Atlanta's Future

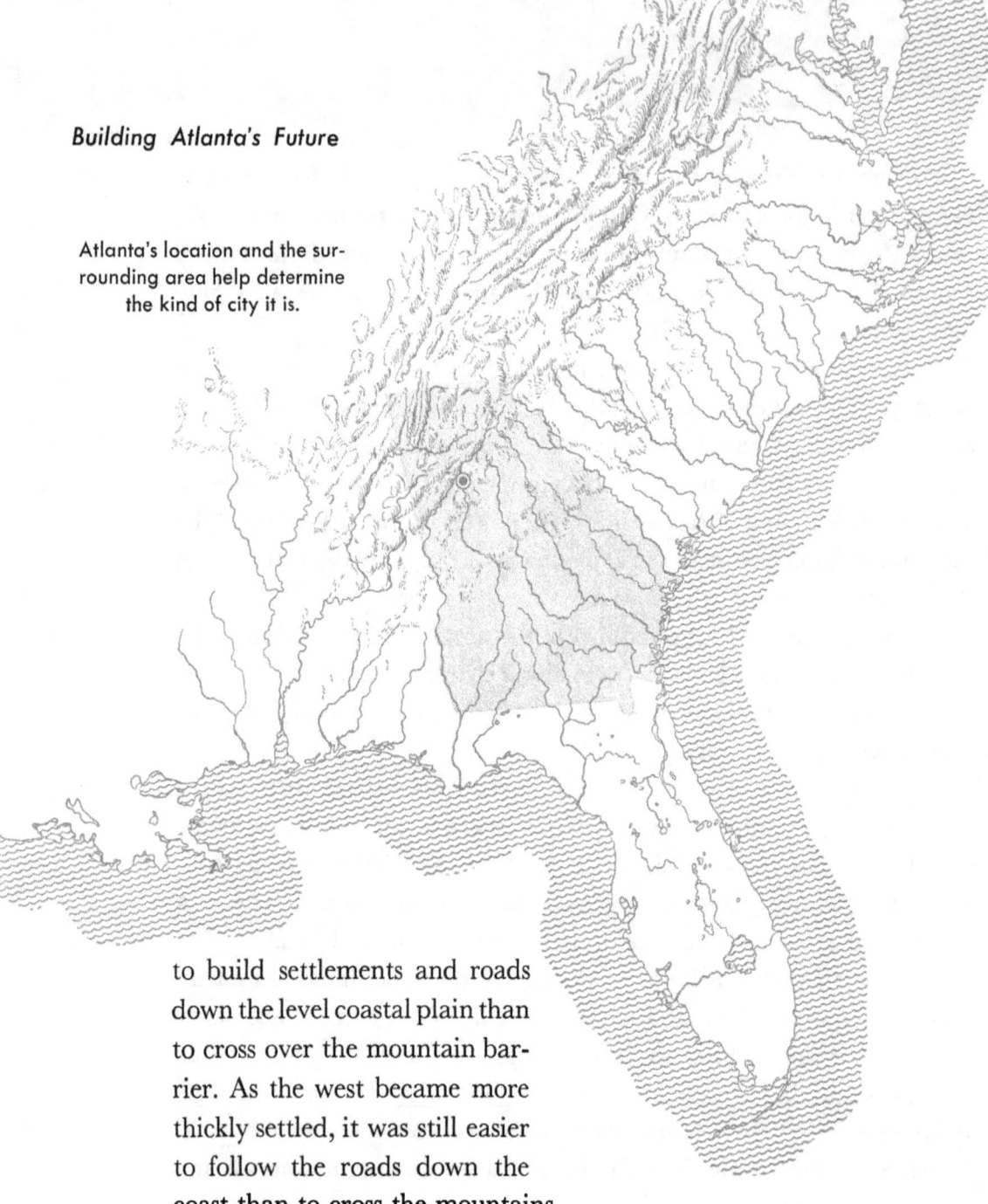

Atlanta's location and the surrounding area help determine the kind of city it is.

to build settlements and roads down the level coastal plain than to cross over the mountain barrier. As the west became more thickly settled, it was still easier to follow the roads down the coast than to cross the mountains.

Atlanta, being near the southern end of the mountain barrier, is in truth the "Gateway to the South." The transportation lanes coming down the coast can here turn west without having to cross the mountains. Goods coming in from the west and other parts of the southeast can gather here and take the level route to the north. They can also

What is Atlanta?

move to any one of several seaports on the Atlantic or Gulf of Mexico. Here they connect with ocean lanes to all parts of the world.

Being the "Gate City" has done much to make Atlanta what it is today. Geography has helped make it a natural hub near the center of the group of southeastern states. Spokes of transportation lines go out in all directions—to other parts of Georgia, to the Southeast, the nation, and the world.

METROPOLITAN ATLANTA

The city of Atlanta extends into two counties: Fulton and DeKalb. About two-thirds of the area is in Fulton County. The city limits enclose 34.7 square miles. Within these corporate limits about 339,000 people live. It is easy to locate these city limit lines on a map. We can also mark the point along a road where you leave or enter the city limits. These limits are definite, set by law. Maps can show these things for all to see at a glance.

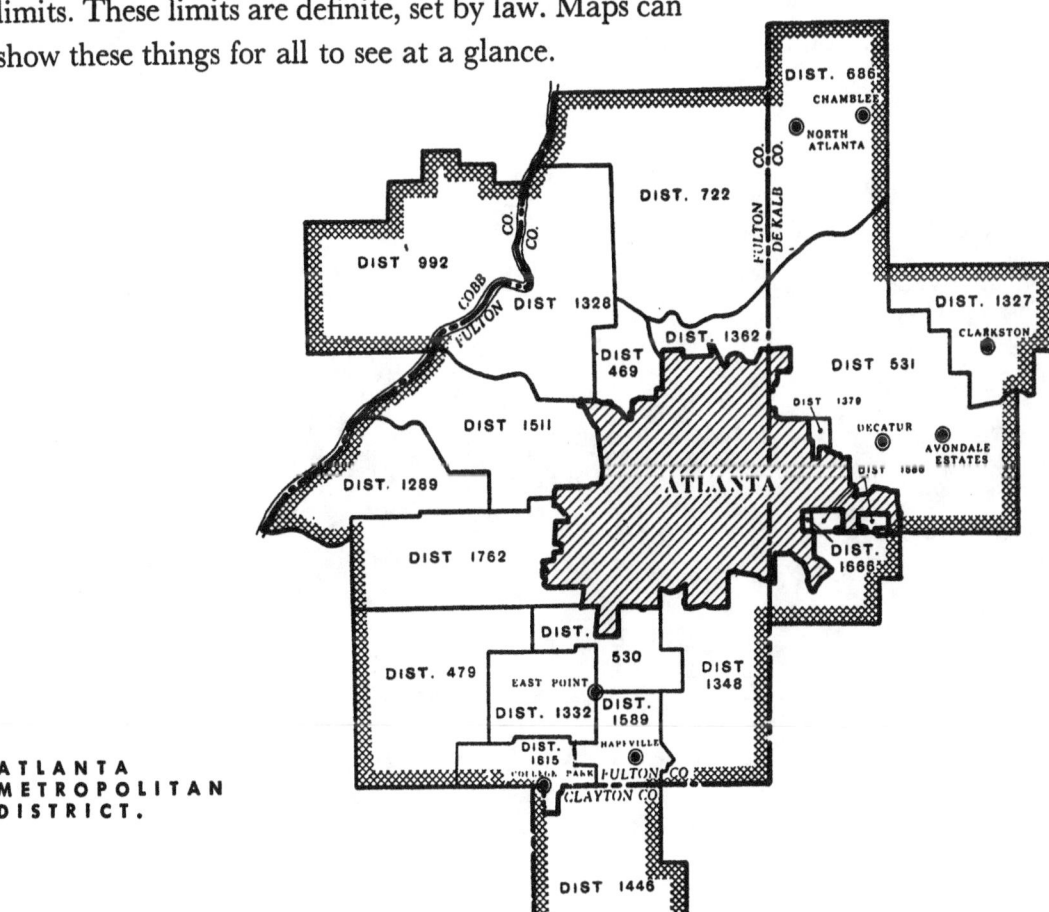

ATLANTA METROPOLITAN DISTRICT.

Building Atlanta's Future

Within the city limits is the area in which people pay city taxes and take part directly in the operation and services of city government. But the city limits do not enclose all that is a part of Atlanta. This is only a sort of *heart city*. The surrounding area is really very much a part of Atlanta too. Several small cities cluster around the larger one. Many of the people who live in them work in Atlanta. Their businesses and interests are in Atlanta, or they are dependent on it in other ways. Many of these people feel that they are Atlantans, and Atlanta could hardly be what it is without them.

As you drive out of Atlanta you would find it hard to decide just where the city ends. Where does the suburban town begin? Where do you leave the city and enter the country? City limits are not noticeable unless they are marked. The houses, streets, and people change very gradually as you go along.

Atlanta and the surrounding "city area" is known as Metropolitan Atlanta, or sometimes as "Greater Atlanta." The United States Census

Each part of a

city has its purpose.

defines a metropolitan district as the area around a central city which has a population of 50,000 or more. It includes all joining minor civil divisions with an average population density of 150 people or more per square mile. Thus Atlanta is the "Metropolis" (which comes from Greek words meaning "mother city") or heart city of the metropolitan district. All the metropolitan district is included when we speak of Metropolitan Atlanta. There were 140 metropolitan districts in the United States in 1940.

Within Metropolitan Atlanta there are about 550,000 people. This includes Atlanta and the surrounding cities and towns: Decatur, Hapeville, College Park, East Point, Chamblee, Avondale Estates, Clarkston, and North Atlanta.

Each of these cities may have its own local government, police and fire departments, and other civic services. But the living and working of the people are very much tied up with the larger city of Atlanta.

Building Atlanta's Future

Atlanta's transportation system reaches out to them. Many of the people work in Atlanta's businesses and industries but go back to these places each night. Without fast, certain transportation to their jobs they could not live there. Thousands of people are needed to do all the work in our city. It would be hard to give all these people the kinds of homes they want within the city limits.

Thus, you see that the people in all parts of Metropolitan Atlanta have common interests in our city. The crowded, rushing hustle of a great city is a fine place for stores, office buildings, banks, restaurants, and theatres. But it is not the best place to have a home, to rest and sleep, and to give children a place to play. These things are often better achieved in a quiet, roomy suburb or in well-planned housing developments such as Techwood and John Hope Homes. People are healthier, happier, and more efficient when they are not crowded into city tenements and slums. Some suburbs are often called "bedroom cities" because so many people have jobs in the metropolis but return to the suburbs each night to sleep. Other suburbs may contain special industries, resort hotels, and so forth.

Metropolitan districts grow up around all great cities. They depend on the central city and the central city depends on them. Each part of the metropolitan district has its place—its job to do. It takes them all to make up a smooth-running unit. Factory and business sections produce goods and furnish work. Residence and recreation districts provide houses for workers and keep them happy. Transportation and communication bring workers together so the work of city life can go on. Each must depend on the other to do its part.

CITY OR COUNTRY ENVIRONMENT

To be sure, other near-by cities and towns such as Marietta and Fairburn are also closely related to Atlanta. But they are farther away. To reach them you must pass through a "rural" area in which the population density is less than 150 people per square mile. Therefore, the census does not include them in the metropolitan district. They

What is Atlanta?

may have many common interests with Atlanta, but they also have more interests of local nature than do those cities in the metropolitan district. They are market centers for near-by farmers as well as "bedrooms" for some Atlanta workers.

Just how does the city differ from the country? We hear jokes and stories about country boys and city slickers, but how much of this is true? We know there are many differences between life in the big city and life on the farm. Leading these different lives means that people learn different things. A country person in a city for the first time is in a new "*environment.*" The same is true for a city person who visits a farm for the first time. The word *environment* means total surroundings. This includes houses, streets, traffic, plants, animals, and all the things we can see. But it also includes behavior of people, ways of thinking and acting, and the importance people put on different behavior.

Of course most people are neither purely "citified" nor "countrified." Some may have lived in both places and nearly everybody has learned something of both types of environment. However, it will perhaps help us understand rural-urban differences if we look at the two extremes. Then we can better see why city people are usually different from those who live in small communities. We will not try to decide which is the better place to live. Each has its good and bad points and

City and country environments teach us different things.

Whether we live in the city or each could be called *better* for certain things. We want to understand, rather than judge, the city and the country.

HOW DO CITY AND COUNTRY LIFE DIFFER?

First, let us look at occupation. The people with the *most rural* environment are the farmers. There are many kinds of farmers but all of them work a great deal in the open. They spend much time by themselves or in small groups. They are often concerned about the weather and its effect on their work. They come in contact with growing plants and animals more than they do with people. In our present system of farming people live far apart in order to have enough land on which to raise their crops. For that reason, visitors are few and are usually welcomed. A farmer may have to work very hard during planting and harvest seasons, then he may have a slack season. He has some variety in his work.

The city worker may work at one of several hundred occupations. He usually works with many people and handles paper or machines instead of plants and animals. His job may require him to do the same things day after day. Much of his work may be indoors where weather is not so important. The farmer has fresh air and sunshine but the city worker has steam heat and sometimes air-conditioning. The city worker gets paid each week or month. The farmer's income is more irregular and may come only once a year.

country, we must work with other people.

Since farming requires land for crops, rural communities contain fewer people. The United States Census classes communities of 2,500 people or more as urban. Some communities of this size are more rural than urban but it would be impossible to classify them exactly in every case. Small communities and scattered population are rural features. Rural dwellers know fewer people but they know these few better. They are more neighborly; they visit and help each other by borrowing and lending. Usually, they also know one another's business and affairs and talk about them more than city people.

City dwellers come in contact with many people every day. It would be impossible for them to know the name of everyone they meet on the streets. Often they do not even know the names of the people next door. Their friends and neighbors are those with whom they work or who belong to the same clubs or churches. Being in the midst of so many people can lead one to pay very little attention to the affairs of any one of them. The rural person often knows everybody in the community—who his kinfolk are and what he thinks about politics, religion, and many other subjects.

A large city is made up of people from many different places. These people may differ greatly in race, language, background, beliefs, religion, occupation, and in many other ways. So some groups remain separate in their social life. We say a city is a "melting pot" in which people are brought together. They all live within the city, but they don't in all ways "melt together."

The church is often a community center. Going to church is both a religious and a social event. City

In rural communities, all the people usually have about the same backgrounds and interests. There is not so much difference in education, religion, and customs as may be found in great cities. We say rural communities are *homogeneous* (made up of like kinds). Urban communities are *heterogeneous* (made up of differing kinds).

Rural people tend to marry younger and to have fewer divorces. Their families are larger. The birth rate in cities is usually not high enough to replenish the population. More people die than are born in most cities. The surplus young people in rural areas who "migrate," or move, to cities keep the population from declining. One reason for this

churches have larger congregations who can hardly be as intimate as the rural churchgoer.

is that as modern machinery comes to the farm, fewer people are needed to raise the crops. The surplus young people as they grow up go to the city to find employment. Thus, we find that many city people come from the country, but few country people come from the city.

These things we have mentioned go into making up rural-urban differences. Of course, there are many more and we can combine some of them into reasons for some problems of each type of community.

For instance, city people are so often strangers to those they meet. They see so many people in a casual way and may never see them again. This tends to make them "impersonal" toward those they do not know well. On the other hand, rural people know everybody in the community. They hold each responsible for his actions. One must be careful what he does or his neighbors will talk about him; they may even refuse to associate with him. He will think twice before he does something contrary to custom. The city person may "get by" in the crowd for doing the same thing. Nobody knows him and he is soon out of sight. Thus, we have more police and more laws and restrictions in the large city than in the country. However, this same "neighbor control" in rural areas may include harmful customs which it would be well to do away with. The strong hold of custom may kill new ideas that would be good.

CITY AND COUNTRY DEPEND ON EACH OTHER

Yes, there are many differences between city and country life. We know that great cities represent some of man's greatest achievements. Though cities afford some of the best features of living, they also present some disadvantages, such as noise, crime, disease, and crowded living. While we may wish and work for correcting these evils, no one wants to go back to primitive life where everyone raises his own food and makes for himself everything he needs.

Even the remotest farmer now looks to the city for his clothes, most of his tools, and for the books and machines of modern living. It would be a poor life by our standards to go back to pioneer methods. We know that a specialist can do a better job than a Jack-of-all-trades. Each can do that which he does best. Then, by exchanging goods through the use of money, we can all live better than by trying to fill all our needs alone. It is hard to make a pair of shoes in a home shop which are as good as those made much faster in a well-equipped factory.

Rural areas and rural people produce food and raw materials. Without them there could be no cities. Have you ever stopped to realize how helpless a city is without the country and without transportation to and from the country? People in Atlanta eat trainloads of food every day. If the farmers stopped selling any food at all, what would city people eat? Cities have been cut off from their food supply in time of war and famine in many countries. Suffering and death are swift and certain.

But the food supply does not have to be completely shut off to be disastrous. If the supply is limited by strikes or by poor crops, the effect is soon seen in food stores. Scarce food means worry, poor health, and less working efficiency. If a farmer raises a poor crop, he sells only that part which he does not need. He must first keep enough for his own family to eat. City people get only his surplus. Therefore, city people are the first to suffer in time of famine. Someone has said, "If the farmer is cut, the city man bleeds." While this, of course, cannot be literally true, it hints at the extent to which the city depends on the country.

There are many other ways in which city and country depend on each other. Large city newspapers and radio stations serve both city and country. News and advertising help the farmers buy and sell things they need for living and producing. They depend on the city to supply them. Great city radio stations reach millions of rural listeners, through networks of local stations. They bring programs to farmers which help them to produce better crops. Cities can prosper only as the surrounding country prospers.

How much city and country depend on each other is well shown by transportation. Roads are built so that there can be easy travel and exchange between cities of all sizes and even to the smallest farm. If transportation stops, everybody is at a loss. Different kinds of farms and different kinds of cities must be able to exchange their products today if man's business of living is to go on.

Transportation plays an even more important part in Atlanta's

Atlanta, the "Gate City"—Hub of the Southeast.

Building Atlanta's Future

well-being than in most cities. In the next chapter we will look farther at transportation as it may affect our future.

A city, then, plays the part of a device—a kind of tool, so to speak—for bringing together objects and forces from far and near. As such a device, a city acts as a unit, or part, in carrying on the work of the nation and world. We must see our city from the point of view of the part it plays in the larger picture. At the same time, other cities over the world are filling slightly different needs.

We must also see our city from the point of view of the individual—you. What can Atlanta offer you in the way of jobs and services? Many individuals go into making up the working force which allows Atlanta to fill its place. Each person sees Atlanta as a place in which to live and work. But that living and working depend also on the larger job which Atlanta plays in serving the South and the United States. Only as the city holds and serves this place can her people, as individuals, better themselves and their living. Keep this larger purpose in mind as we study our city.

DISCUSSION QUESTIONS

1. Why is Atlanta called the "Gateway to the South"?
2. Why do suburban cities and towns grow up around large cities?
3. What are some rural-urban differences?
4. In what ways do city and country depend on each other?
5. How does Marietta differ from Decatur?

HAVE YOU READ?

1. *Atlanta, A City of the Modern South.* "Transportation." American Guide Series. New York: Smith and Durrell, 1942.
2. Citizens' Fact-Finding Movement of Georgia. *Georgia Facts in Figures, A Source Book.* "Natural Resources." Athens, Georgia: The University of Georgia Press, 1946.
3. Stonorov, Oscar, and Kahn, Louis I. *You and Your Neighborhood, A Primer for Neighborhood Planning.* New York: Revere Copper and Brass Incorporated, 1944.
4. *The Story of Georgia, A School History of Our State.* Part II, "Our Bit of Earth." Atlanta, Georgia: Science Research Associates, 1942.

3. Atlanta's Regional Setting

WE have seen that Atlanta is the "heart city" of a metropolitan district. The welfare of all the people in this area depends on how well each part works with the others. But a metropolitan district is a city area. It is a user and converter of raw materials rather than a producer. It can not stand alone but must depend for many things on the surrounding areas. These areas furnish not only materials, but also a huge market—millions of people to buy the things we make. From this market we get the money with which we in turn can buy a living and more raw materials.

One of our first jobs in understanding our city is to learn how we influence and serve people outside its limits. The exchange of goods and money goes on between many cities, states, and nations, both near and far. Without it no city could exist. We must also know how people outside Atlanta influence and serve us in our city.

ATLANTA IS A TRANSPORTATION CENTER

One of the best-known ways in which Atlanta serves this part of the United States is as a transportation center. You will recall that its location is one of the reasons Atlanta has become a great transportation center. How much does the flow of goods through the city affect our business and the surrounding area?

All of us have seen the many railroad tracks leading into and out of the Union and Terminal stations. Trains are moving in the yards at all times of the day and night. We have seen the highway which leads north to Athens, the Carolinas, and to the great cities of the Northeast. The same highway runs south to Newnan, LaGrange, New Orleans, and thence to the western states. Traffic is always heavy on these roads as it is on the east-west highways to Birmingham, Savannah, Jacksonville, Chattanooga, and places beyond.

Atlanta's bus terminal is one of the busiest in the South. Buses arrive and leave every few minutes of the day and night. They connect Atlanta with all parts of the United States. The many truck lines which run through and from the city rival railroads as freight movers. The airport and its growing traffic is the newest addition to the flood of goods and people that come and go. Travel by air brings many cities within a few minutes or hours of travel time. Business can be conducted over a much wider area than was possible a few years ago.

In 1860 it took several days to drive a wagon or ride a horse from Atlanta to Chattanooga. Early trains made the trip in less than one day. Now an airplane can make the trip in a matter of minutes. Chicago is much nearer, in travel time, than Chattanooga was then. Have you ever walked or driven a horse down a main highway? The cars really whiz by you. Airplanes go at even greater speeds compared to automobiles and trains. This speed and ease of travel make Atlanta important to more people over a wider area. Distant cities in the same way become more important to us.

Railroads, bus lines, and air lines connect Atlanta with the region and the world.→

Building Atlanta's Future

Transportation was one of the main causes for the location and the early growth of Atlanta. It is one of the reasons that Atlanta is a great city. Many people in Atlanta earn their living by working at the job of transporting materials and people. Many more work at handling, re-working, and processing goods before they are used or sent out again.

Transportation, then, is still important to Atlanta. Many of the goods and people traveling from north to south or from east to west in this part of the United States go through Atlanta.

ATLANTA AS A REGIONAL CENTER

So many railroads, highways, and airlines going in all directions help make Atlanta a "regional center" in many ways. It is near the center of the southeastern states. Factories here can send their goods over several neighboring states all within a few hundred miles. In the same way those places can send their goods into Atlanta markets easily. Large companies can look after branch offices in several states from headquarters in Atlanta. Telephone and telegraph lines run out in all directions much as roads do. Atlanta is a "switchboard" for the Southeast. Such means of communication also help make Atlanta a regional center.

But what do we mean by a "regional center"? What is a "region"? In what other ways is Atlanta a regional center?

Perhaps you think of a region as a large area. That is true. But all large areas are not regions. "Region" is a general term sometimes used for quite small areas. But it is used here in a special way. It refers to the southeastern United States. Why is this group of states known as a region?

The countryside must be similar throughout to be called a region. It must be an area in which the people have many common interests. By "common interests" we mean interests that are shared by most of the people. If most of the people are to be interested in the same things, they must be alike in ways of working, thinking, and living. They must have similar environments and problems. It is easy to see that the states

Atlanta's Regional Setting

surrounding Atlanta can be classified as a region for it fits this description.

We have seen how Atlanta is a terminal transportation point for the southwestern United States. In this way it serves other near-by states. Atlanta depends on them and they depend upon Atlanta in collecting and distributing the things we need. We have, in this way, a common interest in transportation with our neighboring states.

GEOGRAPHY AND THE REGION

We have many common interests with the states around Georgia. We grow many of the same kinds of farm products, such as cotton, corn, tobacco, peanuts, sweet potatoes, and many others. We have the same kinds of trees—pines, oaks, hickories, and the like; and the same kinds of birds, flowers, and wild life. This is especially true of Virginia, North Carolina, South Carolina, the northern part of Florida, Alabama, Mississippi, Louisiana, Tennessee, and Kentucky.

Why do these states have the same kinds of agriculture, forestry, flowers, and birds? For one thing they all have about the same climate. The temperature, rainfall, humidity, and growing season are all much the same.

These states also have similar soil belts. Some soils are very sandy, while others have a great deal of plant material in them. There are soils of different colors—tinged with red, yellow, black, and white. These soils have different mineral and chemical content. Some are good for growing one kind of plant while others are better for other plants. Soils differ within a state and between states. But in general, each state in a region will have some of the same kinds of soil. This means that since the climate and growing season are similar, the same kinds of crops, trees, and animals *can be grown* throughout the region.

We see, then, that climate, soil belts, types of trees, plants, and wild life are similar in the southeastern states. These things are also closely related to the lay of the land. The lay of the land means the slope of the land and the shape of the surface of the earth. The word for describing the slope of the land is "topography." Georgia and the neighboring states have similar topography. They all have some flat plains, some rolling or hilly land, and some mountain and valley sections.

Geographers say that neighboring states which have the same kind of climate, soil types, and topography are a part of the same *geographic region*. Their geography is so much alike that they seem to belong together. Each part of the region adds something a little different. Together they make up a sort of balanced whole.

The geography of a region has a great deal to do with the kind of life the people live. It sets the limits as to what kinds of crops the farmer *can* grow and the kinds of industries that *can* be set up. The people have wide choice within these limits, but they cannot choose outside of them. For instance, an Eskimo cannot raise sugar cane in his land of snow and ice. Neither will polar bears grow a beautiful coat of heavy fur in Cuba. Because of their geography the Eskimos and the Cubans must choose from the plants and the animals that will grow in their regions. To a lesser degree the same is true of the people in Wisconsin and those in Georgia.

CULTURE AND THE REGION

There are other reasons why the people of Georgia and the neighboring states have chosen similar crops, livestock, and industries. For one thing most of the people are descendants of settlers who came here before 1800. Many of the earlier settlers came from the British Isles and northern Europe. The Negroes were brought over from Africa. These people brought with them the customs from their mother countries. These ways of thinking and doing things grew into our customs today. We say that people over the southeastern states have about the same "cultural background."

"Culture" as used here means more than interest in poetry, good manners, and moral conduct. The culture of a people includes all their knowledge, customs, and possessions—their ways of thinking, acting, living, and the things they think are right or wrong.

The Southwest with its level, arid prairie is a region in itself.

The culture of the United States is different from that of other countries—say of India, for example. Children in the schools of India are not taught the same things you are taught. Their religious rituals and their family customs would seem strange to us. Indian people do not associate with those of another "caste." A caste is a social division—similar to a social "grade" or "class"—to which people belong because they are born into it. Children belong to the caste to which their parents belong. The caste system in India is quite strict. People in the lower castes cannot climb to a higher caste by hard work and good education. Most people there earn much lower wages than people in

The Southeast is also a region with its moist climate and rolling hills.

the United States. They have a lower level of living—for instance, they have fewer automobiles, washing machines, and good homes—than we have. All these things are included in culture as we speak of it here.

The people of the Southeast, then, have similar culture patterns. Our ancestors have been neighbors for many generations and have taken on one another's customs and ways of living and thinking. We differ in culture from the other regions of the United States; not so much as we differ from India or China, but there are differences. The people of the northeastern states think some of our customs strange, and we feel the same way about theirs. When we visit in the northern

Atlanta's Regional Setting

or western states, people notice our language is different. We may find that some of their food is not like ours.

There are more and larger cities in the Northeast and fewer farms. You will remember that rural-urban differences show that city people have a different culture from country people. The cities in the South are small and people see more of rural life. They have a more rural culture than the larger cities in more industrial areas.

In many ways "the South" is considered a region. We often hear people speak of "the South" as a region. However, there is quite a difference between the eastern and western parts of the South. The level and prairie land of the Southwest is more of a region in itself. So is the country of moist climate and small farms in the Southeast.

CULTURE AND HISTORY

Down through the years the people of the Southeast have shared periods of hard times and good times. These memories and the forces that caused them have helped make a kinship of culture. They add to the ties that make a region. Our whole region has struggled with:

1. Cotton economy
2. Slavery
3. War Between the States
4. Farm tenancy
5. Soil erosion
6. Boll weevil
7. Mechanization of farming
8. Racial adjustments

These problems have done much to give the people of our region their outlook on life. Other regions have had different problems and other factors which affect their people. Because of their common background and experiences, the people of a region develop similar government, education, literature, music, and other such things. They have similar attitudes and place the same values on what they believe is right or wrong. They cooperate to meet the needs which are much alike all over the region. For instance, we have in the Southeast such agencies as: Tennessee Valley Authority, Southern Governor's Con-

Building Atlanta's Future

ference, Southern Regional Educational Council, Southern Association of Colleges and Secondary Schools.

These organizations have been set up to deal with problems and interests of the southern states. You may be interested in looking up more information about them. Other regions have their own organizations.

Regions of the United States.

In the Southeast most people speak in a slow soft manner which is referred to by outsiders as a "drawl." Many people in other regions have learned to like the way we cook "Southern" fried chicken, hot biscuits, gravy, black-eyed peas, and corn bread. They are known as our regional specialities. We may like baked beans too, but we still know them as "Boston Baked Beans" if they are cooked in a certain way. We also like tasty cheeses and Kansas City steaks but we give the credit for their origin to the north central and southwestern regions. Customs of speaking and eating are interesting examples of regional differences in people. They illustrate differences in backgrounds of history and culture, as well as geography, plants, and animals.

Atlanta's Regional Setting

We have seen that soils, climate, and topography which are alike make an area a geographic region. Now we see that the people in a region are similar too. They think, feel, and live in much the same way. They work together on common problems. We say they have a common culture.

A region, then, is a group of neighboring states, or parts of states, which have much the same culture and geography. It is because of this common culture and geography that the people have common interests and actions—that they work, think, and feel much the same way. The southeastern region is an area which contains these similar interests and features.

REGIONS OF THE UNITED STATES

A regional boundary does not always follow state lines. Part of a state may be in one region and part in another. People and land belong in the region to which they are closest as measured by the definition of a region.

Along the edge of a region is a fringe which may belong partly in one region and partly in another. In some ways the people and land are like one region; in some ways they are like the other. It is sometimes hard to say just which region they resemble most. Thus regional boundaries cannot be drawn as clear lines like state lines.

A region ends where the people and the countryside begin to be different in more ways than they are like the general character of the region. Then another region begins. No two regions are exactly alike. Each region has its common aspects which set it apart from all other regions.

How many regions are there in the United States? Our nation is so large that there are many differences in climate, topography, and soil belts in its great expanse. There are differences in plant and animal life and in the lives of the people who live there. The people in each part have slightly different cultures and backgrounds. Their problems and common interests differ.

Building Atlanta's Future

Howard W. Odum, a great social scientist who was born in Georgia, divides the United States into six major geographic and cultural regions. They are shown on the accompanying map. These regions depend on one another as the states within a region do. They raise different crops and livestock and have different industries. They exchange their surplus products by buying and selling. The people of the Southwest raise more cattle and sheep than they need. Those in the Middle States raise surplus wheat and dairy products. Those in the Northeast depend more on manufacturing than on farming. They make many things such as clocks, watches, clothing, and machinery. The se are needed in the other regions. They can be exchanged for the surplus foodstuffs the others have.

The culture, historical background, and geography of each of these regions blend to make a region what it is. The common interests and problems of each will be a little different from the others. These differences tie the regions together into our nation. If we did not need each other we could not go together to make up a great nation. By working together and supplying each other with the things of which we have more than we need, each region is better off than it could ever hope to be alone.

The regions of the United States and their people have many similarities. We are all alike in many ways. We speak of our "American culture and traditions." The differences among the regions serve as a basis for cooperation. Through them runs the thread of common interests in the welfare of our nation.

THE REGION AND ATLANTA'S FUTURE

Atlanta is located near the middle of the southeastern region. It is a center for transportation, communication, business, banking, and other services for Georgia and the neighboring states. Atlanta's problems and opportunities are tied up with those of the entire region.

For instance, suppose you are a farmer living somewhere in Georgia or in a neighboring state. You have spent most of your ready cash

Atlanta's Regional Setting

for fertilizer and supplies. Your crop has been cultivated well, but a drought comes and ruins it. You have nothing to sell and no money to live on until next year when there is another harvest. Very likely your neighbor farmers have suffered the same losses and cannot lend you anything.

You must go to the local merchants and bankers and ask for credit. They may not be able to give credit to everybody who needs it. They must look to the wholesale concerns and larger banks for credit too. Otherwise they cannot get merchandise to sell nor money to lend. You see that the farmers' crops affect everybody in the area. Your credit and a chance to make a new start may depend on the credit policies of large banks and firms in Atlanta.

Your local merchant buys his goods from a wholesaler or jobber in a large city. These large business firms exist by selling goods to local merchants in the area. Many such firms have headquarters in Atlanta. If you as a farmer do not buy the things they have to sell, these firms do not prosper. The drought affects the city people just as surely as it does the farmer.

The country general merchandise store is a community trade and social center.

Building Atlanta's Future

Therefore, the businessman and banker in large cities know they must help farmers out of their difficulties or their own businesses suffer in the long run. If they cannot get goods to sell or if people do not have money with which to buy, the whole system breaks down. If the trouble is widespread, we have a "depression."

During a depression the factory workers, merchants, bankers, railroaders, and farmers all suffer. People in cities like Atlanta suffer when the farmers raise poor crops. The farmers and others suffer when strikes come or business firms fail and break up the production and distribution of goods.

It is just as important that credit is available for farmers and businessmen in the region when they need it as it is that crops be bounteous and factories operating. For that reason we have Federal Reserve Banks, each serving a Federal Reserve District. These banks act as clearing houses and as go-betweens for the smaller banks. They help keep credit and business running smoothly. They serve a type of region instead of a state. However, Federal Reserve Districts are not quite like the geographic and cultural regions, but they are similar.

Our states were not laid out to meet farm production and business needs. People do not notice state lines when they go to town to buy and sell. They go to the nearest town where they can find what they want or get the best prices. The region is a more natural area than a

Federal Reserve Districts of the United States. Each Federal Reserve Bank serves several states as a regional agency.

state within which to conduct business. Large firms and federal agencies realize this and are often organized by regions.

Atlanta is headquarters for many regional agencies. They are part of our city and do much to make it a great one. Because of them Atlanta has a great influence all over the Southeast. We must see that these agencies do their job of keeping the region running smoothly. Their quality has a great effect on the prosperity and welfare of the people.

YOUR PART IN OUR REGION'S FUTURE

In the future, Atlanta's progress will, in part, depend on the progress of the region. As a voter you will someday be called upon to help decide what laws and agencies are best for the growth and development of the region. It will be up to you to know how the welfare of the region as a whole will affect your own welfare. Planning for Atlanta's future must include planning for the region also. Good plans

Building Atlanta's Future

for Atlanta must take into consideration the farmers and workers all over the region. You should remember this when you begin to cast your ballots.

Atlanta serves as a central force in bringing together the southern states into a region. As a gateway in transportation and communication, it links the region with the rest of the nation. Here the surpluses of our region are gathered and sent to supplement the wealth of other regions. In turn the products of the nation and world are gathered to Atlanta to benefit the people of our region.

Atlanta serves the nation while it serves the Southeast. It does this and more. Atlanta is very much a city of the world. How we plan and live as citizens of Atlanta affects people in the far distant corners of the world.

Now we are ready to take a closer look at our city. We must not see it as just a place to live and work. It is also a powerful agent of service to the Southeast, to the nation, and to the world. As adults of the future, we must know how to use our city for greater public service, personal welfare, and happiness.

DISCUSSION QUESTIONS

1. In what ways is Atlanta a regional center?
2. What are the factors which make the Southeast a "region"?
3. Why is Atlanta so important to the Southeast as a region?
4. How can you as a citizen of Atlanta help improve the welfare of the region?

HAVE YOU READ?

1. *A Report on Health and Welfare in DeKalb and Fulton Counties.* Part I, Chap. II, "Regional Background of the Atlanta Area." Atlanta, Georgia: Social Planning Council, 1943.
2. *Atlanta, A City of the Modern South.* "Transportation." American Guide Series. New York: Smith and Durrell, 1942.
3. *Building America, Illustrated Studies of Modern Problems.* Vol. VII, "Cotton." Building America Illustrated Studies. New York: Americana Corporation, 1942.

4. Atlanta's Resource Base

IN the preceding chapters we have looked at Atlanta as a place to live and work. We have found that we depend on our surrounding areas and on distant regions for many of the materials we need for pleasant living. Each part of a city, region, or nation plays a part in the world's work. What are these materials which are so necessary and the ways they are used by people? Anything which we use to make a living or to improve living is called a *resource*.

What resources have been used in making Atlanta what it is today? And what resources do we have to work with now and in the future? If you want to build a rowboat or cook a meal, you must first have resources. For the boat you would need tools, nails, paint, and lumber or some other kind of water-proof material. The dinner would require different resources. For a pleasing meal, you would need meat, vegetables, utensils, and a stove.

After you have the materials, you must *know how* to make a boat or cook a meal. Or you must have someone to show you how. If you have someone to help you, the work goes faster. Thus we find that you need several kinds of resources if you are to make a good boat or cook a good dinner. Resources are sometimes divided into three types: natural resources, social resources, and human resources.

THREE KINDS OF RESOURCES

Natural resources are the materials and forces with which nature surrounds man. The sun, wind, rain, and humidity make up the climate—all are part of the wealth which nature holds. They represent forces and materials which affect the earth and man. If man can use them to his advantage, they become resources.

The cave man ate his food as he found it. He had few resources.

There are natural materials which are earth bound. The soil, the minerals—like iron, coal, and oil—these, too, become natural resources as we learn to use them. And then there is the plant and animal life which nature makes possible. Our food, clothing, and many other needs depend upon these gifts of nature.

These materials and forces form the basis of our very existence. Without them there would be no life. Through ignorant use we can destroy those things which can become resources. Through intelligent use we can make them provide more of those materials we need for modern social life.

The iron ore for the tools and nails, the lumber, and the chemicals used in the boat in our example are natural resources. So are the fuel for cooking and the vegetables and meats which go into our dinner.

Atlanta's Resource Base

The materials for food, shelter, and clothing come largely from the land. They are natural resources and are closely related to geography and its importance to city life.

Natural resources do not benefit us until we can use them. Materials for the boat are useful only if they are at hand and we know how to use them.

Primitive man had to depend very much on his natural resources. He hunted fruits and animals and ate them as he found them growing wild. He wore animal skins for clothing and slept in trees or caves. However, as he discovered ways of making living better and easier he taught them to his children. He learned that several men or families working together could do things they could not do alone. One man could never lift heavy building stones into position. A large group of men can, together, build great houses which one man could never possibly build alone. In this way man has learned the resource of *organization*—the sharing and cooperative use of knowledge, skills, and strength.

The ways of organizing people to work and live together are *social resources*. If man had never developed the plan of living and working in groups, he could never have made such progress. Men could not have exchanged ideas and inventions and put them together in new and different ways. Our family, school, community, and business groups are examples of how people organize to cooperate in meeting common wants. The skills and knowledge of the group are passed along from generation to generation. The modern world has accumulated a vast store of such social resources. Without them we would still be living as history tells us that primitive man lived.

Therefore, we use some social resources in building a boat or in cooking dinner. These include the knowledge and skills we have learned from other people. Perhaps we learned by watching them work, or we may have read about how it was done. A great deal of social organization went into inventing and making the tools, blueprints, or cookbooks we use. The materials of which they are made are

Whenever people organize to work together they increase their social resources.

natural resources. But the ways people work together and use ideas in developing and using these things are social resources.

Human resources are people themselves. You and your two hands are the human resources used in our examples. The quality of your human resources depends on your intelligence, strength, health, and your willingness to work. If you have someone to help you, your human resources are doubled.

Human resources are, of course, the most important resource. Things have no value unless man wants and needs them. Neither are there any resources used unless man does the planning and work of putting them to use.

Human resources, then, are of first importance. Man's intelligence allows him to learn how to use nature's resources. But this intelligence must be developed to its highest degree if man is to use his resources wisely. The health of people also has much to do with the vim with which they go about their work. A sick person is a poor human resource. He must be cared for and does no useful work.

Atlanta's Resource Base

The use of all resources depends on our people. A population which is intelligent, well educated, healthy, and happy is the kind of human resource we desire. If you are not healthy, the chances are the boat you make or dinner you cook will be poorly done. The same may be said if you are not interested in doing a good job or if you never bothered to learn the best way of doing it.

USING RESOURCES IN LIVING

It took thousands of years for today's ways of doing things to develop. Primitive man would think our boat or modern dinner wondrous things. Our tools and stoves would be like magic to him. And they *are* wonderful compared to his method of gathering and eating food or of floating on a log. Anthropologists believe that we are perhaps no stronger and have no more native intelligence than primitive people. But through our social resources we have become able to make more and wiser use of our resources. Through knowledge, skills, and organization, we now gather materials from all over the world.

Many resources are used in putting the goods into this store.
The cave man had no such convenience.

Building Atlanta's Future

We now get many things by the simple act of going to a store and buying them. We seldom realize how many social resources go into putting a loaf of bread on a grocer's shelf.

It took thousands of years for men to invent steam engines, airplanes, telephones, radios, and electric power. We have had, also, to learn how to work together in using these devices. Each new invention must be used so as to contribute smoothly to the operation of the others.

Everyone is concerned with the process of living. We must change the raw materials and the forces of nature into food, clothing, and shelter. All of the needs and wants of men are met by using our resources. Of course, today we want more than just enough food, clothing, and shelter. Our wants include recreation, art, music, books, and

Our wants include recreation as well as food, shelter, and clothing.

many other things. We must do more useful work and use more resources in order to have these things. As we learn to use them better we will have more leisure time to enjoy luxuries.

Cities are examples of what man can build by using his natural and social resources. They are "super" social resources. In them large groups of people—human resources—are gathered together. By gathering together, they can work in closely organized groups. A city is thus a central point in the network of social resources and human resources.

Atlanta, for instance, is headquarters for many organizations which serve and direct people in their work with natural resources. Transportation companies, banks, factories, wholesale stores, and the like are organized groups—social resources. They make it possible for natural resources to be changed into things people use. They are also a means for distributing these things to the people who use them in living.

WHAT ARE ATLANTA'S RESOURCES?

What can you find in Atlanta which will give you the things you want in life? This will be a very important question when you start to make a living. Remember that all the things you will own and use come from resources. How well we use our resources determines how many of the things that people want will be available. Some people in Atlanta do not have enough of the things they need. We say they make a poor living. Do we have the resources to allow all the people to live better?

Cotton becomes a more useful resource as it is picked, ginned, woven, and made into clothing.

Building Atlanta's Future

Atlanta's resources are those things which our people use in living. A city contains few natural resources. Farm land, iron, coal, oil, forests, rivers, and other producers of raw materials are found outside the city. However, these things are not really resources until man uses them.

Land—the soil—is a resource to the farmer in raising cotton. The cotton is a resource developed from the earth. Cotton is useful only when it is made into things like a mattress to sleep on or a dress to wear. The farmer cannot use the raw cotton in living. It must go through the social resources of manufacturing before it is changed into useful things. Then it becomes a resource for the merchant. He sells it to someone to whom it is a resource for use in living. It then serves its purpose by supplying the needs of life and comfort.

A city like Atlanta is a great network of human and social resources. These work together to put the natural resources—materials and forces of nature—into form which man can use for life, comfort, and enjoyment.

We cannot divide the kinds of resources in actual practice. Soil, minerals, and forests will not produce food, clothing, and shelter by themselves. Man must cultivate, change, and adapt their products to his needs. To do this he must develop inventions, knowledge, and skills. Then he must work with organized groups to keep resources moving along the production line from nature to the people who use them.

Neither natural, social, nor human resources can supply man's needs alone. All must come together in the right way if we are to live as we desire.

WHAT IS CONSERVATION?

There has been much interest in *conservation* of our natural resources during recent years. Conservation means more than "saving" our resources. They would not be resources if we did not need and use them. Conservation means making the *best possible use* of resources. We should use our land but conserve it by growing the kind of crops best

Atlanta's Resource Base

suited to each field. We should use soil building practices which restore the fertility as fast as it is used. By wise use of the soil we can grow greater and better crops without harming its fertility.

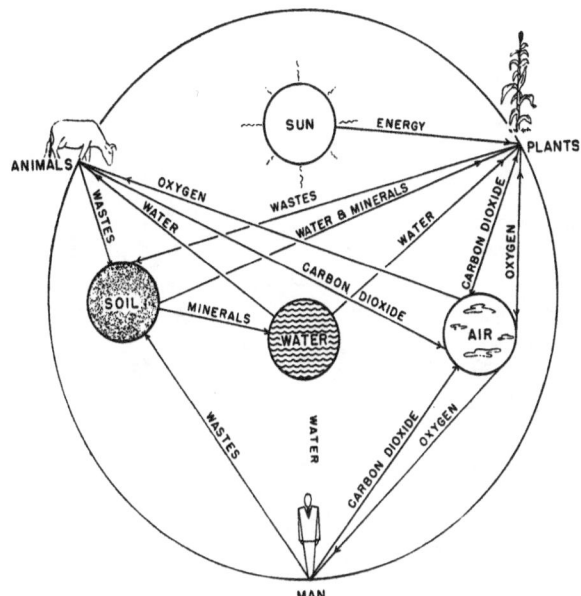

Man can use nature for his benefit, or he can disrupt nature's forces to his sorrow.

Soil is thus a *renewable* resource. We can use it over and over. But we cannot keep taking out without putting something back. Nature provides that plants and animals take food from the soil. But nature balances this taking out by returning materials when the organism dies. Dead leaves and stems fall back onto the soil. Animal bodies "return to dust." This process is vital to nature's soil-building action.

When man reaps his crop and hauls it away, he breaks up nature's balance. If he keeps doing this, he finally robs the soil of its life-giving fertility. If he is to keep getting good crops, he must *renew* the soil by returning the elements he takes out. He does this with soil-building crops and fertilizer. In this way he restores nature's balance—or even improves on it.

Our forests, wildlife, and water power are also renewable resources. Nature replenishes them so long as man does not interfere.

Forests grow up again after being cut and burned. But the kind of trees we want may not grow unless we plant them and protect them from being crowded out by less desirable kinds. Man must work *with* nature instead of *against* nature if he is to get the best results.

Our mineral resources, such as iron, coal, oil, copper, and aluminum are *nonrenewable resources*. Once coal is burned it is gone forever as a source of heat. Metals may be remelted and used again and again, but when the ore vein is exhausted, the mine is useless. These things will not "grow again" as will plants and animals.

Conservation of our mineral resources does not mean that we must stop using them. It does mean that we must improve our way of mining

Atlanta's Resource Base

and extracting them and prevent waste. We must use substitutes whenever we can and reclaim scrap metals to use again. By study and experiment we can discover new ways of conserving our supply of nonrenewable resources so that they last on and on.

For instance, industry must have power to turn all the machines in the factories. That power has long been supplied by coal which produces steam for steam engines. Oil is also a source of power for automobile, airplane, and factory. Both coal and oil are nonrenewable. Scientists say that the known sources of oil and coal will last the world only a few generations at our present rate of use.

However, science and technology have given us inventions—improved engines which get more power from the same amount of fuel. Then, too, we have learned to dam the streams which nature provides. This gives us a source of great power from falling water. We can convert it into electricity and send it for hundreds of miles over wires. This *hydroelectric* power may run machines in factories, light our homes, cool us in summer, and warm us in winter, as well as cook our food and

We have often wasted our natural resources.

supply many other uses. Water is renewable. Rain keeps the reservoirs filled. The dams and power lines are expensive at first, but their hydroelectric power is cheap in the long run.

These are only a few of the ways we can apply social resources—science and technology—to making the world a better place to live. Scientists tell us that we will soon develop atomic energy as a source of power. We will have a great chance to develop new social resources with which to use this new power resource for meeting man's needs. Many people will be slow to realize how we can put these resources to their best use—just as people today are slow to see how conservation of resources can lead to better living. They will be of no benefit except to

Coal, oil, and forests must be used—but used wisely.

Building Atlanta's Future

serve man. It is up to you to see that they do serve man in the "best possible way."

RESOURCES IN EVERYDAY LIVING

As you walk about your city you can see much evidence of waste and poor use of resources. Black smoke pouring from a factory or locomotive smokestack means that coal is being poorly burned. Millions of years were required for the coal to be formed in the earth. In a few minutes its usefulness is spent in the furnace. This heavy black smoke contains useful gases which are not being used at all. They are being wasted and are also making soot and odors in the city. Can we find new ways to use coal more efficiently?

Look about you at the throngs of automobiles, trucks, and buses on the streets and highways. Think how much gasoline and oil they use in a day—in a year. These oil products were eons in the making. Gasoline wasted while engines run impatiently in a traffic jam serves no good at all. That much of nature's store of energy has been wasted. It cannot be renewed. Can we make a street and traffic system which will help prevent this waste? Can we invent engines which will run a car more miles on a gallon of gasoline? These are questions facing our scientists and citizens today.

Think of all the materials and work that went into making the buildings and streets of Atlanta. Where did all this lumber, steel, stone, cement, and labor come from? How much was wasted in the process? Have we made provision to see that we can get more of them as we need new buildings? Where is our future timber supply and are we making sure that it is being renewed?

A building represents materials from many places. We cannot build one unless we have these materials. Men and machines must depend on each other in gathering the materials and making them into the building. Organized work by men is as important as are the materials. The food which the workers eat is also a vital part.

Black smoke is a nuisance and a waste of coal by-products.

Our city would be quite helpless—indeed, would never have grown up—without materials, people, and information from other places. Our interest in resources must include all these places. Since we get tin from Bolivia in South America and iron from Minnesota by way of Pennsylvania, we must be interested in the welfare of people there. If they waste their resources it is harmful to us. Our supply depends on them.

We must use coal, oil, and electricity to produce power to run our city's factories. City people must ride to and from work. Goods must be transported. Our living depends on it just as we depend on farmers for food. We do not want to "save" our resources but to use them well and wisely.

The way our government and other organizations affect our use of resources is very important. Natural resources can be long-lived and may be used by many generations of people in the future. Public and

Building Atlanta's Future

governmental policies, attitudes, and laws also exist past any person's lifetime.

We can best assure good use of resources if we set up proper laws and organizations to look after them. We, as voters, tell our government what we want done. City people do not work directly with all kinds of resources. But their votes and their knowledge will have a great deal to do with the way resources are used. It is up to city people to see this and to work for the best use of all resources for the good of all people.

ATLANTA AND OUR REGION'S RESOURCES

Atlanta is a regional center of the Southeast. The resources of the Southeast are Atlanta's resources, and Atlanta people must see that they are used wisely. How well are we using these resources? Are we wasting any of them?

First, the human resources. Atlanta has a population of 339,000; Georgia has 3,200,000; the Southeast, 28,600,000. We have excellent human resources. However, many of our people are often far behind other regions in health, education, and income. Their skills and intelligence are being wasted because they do not have a chance to use and develop them. Why is this true? Is it because we do not have enough natural resources?

No, the Southeast has an abundant supply of nature's gifts. We have good soil, many minerals, and rivers for hydroelectric power. The problem is to use them to produce the things we need for better living. That means we must use better social resources in putting our natural and human resources to their best use. Again, it is not enough to furnish food, clothing, and shelter. To be sure, we should have enough of these for everyone. Many people do not have enough. But we must have more than barely enough.

The wants of Atlanta people include also such things as better schools, colleges, churches, hospitals, libraries, music, art, and govern-

Through their votes citizens in a democracy plan for wise use of all our resources.

ment. These are social resources which help people achieve a better life. But they cost money. If we are to have them in abundance, we must use our resources so that we produce more wealth than is required for a bare living for all the people. We have the resources. We must learn to use them and learn how to get everyone to put into practice the ways of wisest resource use.

Using our resources wisely concerns not only farmers who till the soil, nor miners who dig the ore, nor lumberjacks who cut the trees. The people in Atlanta and in all cities are concerned too. Many people live in cities. Their votes help decide which laws are passed that affect resources. Their attitudes do much to shape public opinion as to what is best in the long run. If Atlanta, Georgia, and the Southeast are to profit from the results, city people must know all the facts. They must

Building Atlanta's Future

realize that since city and country depend on each other, neither can progress alone. A bird's-eye view shows many things which are hidden from a worm's-eye angle.

DISCUSSION QUESTIONS

1. What are resources? Give examples of using each kind of resource.
2. What kind of resource is found mostly in cities? What kind is not usually found in cities?
3. What is the real meaning of "conservation of resources"? Give examples.
4. What is the difference between conservation of renewable and nonrenewable resources?
5. What resources were used in producing the food you ate for breakfast and in getting it on the table?
6. Where do most of the natural resources used by Atlanta people come from?

HAVE YOU READ?

1. Citizens' Fact-Finding Movement of Georgia. *Georgia Facts in Figures, A Source Book.* "Natural Resources," "Human Resources." Athens, Georgia: The University of Georgia Press, 1946.
2. *Georgia's Human Resources.* Report of the Georgia Citizens Council. Atlanta, Georgia: Georgia Citizens Council, 1946.
3. *Georgia on the March.* Industrial Department, Georgia Power Company. Atlanta, Georgia: Georgia Power Company.

Part Two

CITIES SERVE PEOPLE

5. Atlanta's People

IT is Saturday. The football teams from Georgia Tech and the University of Georgia are to play today at Grant Field. You are trying to walk from the Henry Grady Hotel to the Piedmont Hotel.

Look at the people! The streets are almost overflowing with cars; the buses are crowded. The sidewalks seem to be a solid flow of men and women, boys and girls. You and your classmate are selling "colors" for the two teams.

It's only ten o'clock in the morning; the game doesn't start until two. But already Atlanta is swamped with people; more people than can find places to eat, walk, or even stand. All of a sudden they seem to have descended from nowhere. Almost mob-like they mill to and fro, some shouting, some singing, all excitedly waiting for the big game.

Here we have the bright pageant of holiday. Atlanta's normal population is greatly swelled by visitors from neighboring communities and rural areas. Our streets and buses, our sidewalks, our cafes, and

Building Atlanta's Future

hotels just cannot absorb this rush of humanity. We have more people than we have room for or resources to serve.

You are seeing in one mad rush a process that is always going on in a city. People, space, and the living facilities needed are always changing to adjust to one another. In normal times, this process may go so smoothly that we hardly notice it. Even so, there are always large numbers of people coming to Atlanta to live, visit, or trade. Likewise there are large numbers leaving our city.

We have already learned that every city has three major resources: human, natural, and social. The city is a super social resource. Its job is to furnish space and facilities for people to live and work together. At any given time a city can provide a comfortable living for a certain number of people with certain kinds of skills and health conditions. Today, with the football game in Atlanta, we are seeing the spectacle of a city almost choked with a flood of people.

It is important for us to know all we can about the people of Atlanta. We can imagine a steady inflow and outflow of population. But how does this stream of people affect the ability of Atlanta to give opportunities for work, recreation, education, and other services which we need? To get the answer we must take a closer look at our people, where they come from, how old are they, and many other such questions.

PEOPLE USE RESOURCES

For the moment let us suppose that we are in a land of make-believe. We live in a dream community cut off from the rest of the world by a great wall. Everyone is very wise and no one is at all selfish. In this wonderful country there is enough land, minerals, trees, and animals to meet all our needs. If we put ourselves to work, we could build all the houses, raise all the food, make all the clothes, and have all the nice things of life that we want.

Of course this would require that all the people have the right knowledge and skills for this work. They would have to know and do exactly the right things all the time. Everyone would do his part; there would be no shirking. If that were true, the only thing that the people would have to do in order to enjoy a healthy, happy life would be to use their time for productive work. No one would have ugly, unhealthy houses. Everyone would have the right kind of clothes to wear.

The kind of community in our dream world would thus depend on what we did with our natural and social resources. We, the people, would have to have the desire, the skill, and the health to use the resources around us. First we must *want* the good things of life. Then we must *know how* to get or make them. Otherwise we would not be any better off for having so many resources. The whole thing depends on the people themselves.

Many writers have described such ideal places. Some "Utopias," as they are called, have been tried out. They failed to work because the people, the human elements, can hardly be so perfect. Also no one community can have *all* the resources to produce the many things we

want today. We must depend on others for some of them. But our dream world may help us understand some points about our real environment. Atlanta and the Southeast are in a nearly ideal situation in many ways. We have a great many natural and social resources as well as human resources. We can improve our city and our region by first improving the desire, the skill, and the health of the people toward using their resources wisely.

KINDS OF PEOPLE

What do we mean by "kinds of people"? We can class them in several ways. We know that there are old people, middle-aged people, young adults, and children. The size of each of these age groups in a community is important.

Children and very old people do little work. If there are many very old or very young people, the community will differ from one that has many middle-aged people. There will be more schools for the young. Hospitals and recreation places will be made to suit the elderly group.

Young adults and middle-aged people are the productive groups. They do most of the work. Their likes and dislikes differ from those of the younger and older age groups. Compare a quiet resort city for retired elderly people with a hustling factory city. The two are quite different.

Some places have more men than women; others have more women than men. In mining towns there are many men to do the heavy work of mining. In trade and business centers or in textile mill towns, there may be more girls and women working in offices and doing light fancywork. Recreation and shopping centers will be made to fit men's or women's tastes, as the case may be.

We also know that in most communities there are people with different physical appearance. They differ in height, weight, facial expression, kind of hair, color, and in many ways. Look around at your

Office work employs many women workers.

friends. You can see examples of blonde and brunette, tall and short, and many in-betweens. These are differences which we do not often notice.

The two major physically different groups in Atlanta, and in the South in general, are the white and Negro. We have built a great many of our customs around this difference. Whites and Negroes live in different neighborhoods, attend different schools, work at different jobs. These customs mean that we have separate facilities for the two groups. As the size of each group changes, the city changes to adjust to them. About one-third of our population is Negro, two-thirds white. There are also a few Indians and Oriental people but not many.

Later in this book, we will discuss the kinds of people as to the

Building Atlanta's Future

work they do, how much education they have had, their income, and other factors. These are called the "social elements" in the kind of population a community has.

HOW POPULATION CHANGES

So far we have mentioned age, sex, and race. These are important elements in the study of the human resources of a community. Let us look at three other important elements. These have to do with what are called "dynamic forces" in population change. "Dynamic" means active—moving or changing. Dynamic forces, then, are those forces which make our population change. They may make it grow larger or smaller. Or they may make the kinds of social groups change.

What are these dynamic forces? How do they make population change? One of these forces you can see everyday—the new babies. One way in which population grows is through the birth rate. If no babies were born in a community, the people would keep getting older

New Atlanta Citizens.

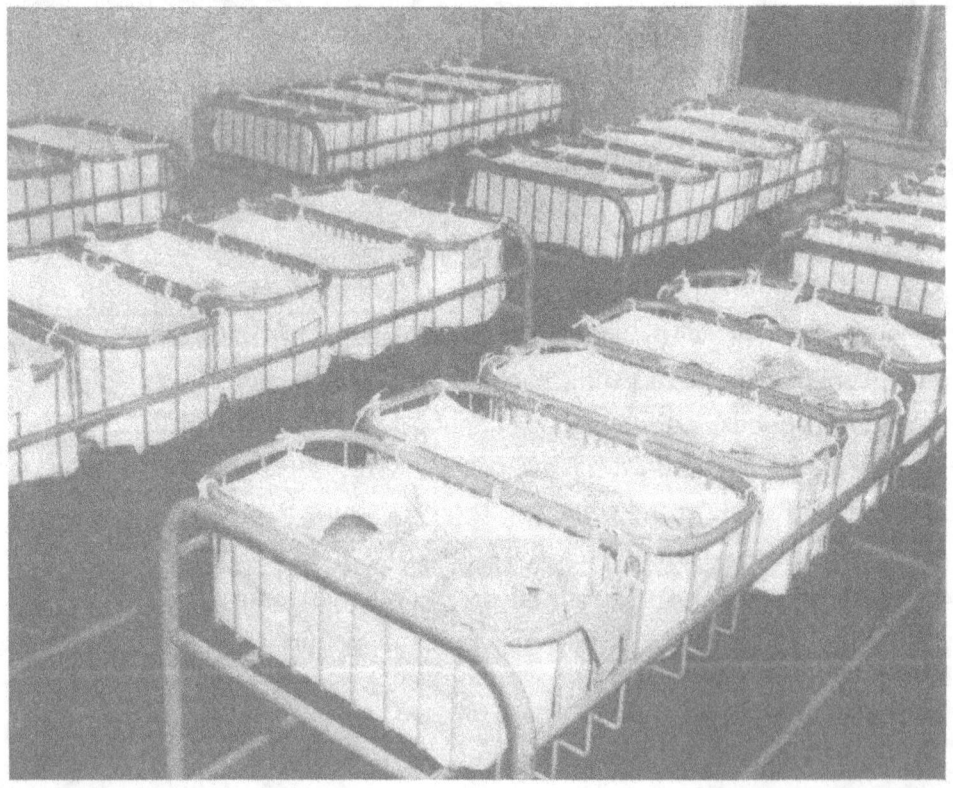

Atlanta's People

all the time and no young ones would be growing up to take their places. Soon there would be only old people in the community. When they died there would be no community left unless new families moved in.

Births and deaths in a population are usually expressed as birth rates and death rates. Just as the rate of speed of a car or airplane is expressed in miles per hour, so births and deaths are expressed as number per 1000 people. The most common use is the "crude" birth and death rates. It is given as the number of babies born each year for each 1000 population. If the population of a town is exactly 1000 and there is an average of 20 babies born each year, the birth rate is 20. For a town of 2000 population there would have to be 40 babies born each year for the birth rate to be 20. In a city of about 300,000 such as Atlanta, there would have to be 6,000 (300 times 20) births a year to give the same birth rate. Of course these figures should be averages for several years. There may be a few more or less in any one year.

One great population problem is that families with lowest incomes often have the most children. High income groups who can afford to support many dependents quite often have the fewest to support. This is true of most places in the United States. Many of our problems of poverty and health are caused by this upside-down situation. It means that the groups containing the largest number of children have less money to spend. The children have less opportunity for good education. They do not get the best of food and medical care which would assure good health. Many of our future citizens are not getting a good start in life. Is this good for the future of a city?

The death rate is expressed just as births are. The number of people who die in a year per 1000 population is the death rate. In an ideal community the births could be expected to replace the deaths each year. There would be enough babies to take the places of the people who had finished living. However this seldom happens in cities. Atlanta is one of the few large cities with a birth rate higher than the death rate.

People move into and out of our city.

The birth rate in Atlanta from year to year is usually about 18 per 1000. The death rate has not been higher than 14 for several years —some years it has been as low as 9 per 1000. Thus more people are coming into our city by births than leave by deaths. Our population is growing from these causes. But is that the only way it grows? It would be if people could not get in and out of the city. We know the small increase caused by excess births over deaths does not account for the rapid growth of Atlanta and other cities.

MIGRATION

Most of our large cities have low birth rates and high death rates. Their population would grow smaller and smaller and finally dwindle away if births were the only source of people. But many cities grow very fast. That brings us to the third dynamic force of population change. It is called *migration*.

Atlanta's People

To migrate means to move residence from one place to another. People who come to a city just for a football game are not migrants. They may leave again the same day and are only visitors. Our nation got its early settlers through migration of people from Europe to America. Where once were a few Indians, there now are many kinds of people. Those migrants caused a *gain* in population in America.

In the same way, people migrate from rural areas to cities. Remember that in Chapter 2 we said that large families are more often found in the country than in the city. Some of the children from these large families are the young people who migrate to the cities to live and find work. Tractors and other farm machinery allow one farmer to raise as large a crop as several farmers raised by hand. The surplus farm population thus goes elsewhere to find work. The high birth rate in rural areas is one factor which makes it necessary for people to keep moving from the country to the cities.

People also move from city to city. American cities are constantly changing because all the time some people are moving out and others are moving in. This migration makes the age, sex, and racial groups in a city change from year to year. Usually it is a slow change, but such forces as war, depression, or gold rush may cause rapid change.

We may compare a city with a water barrel. The water in the barrel represents the population. The water level rises and falls as more water runs in or out. In a city, births and in-migration increase the number of people; deaths and out-migration lower the number of people. Whether inflow or outflow is the larger will determine whether the water, or the population, will increase or dwindle.

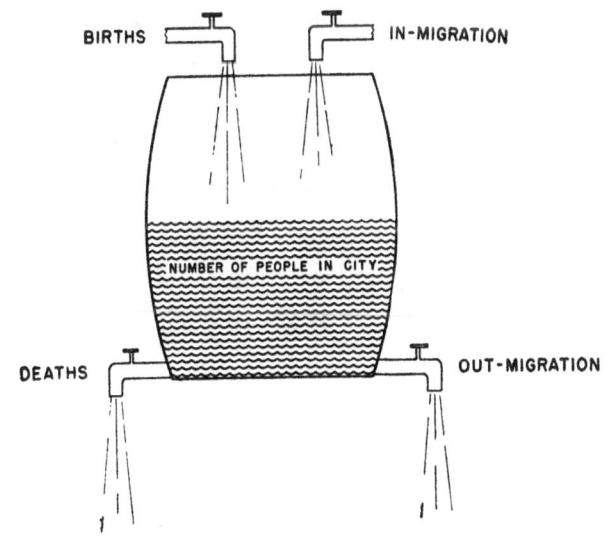

The water rises or falls in the barrel, depending on whether in-flow or out-flow is greater. Population also increases or decreases through in-flow and out-flow.

WHAT IS A CENSUS?

The way we find out about population is through the "census" and "vital statistics." Vital statistics are records kept of each birth, death, marriage, and divorce. A census is a complete population count. The United States government takes a complete census every ten years. The last one before this book was published was made in 1940. Less accurate "estimates" are made more often by counting a small sample of the people. Perhaps you have never seen the census taker come to your house. But they do go to all the houses and get the information needed to count all the people in the United States. They ask several questions about each family in order to find out the things the government wants to know about our population.

Atlanta's People

The results of this grand count of the people in the United States are published in books which may be found in most libraries. They contain tables showing the number of people, their age, sex, and race groups, the work they do, and many such things. We can use census figures to find out how large each kind of group is in Atlanta, in Georgia, and in the United States. What do they tell us about Atlanta's population?

We have said that the kind of population a city has is reflected in the kind of city it is. Age, sex, and race groups are important elements of the population. Census figures tell us how much of Atlanta's population falls into each of these groups.

How does Atlanta compare with other places as to the per cent of the people who are of working age? By the 1940 census, 64 out of every 100 people in metropolitan Atlanta are between the ages of 20 and 65. Only about 54 out of 100 people in Georgia as a whole are between these ages. This is caused in part by the migration of young adults to Atlanta to work. The very young and very old do not migrate so readily.

People between the ages of 20 and 65 are looked upon as our "working group." Under normal conditions, they can be expected to support themselves and their dependents. Thus Atlanta has a greater proportion of population in the "working group" than Georgia as a whole.

This fact also means that a person between the ages of 20 and 65 in Atlanta probably has a smaller number of dependents than in most other areas in Georgia. This is important. Atlanta workers are not

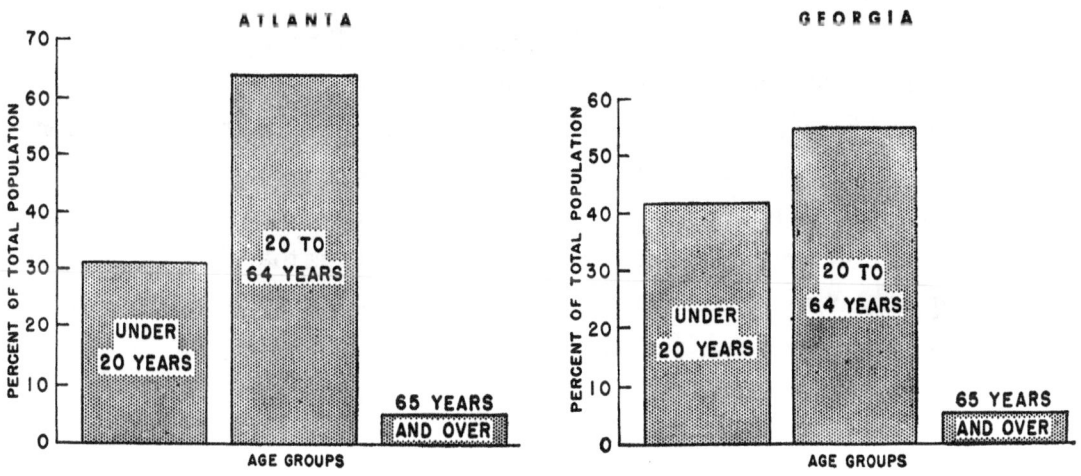

Building Atlanta's Future

supporting as many people who are too old or too young to work. They have more money to spend on the extra things they want, recreation and luxuries, than if they had many dependents.

As Atlanta becomes an older city, however, the proportion of older people will probably increase. The large group of workers grow older, on the average, each year. They retire from work as they reach old age. There must be a constant flow of young people into Atlanta from other places if the size of the working group is to be kept as it is. We may then continue to have a favorable balance between workers and dependent groups. In looking toward the future, we must keep in mind this need for young workers from farms and villages.

Ratio of Men to Women in Metropolitan Atlanta

Ratio of Men to Women in the State of Georgia

MEN AND WOMEN WORKERS

How about the ratio of men to women in Atlanta? Do we have more males or more females? Census figures tell us that we have more females. Metropolitan Atlanta has about 89 males for every 100 females. For white this is given as 92 males to every 100 females, and for Negroes, about 82 males per 100 females. For Georgia as a whole, there are 96 males per 100 females. While this does not seem to be a great difference from these small figures, it means that there are about 25,000 more females than males in metropolitan Atlanta. How does this affect the city? How can we explain it?

Atlanta's People

In discussing the mining towns, we said that women were not attracted by such work as mining. They are not attracted by the work of farming to as great a degree as are men. Therefore many women leave rural areas and small towns and go to larger cities. Since Atlanta is one of the largest cities in the Southeast, women come from a large surrounding area to find work in the offices, stores, and mills. This kind of work is pleasing to women and they do it as well or better than men. Thus the jobs available in Atlanta are a cause for there being more women than men here.

The ratio of males to females also affects the proportion who are married and the birth rate. If males are scarce, there will be fewer marriages. There will be, therefore, more unmarried females who may seek jobs. Under present employment patterns in this country, women earn less income than men. The total income of a city may be affected by the ratio of males to females.

POPULATION PYRAMIDS

The "population pyramid" is a device for showing the age and sex composition of a group of people. Each "layer" in the following pyramid for Georgia people represents an age-group. The youngest group is at the bottom, the oldest at the top. Males are shown to the left of the center line, females to the right of the line. We can thus compare the size of any age group with any other; and also compare the number of each sex in a group and between groups.

In a normal population which is affected only by births and deaths, we can expect the youngest group to be the largest. Some of this group can be expected to die during each year. Thus as the group gets older, it becomes smaller through the death of its members. Each layer becomes shorter as it moves toward the top and represents an older group. The population of a primitive tribe with no migrants, therefore, would be represented by a pyramid shaped very much like the peaked pyramids of Egypt.

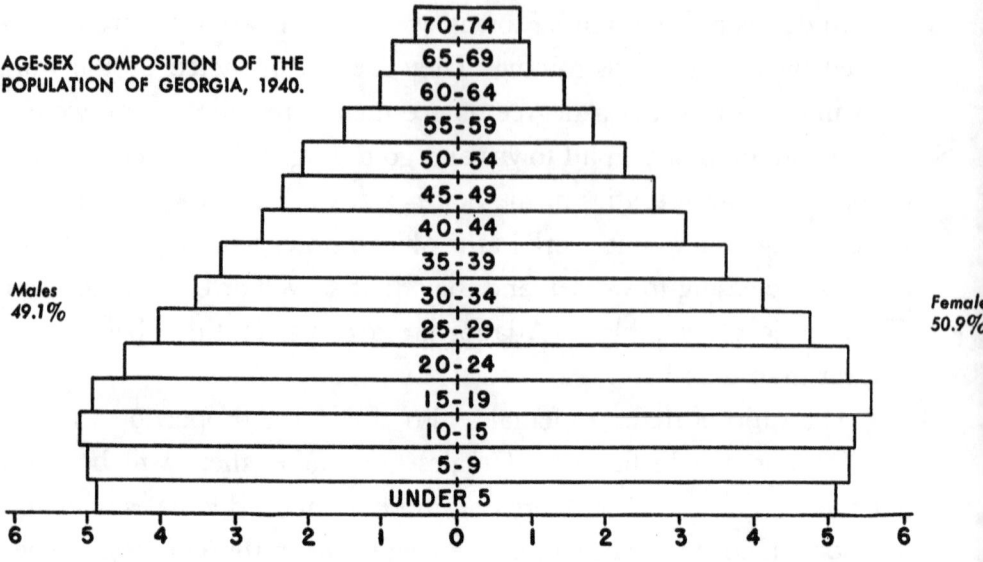

The population pyramid for Georgia is almost a perfect one. It is broad at the bottom and narrows almost to a point at the top. For the city of Atlanta, however, the pyramid is more irregular. It is small at the bottom and at the top, with a bulge in the middle. This shows that there are fewer children than there are middle-aged people. Why is this? You will remember that the birth rate in cities is lower than in

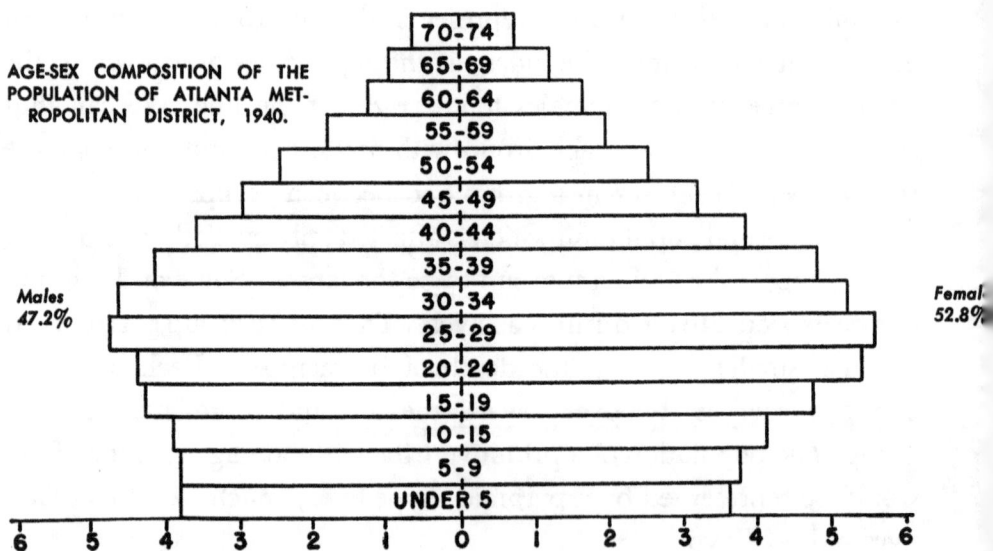

Atlanta's People

rural areas. The low birth rate accounts for the few children. Remember also that many young adults move to the city to find jobs.

The young adults who move to Atlanta are the cause of the bulge in the 20 to 40 year ge groups. Notice also that the bulge in the middle

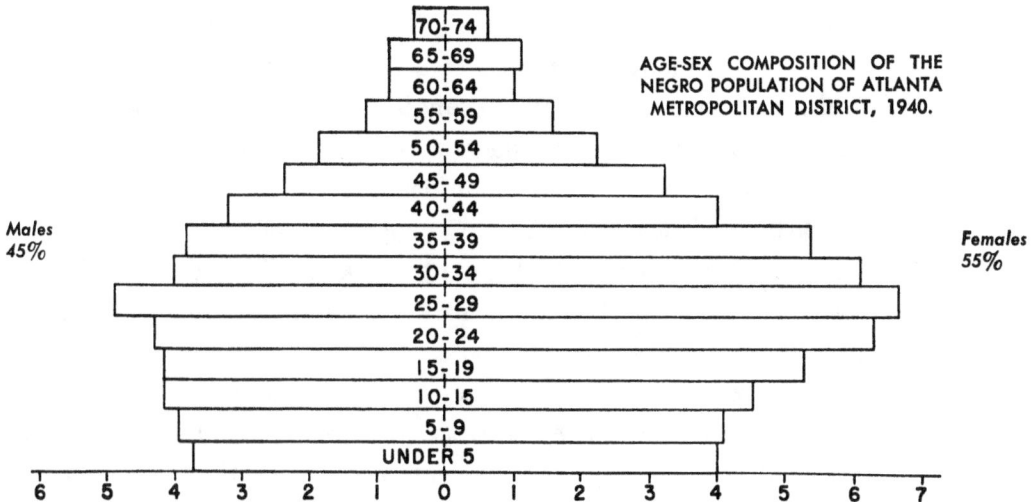

group is larger for females than for males. This represents the large number of females who come to Atlanta because they are attracted by the kinds of jobs in cities but not by farming and other rural jobs. If you study it closely you may find that the pyramid illustrates many facts of population composition.

Another important aspect of Atlanta's population is its racial composition. According to custom, Negroes, in the southern states especially, work at jobs that do not generally pay the highest wages. This means that the Negro one-third of our population does not have the opportunity to contribute one-third to the total income in Atlanta.

In looking toward the future of Atlanta, we must think of the educational, health, welfare, and general security of the whole population. The needs of both races must be considered and each encouraged to make the fullest contribution.

Building Atlanta's Future

Now let us look at the "dynamic factors" in population change: birth, death, and migration. Atlanta's population is constantly changing because of the relationship among these three factors. Figures for the first two are on a county basis for Fulton and DeKalb.

In both these counties the birth rate exceeds the death rate. Fulton County shows a birth rate of 20 to a death rate of 12 persons per 1000 population. DeKalb County shows a birth rate of 16 to a death rate of 10 per 1000 population. This may be because DeKalb County has more rural area than Fulton. Without any in- or out-migration of population, we could say that metropolitan Atlanta's population is increasing because there are more births than deaths.

Births and deaths operate to change the population of Atlanta. While people are moving to Atlanta to work and live, other people are moving away from Atlanta. This "out" and "in" migration also operates to change the population of the city.

A large number of people between the ages of 20 and 35 have moved into Atlanta to live and work. It is this group of young adults, both white and Negro, which seems to account for the large increase in the city's population in the last two decades. The excess of births over deaths is not great enough to cause nearly so much increase.

We found from the population pyramid that there were more females than males in Atlanta's population. This difference shows up most in the 15 to 40-year-old group. It may be explained by the fact that a larger number of women than men are coming into Atlanta looking for jobs. It may also be true that a larger number of men than women are leaving the city to look for jobs elsewhere.

The Negro migration pattern seems to show the greatest "in" migration in the 25–29 age group as shown in the pyramid for Negroes.

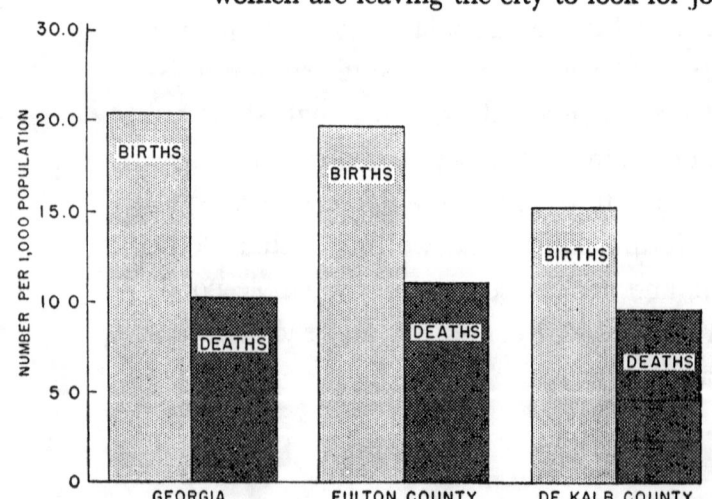

BIRTH AND DEATH RATES, 1940.

The ratio of females to males increases through the age groups from 15 to 34 years.

These migration figures mean a great deal in planning the future of Atlanta. They show that the great population increase for the city will come from in-migration of young adults. Most of these migrants will not know too much about our city. Those of us who grow up to live in Atlanta must be responsible for assisting these people to see how our city can be made a better place to live and work. We must be leaders in such efforts.

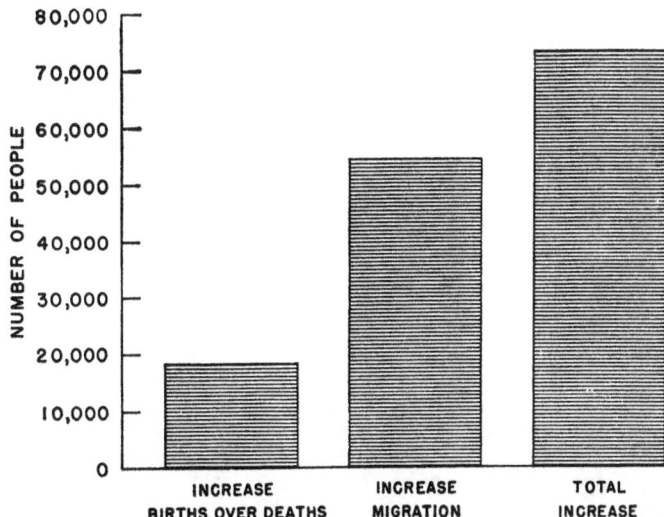

INCREASE OF ATLANTA'S POPULATION, 1930–1940.

A CITY FOR ALL THE PEOPLE

The different groups within our population and the dynamic factors of population change affect our plans for the future of our city. Trends in birth and death rates, in migration, and in racial and age groupings must be included in future plans. We must expect Atlanta to change in keeping with the changes in these factors. Plans should be made to keep the city in step with the nature of the people in it.

The plans must also include other forces which go along with those just mentioned. Social forces are closely related to dynamic forces. This means that migration depends in part on the social force or "pull" exerted by the jobs which are available in Atlanta. The right kind of job must be available to get a person to move to Atlanta. Then he must be able to find the right kind of a house to live in when he gets there. People look for community services, recreation, housing, neigh-

Young people migrate to Atlanta to find jobs.

borhood organizations, and the like before deciding to move into a city. These things also affect the family life in the birth and death rates, the sex ratio, and the customs of the people. The birth rate is more likely to increase in an environment which is good for children. The death rate may decrease if we have fine health programs.

Thus we find that the dynamic forces are in large part a result of the social nature of a city. If we want our population to grow we must make the city attractive to people in other places. We must plan for the development of business and industry which will provide jobs better than elsewhere. A pleasant environment also entices people to come to our city to live. Of course the *number* who come is not the only thing to consider. Good social environment also attracts people with higher skills and more education. It encourages and assists them to improve their level of living after they get here.

Atlanta's People

We can change our population trends by changing these factors which affect it. If we make our city a better place in which to live, people will want to live here. The quality of their living will improve. It is upon this quality of better living that a finer city can be developed.

DISCUSSION QUESTIONS

1. How do dynamic forces operate to make population change?
2. Why do young people, especially women, migrate from country to city?
3. What causes the bulge in the center of a population pyramid for a city?
4. What are some social forces which are behind population changes? Do inventions affect these social forces? Give examples.
5. Were your parents born in Atlanta? If not, where did they live before? Why did they move to Atlanta?
6. Do you know someone who has recently moved away from Atlanta? Why did they move?

HAVE YOU READ?

1. *A Report on Health and Welfare in DeKalb and Fulton Counties.* Part I, Chap. III, "Some of the Characteristics of the Population of the Atlanta Area." Atlanta, Georgia: Social Planning Council, 1943.
2. *Atlanta Centennial Year Book, 1837–1937.* "City Population Growing Rapidly." Atlanta, Georgia: Gregg Murphy, 1937.
3. Citizens' Fact-Finding Movement of Georgia. *Georgia Facts in Figures, A Source Book.* "Human Resources," "Health." Athens, Georgia: The University of Georgia Press, 1946.
4. Pierce, Joseph A. *The Atlanta Negro, A Collection of Data on the Negro Population of Atlanta, Georgia.* Atlanta, Georgia: American Youth Commission and The National Youth Administration of Georgia, 1940.
5. U. S. Bureau of the Census. *Current Population Reports, Population Characteristics.* "Population Characteristics of the Atlanta, Georgia Metropolitan District." Washington, D. C., 1947.

6. The Economy of Atlanta

AS you stand and look down on a large ant hill in the summer, you can see that something is making the ants scurry around at a great rate. Some of them may be dragging huge loads of food into their village. They go on and on hurrying to gather food—tirelessly, even almost frantically. A beehive in the spring exhibits similar activity. The energy these insects spend in making a living is very great compared to their size.

If you could look down upon Atlanta from the same position, the scene would be very like that of the ant hill. Cars, trucks, and trains scurry in and out. People hurry around. We even imitate the bee's advantage over the ant by taking to the air in airplanes. Everybody is interested in making a living, in making sure they have food and other things we want and need. A few centuries ago people actually stored up food and materials in their homes and villages to last through the winter just as insects do.

The Economy of Atlanta

In those days, if you worked for someone, he paid you with some useful article. You might get a bushel of potatoes, or a cowhide to be made into shoes, in return for your work. But suppose you already had potatoes and shoes. Then you could go hunt someone who needed these things and exchange them for—say a bag of wheat. If you couldn't find anyone who had wheat and was willing to trade it for potatoes or a hide, you were out of luck. This process of trading one product for another was known as "barter." It was often most inconvenient.

In order to make it easier to trade, people started using trinkets—beads, rings, pebbles, and other kinds of "receipts" for the value of goods and work. These were easier to carry around and could be used to represent many things. Of course they were not always worth the same amount to everybody, but from these things have come our system of using money.

WORK AND MONEY

Today almost all our trading is done through the use of money. How much we can buy for a dime or a dollar varies from one year to another. But one person's money can buy as much as another's. So we work and store up the money we get as pay. We know that we can exchange it for things we want. It can be used over and over and is convenient to handle. 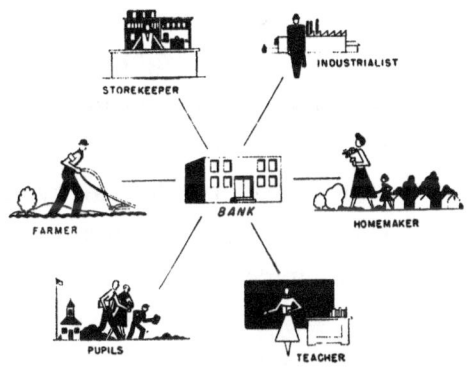 Imagine going to the store to buy new clothes with a bag of potatoes over your shoulder!

Instead of the actual articles, we think of our rewards for working in terms of money. But money is not useful itself. We cannot eat it, nor wear it, nor even enjoy looking at it. It is useful only because it can be exchanged for other things. It can be easily saved and kept. But the things which have the actual value are the things we can use in living.

Building Atlanta's Future

Food, shelter, and clothing are the first necessities of life. They are valuable because it takes work to obtain them.

Through your own work—the efforts of your hands and mind—you expect to make a living all your life. The money you receive for this work can be exchanged for the products of the work of other people. Thus everyone should do the things he likes to do and can do well. He produces more by concentrating on this one job. Yet he gets the benefit of other people's work through the system of money exchange.

Look at all the useful things in and around your home. Think of all the work that went into making them. It would take you a long time to make them for yourself—even for your whole family to make them. You would lose a great deal of time learning skills you might never need again. You would have trouble getting the right materials.

The furniture in your home, the food in the refrigerator and pantry, the house itself, and your clothing all represent the work of many people. Even the decorations, which are valuable only because you think they are pretty, are the results of someone's work—the putting of knowledge, skills, and materials together. People have made a living by combining natural and social resources to produce these useful products. How many of these articles in your home were made or sold in Atlanta? Do most of the people in Atlanta make their living producing such things?

GOODS AND SERVICES

The articles, things you can see and feel, which are used in living are called "goods." Many people in Atlanta have jobs in which they help produce goods ranging all the way from sausages to automobiles. We want many things in modern living. There is seemingly no limit to the kinds of goods we can use to make life more interesting and comfortable. But goods themselves do not serve all our wants and needs. How about the times when we get sick? The doctor does not produce anything in the way of goods. The people who work in stores

The people who sell and deliver our food perform useful services as well as those who actually produce it.

and sell us goods, the men who deliver our mail, and the teachers who help us gain knowledge do not actually produce any goods.

Our needs and wants, then, go beyond visible articles. Besides goods we need "services" of many kinds. How many of these services do you use and pay for in your home in daily living? You would need a long list to name them all.

We have seen how Atlanta performs services to the region as a collection, distribution, and transportation center. These are services of getting goods to people so that they can use them. A large part of Atlanta's workers make a living at this kind of job. The farmer and miner produce goods in the form of raw materials. City workers change these goods into more useful form in factories or work at distributing them to people who want to buy them. The bankers who serve by assisting with money exchange perform services that are just as valuable as other work.

All the jobs by which people make their living have to do with producing and distributing goods and services. No matter what kind

Building Atlanta's Future

of job you select as your life work, you must help produce goods or services that other people want or need. You should be careful to select a job that you like to do, that you can do well, and that will serve the needs of the most people. As a general rule you will be rewarded in terms of how well you produce, your skill at your job, and the usefulness of your work.

What are your chances of getting a good job in Atlanta? How much choice will you have in selecting one? These are things you should begin to think about now, even though you will not start to work for a few years yet.

WHAT ATLANTA WORKERS DO

Atlanta offers a wide variety of kinds of work. It has no one great industry as some cities have. Most people in Detroit, Michigan, for instance, work in the automobile industry. Most of the workers of Washington, D. C., are government workers; textile mills employ a majority of workers in many small southern cities. Atlanta contains several kinds of factories, large commercial distributors, packing and processing firms, government and business office headquarters, and numerous other kinds of employment. It is not a highly specialized city. However, some of these employ more people than others.

There are so many people and so many different kinds of jobs in Atlanta that it would be almost impossible to list the number employed in each. By grouping similar jobs together, however, we can show the percentage of workers in each. The following pictogram shows the percentage of the 228,288 workers in Atlanta over 14 years of age who were employed in each type of job in 1947. The largest group is clerical, sales, and kindred workers—those in "non-manufacturing" work. (Kindred means similar or related.) This group is large, of course, because there are so many stores, headquarters, and offices in Atlanta. Atlanta is a center for retail shopping and people come from great distances to buy in the city. The services given by the clerical and sales workers are important to people all over the region and nation. This

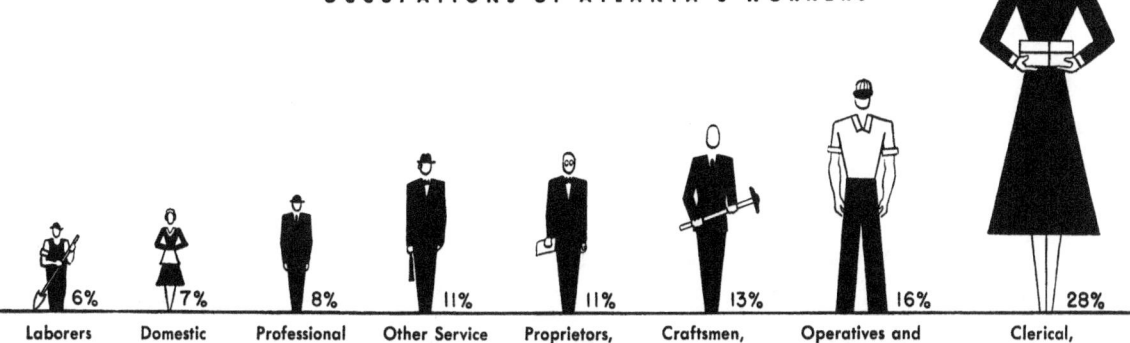

OCCUPATIONS OF ATLANTA'S WORKERS

6%	7%	8%	11%	11%	13%	16%	28%
Laborers	Domestic Service	Professional and Semi-professional	Other Service Workers	Proprietors, Managers, and Officials	Craftsmen, Foremen, etc.	Operatives and Kindred Workers	Clerical, Sales, and Kindred

group works in the businesses which are uppermost in making Atlanta a regional center. They do not work with their hands making objects from natural resources. Rather they represent the "social resources" for getting goods and services to people—the distribution work.

The next largest groups of workers are those who do manual work —work with their hands and machines at building and making things. They make up both the "craftsmen, foremen, and kindred" and the "operatives and kindred" worker's groups. These "manufacturing" jobs represent great variations among types of work. Among them we find carpenters, mechanics, jewelers, motormen, operators of machines in factories, and many other highly skilled jobs. For the most part, these workers change natural resources into finished products which we can use. They work with raw materials to produce finished "goods."

The other groups, while smaller, are none the less important. The professional and semi-professional group includes doctors, lawyers, teachers, engineers, actors, radio announcers, and others. Their professional services are used by everyone at times. The same may be said of the managerial group. Without them, the economic system would become a madhouse in which everyone pulled against each other. Managers are somewhat like the captains, coaches, and officials in a ball game. They train, organize, and direct the members of the work teams which produce the goods and services we demand.

In Atlanta we see that the largest number of workers have jobs producing services. There are more clerks, salesmen and salesladies,

Building Atlanta's Future

and stenographers than any other type of worker. Atlanta as a regional center and headquarters city produces more value in services than in goods. Thus the chances are that if you were looking for a job, you would find more of this kind than any other.

However, there are also large numbers of people in other kinds of work. You may happen to have special skills in one of the jobs in a smaller group. If so, you might have a better chance of finding a good job in one of them. The number of jobs available is only one factor in choosing your vocation. You must think of your chances of success, your happiness in your work, and your skills and talents before making up your mind.

THE INDUSTRIES OF ATLANTA

The types of jobs in Atlanta tell us how we make a living. But they do not tell us all there is to know about the work that goes on in our city. Industrial workers may have jobs in many kinds of factories. Service workers may serve tourists, factory workers, sales people, or other workers. What kinds of businesses and industries do Atlanta workers serve? How many workers of all types are employed by each kind of industry?

Industries such as this steel plant employ many types of workers. They require office workers, managers, craftsmen, and laborers.

The Economy of Atlanta

The following pictogram shows in a different way what Atlanta workers do. Again we must group the kinds of industry into types in order to put them into a table.

The largest group is "Service Industries." It includes such service

PERCENTAGE OF WORKERS IN MAJOR INDUSTRY GROUPS IN ATLANTA
Each Figure Represents 5% of Atlanta's Workers (Rounded Totals)

Industry	Percentage
SERVICE INDUSTRIES	30%
WHOLESALE, RETAIL TRADE	25%
MANUFACTURING	17%
TRANSPORTATION, COMMUNICATION, AND OTHER PUBLIC UTILITIES	11%
CONSTRUCTION	6%
ALL OTHER INDUSTRIES	9%

industries as: finance, insurance, real estate, personnel, recreational, professional, and other related services. These industries employ people in most of the groups shown in the previous table. Any industry needs managers, clerks, and stenographers for their offices and other service workers to serve them.

In fact, the only groups which produce goods—actually change raw materials into finished articles—are the "construction" and "manufacturing" industries. Practically all the other businesses are service industries. Less than one-fourth of Atlanta's workers work in factories or construction work. This is a very important one-fourth, however, and many of the services depend on its production to give them jobs.

You must keep in mind also that the transportation, communication, wholesale and retail trade, and many other service industries serve the entire region. One of the major reasons Atlanta is a great city is that these services are needed by the people all over the Southeast. Many of our goods and services are for markets in far places in the nation and the world. We would have a poor economy indeed if we only produced enough for ourselves. We would have nothing to trade for things which come from other regions and nations. As you look at the articles in your home, you see that many useful things come from distant places. We do not have the resources to produce everything we need.

The way people make a living, their jobs, industries, money, and finance, make up the economy of our city. "Economics" is the study of the earning, distributing, and using of wealth. Atlanta's economy is thus tied up with the economy of the region and the nation. We depend on outside areas for most of our raw materials and also for a market for our surplus goods and services.

If people outside our city do not produce raw materials, or if they do not have money to buy our products, our economy suffers. Our factories must close down for lack of materials or for lack of a market for products. The service workers lose their jobs because there is no

The Economy of Atlanta

manufacturing and trade to bring income to the people who buy their services. Manufacturing and trade are the base upon which our economy is built.

The kind of job you expect to get when you begin to make your own living will depend in large part on the economy of Atlanta at that time. The amount of money you will earn for your work may depend on how well goods and services flow from Atlanta to the people who need them. This out-flow must balance with the in-flow of raw materials and money from all over the Southeast. Most of our goods and services are sold in the Southeast. Only a small percentage goes to distant places. Your future job may depend on the economy of the Southeast as well as of Atlanta.

WHAT ATLANTA WORKERS PRODUCE

What are some of the goods which we produce in Atlanta for our own use and to be sent to other places? What do the 17 per cent of Atlanta workers employed in manufacturing industries contribute to the goods of the region and nation? If we take the manufacturing group from the preceding graph and divide it into the types of manufacturing industries, we get the following graph:

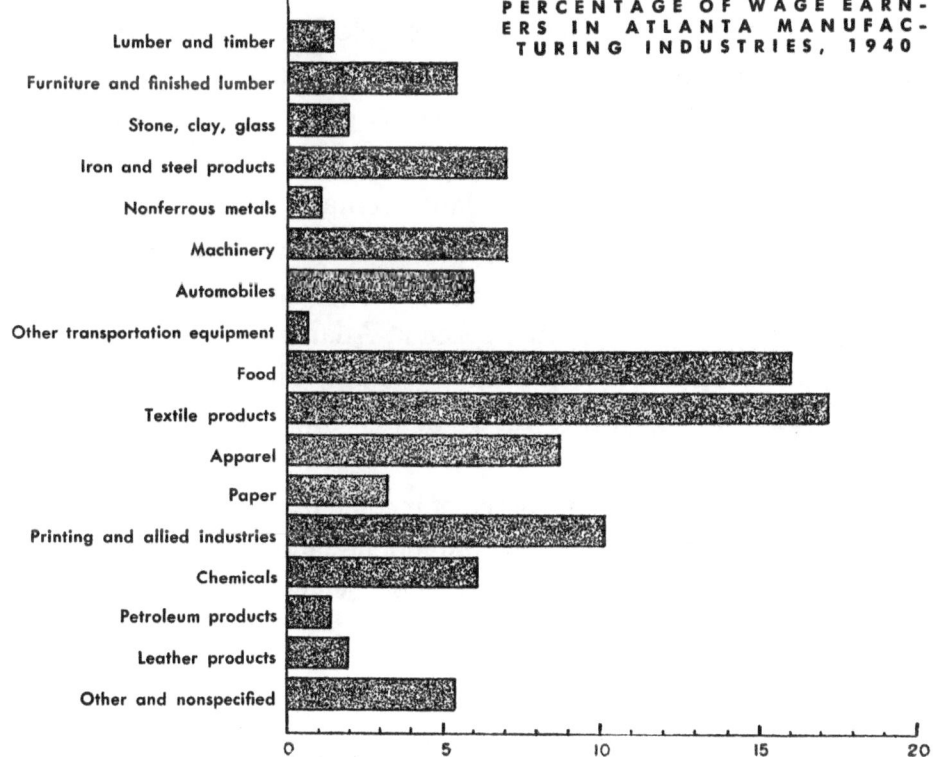

PERCENTAGE OF WAGE EARNERS IN ATLANTA MANUFACTURING INDUSTRIES, 1940

Building Atlanta's Future

Food processing and textile manufacturing industries employed more people in Atlanta in 1940 than any other type of manufacturing. However, other industries such as printing, iron and steel, machinery, chemicals, automobiles, and furniture manufacturing employed a sizeable number. New industries are coming to Atlanta all the time and these figures have probably changed since 1940. They may change even more by the time you start looking for a permanent job. You may find new information about products and jobs in the new census figures as they are published, in newspapers, and other publications from time to time.

Producing these goods gives jobs to a part of Atlanta's workers, but the majority of them work at producing services. Think over all the people you know. How many of them have jobs in which they actually work at producing goods? Perhaps you know some who work in factories and at building trades. The chances are you know more who produce services. The man in the corner drugstore, the bus or trolley drivers, policemen, bank tellers, dentists, cooks, and filling station attendants are all service workers. The insurance salesmen, telephone operators, wholesale grocers, brokers, hospital staffs, and the many office workers serve not only Atlanta people but people all over the southeastern region.

Manufacturing is done in factories. A great many service industries are housed in office buildings. As a center of service industry for this part of the United States, Atlanta contains a great many large office buildings. No wonder its skyline is so impressive. In order to get space downtown for so many offices, buildings have been built higher and higher. There is more office space in Atlanta than in many cities three or four times larger. The renting of office space is one of Atlanta's biggest businesses. It brings much money into Atlanta from other regions.

Another very important source of income in Atlanta is the wholesale and retail trade. Look at the automobiles and trucks that come to the city bearing out-of-state license plates. Many of them have come

Transporting and distributing goods to people who will use them is an important part of our economy.

to buy goods and services. If you could talk to all the people in the department stores, the clothing, and hardware stores, you would find that many of them live outside the city. They come to Atlanta to shop for things they cannot get in their local stores. Visiting shoppers come to buy only a few small articles—others come to order truck and railroad carloads wholesale. The business of gathering and selling the things people need is one of the foremost in Atlanta's economy

INCOME AND PURCHASING POWER

Atlanta people produce and distribute many goods and services. They work long and hard at their jobs. What do they get in return? How many goods and services can they buy with their rewards for working?

Of course you are interested in the kind of living you can buy with the money you earn in the job you choose. The answer will depend on two things: the amount of money you receive and the "purchasing power" of that money. By purchasing power we mean the value of the money in terms of what it will buy. You can make a good salary and still be poor. A large income is of no benefit if prices are so high you cannot pay for the things you need. "How much money do you make?" is not nearly so important as "How much will it buy?"

Workers receive wages, salaries, or profits for their work. "Wages" refers to money paid at a certain amount per hour or per number of units of work done. A bricklayer who is paid at $1.25 per hour and the factory hand who gets $2.00 for every hundred articles he finishes are wage workers. "Salaries" are paid by the week, month, or year. A bookkeeper or a teacher who gets $250 per month, or $3000 per year, is a salaried worker.

"Profits" come from buying goods and services and selling them at a higher price than they cost. Proprietors and owners of selling businesses receive profits in return for their work. Other profits come from processing goods and raw materials to make them more useful. There are other kinds of income, such as interest and rents, but most workers are paid in wages, salaries, and profits.

With their incomes Atlanta people buy a living. If you make the same income year after year but prices go down—then you can buy more with each dollar. Your money has increased in purchasing power. You make a better living but make no more money. However if prices of food, shelter, and clothing go up and your income remains the same —you can buy less with your money. You live more poorly.

As a general rule, prices and income tend to go up and down together. If prices go up, most people get a "raise" in income. When prices come down, their incomes are "cut." Whenever prices and income get out of balance with each other, economic problems result. Then we may have times when money is "cheap." Incomes are high and everyone has plenty of money—but it will not buy much because prices are high too. This is known as "inflation."

When money is scarce and income low, we have times of economic

An automobile coming off the assembly line is the product of the work of a great many people.

"depression." Prices may be low, but if people have little money they cannot buy. Whether for lack of money or because of high prices, if people cannot buy the things they need our problems increase. You may remember the times of inflation which followed the war years after 1945. Money was plentiful and prices rose swiftly despite efforts to control them. People whose incomes did not rise suffered greatly. Older people remember the years during the 1930's when there was a great depression in the United States. Many people had no jobs and no money and had to have relief work provided by the government. Unemployment always comes with depression.

Thus the level of living you can buy will depend on many things. Many people are working on the problem of keeping a balance between incomes and prices. Perhaps by the time you are old enough to vote new methods of preventing inflation and depression will be found. Surely you will want to do all you can to see to it that your income buys a comfortable living.

ECONOMY AND LIVING

Money is worth a great deal to most people. Some seem to forget that it is worthless unless it can be exchanged for goods and services. The quest for money brings many problems to our economy. Instead of working to gather useful materials we need, as ants and bees do, our work often becomes a race to get all the money we can store up. The "social prestige" of money may overshadow its use to bring better living.

As you ride down the street in an automobile, you are concerned with going somewhere swiftly and easily. The car was bought and paid for with the rewards for considerable work. But behind this car, all the other cars, and most of our manufactured products is a long story of workers and materials. It is a story of toil and cooperation, of wages and prices, and the striving of people for money.

The story of the purring motor, polished finish, and shining metal begins with the raw materials. Miners, deep in iron and coal mines,

The Economy of Atlanta

dug out the ore. Native laborers in tropical jungles gathered the sap from rubber trees. Farmers raised the cotton and wool and perhaps the plants from which plastic materials are made. Owners, managers, laborers, and their families in each of these industries lived on the incomes from their work.

Railroads, truckers, sailors, service workers of many kinds helped move the raw materials to foundry, machine shop, factories, and to the assembly plant. At every stop more workers added their bit of skill and energy to changing the materials into new forms. Finally the car rolled off the assembly line—beautiful and useful. It was taken to the sales office to be sold and delivered.

Thousands of people make their living by working at producing the hundreds of parts that go into making automobiles. The same may be said about any one of many products—radios, clothing, houses. Most of these workers are very much interested in making a living. They want the most money and the most of the good things of life they can get. Quite often they have to compete with one another to get as much as they think they deserve. To make more money than the other fellow becomes almost the first thought. "Keeping up with the Joneses" may become more important than our general welfare.

Owners and managers seek more profits; skilled and unskilled workers want higher wages and salaries. Working groups organize into "labor unions" in order to work together in getting more income, better working conditions, and shorter hours. Owners and managers organize into groups to oppose them. "Strikes" and "shut-outs" may occur as each group tries to get a larger share of the value of the products. People who work for wages and salaries are known as "labor." Those who work for profit are known as "management."

Perhaps you have seen "pickets" parading before a business with signs telling that the establishment is not treating them fairly. "Labor" is on strike. That is, they have stopped work to try to get "management" to meet their demands. Sometimes these strikes last for months before an agreement can be reached and both sides can go back to earning a living. During that time both labor and management lose their incomes. The business must close down entirely if all the workers are on strike. Shut-outs occur when the owners or managers refuse to let the workers stay on their jobs. They result in the same loss of time and production.

As you ride in an automobile, listen to the radio, grab a snack from the refrigerator, admire your new shoes, or polish the floor—think of the people who helped produce the things around you. Wherever they were produced and sold, many people made their livelihood by helping produce them. Factory owners, foremen, office boys, stenographers, machinists, and salesmen, all want the highest level of living they can get. Each in his zeal for his own interest may forget the others.

Such selfish and shortsighted conflict, however, may cause loss to both sides in the long run. If labor demands too high an income, management cannot make a profit unless very high prices are charged for the product. If they do not make a profit the business must close. If prices are so high that people will not buy the product, then everybody's income stops.

The labor groups contain a majority of the people. If they are paid very low wages they cannot afford to buy many of the goods and services produced by industries. Those who work for profits thus should keep this need for a large well-paid labor group in mind. They make up a great market for the products from which wages, salaries, and profits come.

The struggle to get what you think is a fair share of the returns for work may be a problem to you when you get a job. Whether you work for profit or wages, you will be in the struggle—unless you can help devise a way to settle the problem of a fair share for all. Perhaps there are ways which have not yet been discovered.

It would seem that a system in which everybody could come to an agreement without so much loss of time and production could be found. Instead of pulling against each other, it would benefit all of us if we could see that giving the other fellow a fair share is sometimes the

This great vat of molten metal is the raw material for many kinds of finished goods which will be handled by workers in several other industries.

Building Atlanta's Future

way to raise everybody's level of living. One problem here is to find a way to keep people from wanting more than their share. Human selfishness is one of the problems we have not yet learned to solve.

DEMOCRACY AND OUR ECONOMY

We have required our government, especially our federal government, to regulate more and more of our economic activities. Just how much governmental control we should have is one of the great questions of our times. Can we have a democracy without controls? How much should government control business? These are great and serious problems. What do you think?

You know that you work harder and enjoy doing a job more if you decide for yourself what you want to do and how you are going to do it. Most of us resent being forced to do things. In a democracy everyone has a voice in deciding what we have to do and we should feel responsible for seeing that it is done.

In democracy we have *freedom*. We help to plan our own destinies. But we also have *responsibilities*. If we are to be free we must see to it that we do not take advantage of others. Otherwise we are not practicing democracy. Freedom does not mean doing as we like without regard for others. It must include fairness and justice. An old saying about fighting puts it well—"Your freedom stops where the other fellow's nose begins." Can you apply that idea to our economy?

People in labor groups must, of course, look after their own interests. Management must see that it gets a share also. But there is a "public interest" which comes above both of these. The "public" includes all groups. No one of them should endanger the welfare of all the others—themselves included—by short-sighted actions. In order to insure the public welfare, we have public regulations—laws set up by a majority of the people. These regulations are enforced by the government in which we all have a voice.

Through our government we can do much to improve our economy. We will perhaps always need police to protect property and to

The Economy of Atlanta

protect the weak from the selfish strong. But to do away with labor unions entirely is a step toward totalitarianism. So would be laws which put business management under complete control of government. We have fought a great war against the ideals of totalitarianism and dictatorship. The democratic way is to get together and work out a solution of our own.

Our economic system is one of our greatest social resources. It is organized to permit us to produce better living. Like any other resource, it must be used and improved to serve its purpose to best advantage.

Totalitarianism thrives on depression and unemployment. Democracy does not. When people are poor and hungry, they may follow a leader who promises them better living. That is the way dictators gain their power. To assure our freedom from such, we must strive for a prosperous economy. Prosperity is built upon a fair income for all people. Poverty among some groups puts a burden on the welfare of everyone. Atlanta as a city will prosper only to the extent that all groups receive a fair and just share of the income from our efforts.

An improved economy will allow all of Atlanta's people to rise to higher levels of living. Through democratic effort we may find ways to make a better economy. A better city and a better world are the goals for our working together to achieve more democratic cooperation.

Final preparations and serving of food requires skills hungry people appreciate immediately.

Building Atlanta's Future

DISCUSSION QUESTIONS

1. What kind of work employs the greatest number of people in Atlanta?
2. Do Atlanta workers produce more value in goods or in services? What effect does this have on the kind of city Atlanta is?
3. What determines the real, or actual, income of a worker?
4. Why is Atlanta's economy dependent upon the resources of the region? Is the reverse of this true also?
5. Where do your parent's jobs fit into the graph on kinds of work?
6. Ask your mother or father how much they can buy for a dollar today. How does it compare with 1940? 1947?
7. How do depression and inflation affect people? Ask some older friends who remember the 1930's.

HAVE YOU READ?

1. *Atlanta, A City of the Modern South.* "Commerce and Industry," "Labor." American Guide Series. New York: Smith and Durrell, 1942.
2. Citizens' Fact-Finding Movement of Georgia. *Georgia Facts in Figures, A Source Book.* "Agriculture," "Industry and Commerce." Athens, Georgia: The University of Georgia Press, 1946.
3. *Key to Atlanta.* "Diversified Industry." Atlanta, Georgia: The Industrial Bureau, Atlanta Chamber of Commerce.
4. *Building America, Illustrated Studies of Modern Problems.* Vol. XI, "Labor and Management." Building America Illustrated Studies. New York: Americana Corporation, 1944.
5. U. S. Bureau of the Census. *Current Population Reports, Labor Force.* "Labor Force Characteristics of the Atlanta, Georgia, Metropolitan District: April, 1947." Washington, D. C., 1947.

7 Our Common Wealth

IF we are to make a living by producing goods and services, we must have work space. Workers must have shelter from the weather. So must the equipment and tools with which they work. This means buildings. Buildings require space on land. Buildings and land thus become of great importance in a city—not only to the workers, but to all those who depend on the products of the work. The land and buildings in the city are "wealth" for all those in the city and those who are served by it. We might say that this is "common wealth" in the same sense that we have common interests and common problems.

Land, buildings, streets, and other improvements made on land are the *physical structure* of our city. They are common wealth to all of us. We would have no city without them. Why do people come to our city to build stores and factories? They come because the other stores, factories, and dwelling houses are already there. They know a great deal of business comes to Atlanta. It is already known far and wide as a good place to buy.

Building Atlanta's Future

It is a great advantage to people to locate their businesses in Atlanta. It is an advantage to those of us already here to have good businesses in Atlanta. The whole welfare of Atlanta is a common interest to us all. Not only the buildings in the physical structure, but also the kinds of activities within them are important. The *social relations* and the wants of the people who are to live and work within the physical structure are the reasons it is built.

The physical and social city is built to serve group needs—the needs of all of us. Each is responsible for doing his part in helping to meet these needs. We are responsible for seeing that we do things which will be good for our city. We are just as responsible to ourselves and to others for not harming the physical and social structures so that they will not meet our needs. We have common responsibilities and common needs in regard to developing our common wealth.

Have you ever thought of Atlanta as being like a great house? Its sections are much like rooms, each filling a special need. In a model home you have a living room, bedrooms, kitchen, dining room, bath, and perhaps a workshop, play room, study, and library. Each is used for a certain purpose. The house must be designed so that each room can best be used for its purpose or it is a poor home. If the kitchen and dining room are at opposite sides of the house, for instance, we do extra work in carrying food and dishes to and fro.

The "rooms" in Atlanta are not quite so clearly marked off as in our homes. But we find definite shopping districts, office and banking sections, transportation terminals, industrial sections, residential sections, recreation districts, and others. These may not be laid out in blocks and they may overlap one another, but the special function of each is often easy to see. A city cannot be complete without all these parts any more than can a house which lacks some of its rooms.

Likewise, some parts of a city go together just as some rooms in a house. In the same way that you need a door between the kitchen and dining room, you must have streets connecting the warehouse district with the shopping districts. It is better if they are not too far apart.

We plan our houses with great care. Have we planned as well for our cities?

Your bedroom should be in as quiet a place as possible and should allow for privacy. The residential sections of our city are quieter and more private if away from the heavy traffic arteries. The living room should be easy to enter from all parts of the house—the business sections also need easy access for many people.

Architects work hard at trying to give us more efficient, more liveable, and better designed homes. Have we done as well for our cities? It would seem not. In our city-house we often eat in the bedrooms, sleep in the workshop, play in the kitchen, and store food in the living room. Sometimes the rooms get all mixed up. It is hard to tell what they are supposed to be.

Building Atlanta's Future

Our city is not only the place in which we live. It is also a set of facilities which can make for better or worse living. Are the parts of Atlanta designed to promote better living? Are we using our natural and social resources to give the highest development of our human resources? As we look at the parts of Atlanta, try to see both the possibilities and the faults in serving all our people.

FITTING THE PARTS INTO A CITY

Factories, office buildings, stores, banks, warehouses, freight terminals—large and small, old and new—are all part of our common wealth. Their size and shape, inside and out, reflect the social purposes which they serve. Usually these buildings are not built to be ornamental but to fill a need for shelter and work space. Some of them, however, are handsome as well as efficient. Their very size and shape lend themselves to magnificence and dignity—to strong lines without useless ornaments.

It is often said that these buildings fit the needs they serve better than the houses we live in. Many people believe that much of our best architecture is found in factories, stores, office buildings, and public buildings.

People must also have houses in which to live while off the job. The wants and needs of individual and family life require buildings which give comfort and convenience. We spend a great deal of time in our homes. Our welfare is very much affected by the kind and quality of the house which we call home. Homes, or "housing" as residential shelter is often called, take up about 60 per cent of Atlanta's developed land area. We will look at housing in detail in another chapter.

Besides sheltered space for work and home, we have schools, hospitals, churches, parks, recreation facilities, and government buildings. These are space and shelter for the more personal "services" which only indirectly help produce "goods."

The final space given to the common wealth of our city is that

The purpose of office buildings is to give as much work space as possible on small land area.

covered by the communication and utilities network. Streets with their public and private transit, telegraph and telephone wires and cables, water and sewerage mains, gas and electric conduits make up this network. The streets form the general framework of a city. The other facilities tend to follow the streets. Thus we have a network similar to veins, arteries, and nerves in our bodies. These lace together factories, homes, schools, shopping places, and all the others.

A cross section of a city street reveals a maze of hidden cables, pipes, and wires. These unseen systems of "nerves" and "arteries" are as important as the streets and transit systems above the surface. They

are the necessary part of our common wealth which enables the intricate organization of a city to function. The development of new communication, water, and sanitary techniques is one reason we can have larger, cleaner, cities than ever before.

The street pattern of a city and its utility systems help decide the location and nature of the buildings. Stores and office buildings should be close to the main transportation lines so that people can come and go with ease. Trucking terminals should be on wide streets but should not be in the midst of heavy traffic. Some industries require extra large water and sewer service. Schools and residences are more safely situated away from the main traffic avenues. Streets and buildings thus can be arranged to fit the needs in each instance. This close relationship among streets, utilities, and buildings is a major concern in the growth and development of cities.

This, then, is the physical and material Atlanta which we can so readily see—the concrete and brick, the lumber and steel, glass and stone which make up the theatre for our city's activities. Our public and private lives are lived among these facilities. They are built to serve our needs. Can we find ways to make this physical city serve our needs better?

THE SECTIONS OF ATLANTA

As we look at a map or ride through our city, we can see how different uses of land tend to divide the city into various areas or sections. The downtown shopping and business district is clustered near the center of the city. The court house, city hall, and office buildings are near by. Several groups of residences are scattered over the city. The edges are given almost entirely to residential districts.

Within Atlanta proper we find four major types of areas:
1. Industrial
2. Commercial
3. Residential
4. Parks, cemeteries, public buildings

← Atlanta's street pattern is the frame within which buildings and other land improvements must fit.

Building Atlanta's Future

As the land-use map shows, the industrial area appears as small knots or clusters along the main thoroughfares and the railroads. Factories and mills perhaps started here because of the ease of shipping raw materials and finished goods in and out of the city. Others were added near by because of the same reasons and also because these were now "industrial areas." Workers could live near by and other facilities needed were handy. The industries have expanded and crowded into other areas as the city has grown.

The commercial or "business" district is more compact than the industrial. It is centered around Five Points in the oldest area of the city. This was once the main market and trading center when Atlanta was but a village. As the trading center, it has continued to grow and

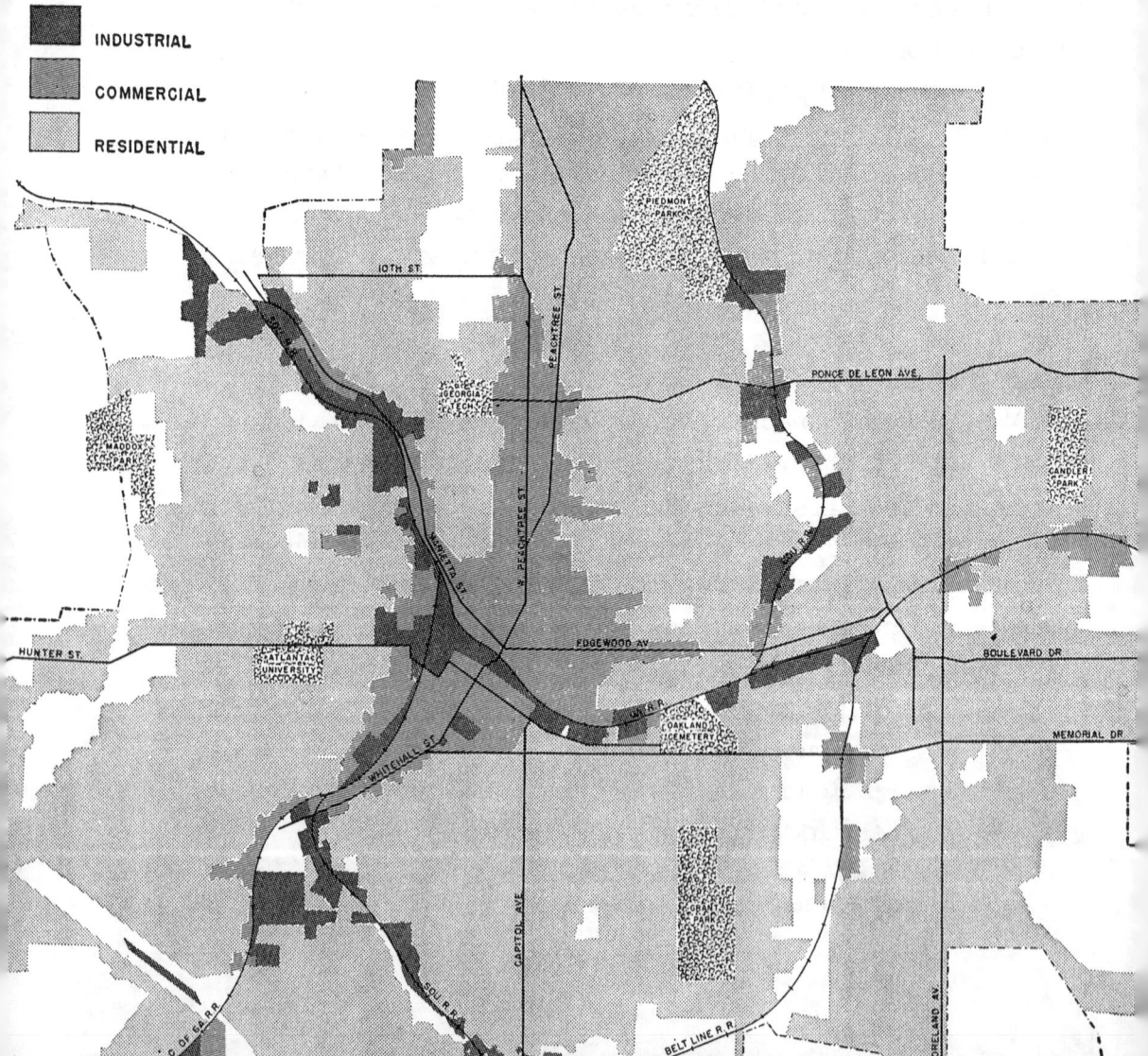

Five Points is the center around which Atlanta has grown. Here land values are very high.

spread and change. Now there are sections within it which contain more specialized establishments. For instance, the area around Five Points and along Marietta Street is taken up by financial agencies.

To the north along Peachtree is the section of larger stores and the newer shopping centers. Here also are the large theatres and restaurants and some hotels. To the south is a section of low-cost clothing shops, five and ten-cent stores, other shops, and one large department store, Rich's. Throughout this area are scattered office buildings. Five Points is the central hub around which Atlanta has been built. The highest land values in the city are found here.

The residential areas make up the largest part of the city. There are several residential sections such as Morningside, Kirkwood, Sylvan Hills, Grove Park, and East Atlanta. These are set apart from each other by industrial and commercial districts. There are sections of small, single-family houses. Others have larger two- and three-family houses, and still other areas contain large apartment houses. Along Piedmont Avenue, for instance, is an area of apartment houses. More women workers live here than men. In the rooming house area nearer the center of the city, most of the roomers are men.

Many homes in Atlanta are being crowded by commercial buildings. Land use in some sections is changing.

As the city changes, the nature of the residences change also. You can still see spacious old homes in central parts of the city. These are now crowded in by business and industrial establishments. The families who first lived there have usually moved out to the newer residential sections or to a suburban area.

Older residential sections which become hemmed in by other land uses tend to become slums. Sometimes they become centers of crime and disease. Transient workers and people who are "down and out" use them as temporary homes. They take little interest in them. Many

Our Common Wealth

slum areas in Atlanta have been replaced by "housing projects" such as Capital Homes and Eagan Homes, sponsored by the federal and local governments. This is a fairly new land use. It has been a great help to the appearance and common good of the city. We will take it up again later.

The public parks, schools, and government buildings are scattered over the city. These usually occupy small areas but are important. They are "public" and should serve the needs of all the people living near them. Schools, parks, police and fire stations, and other

As a city grows and changes, land use changes. The location of new residential sections such as this is very important to the people who live here.

public or government owned facilities are for the use of all the people. Putting them in the places where they are needed is an important part of land-use planning in a city. Are the schools and parks near your home placed so that they serve the needs of the neighborhood? How about the other public buildings?

Land uses in the city limits thus follow a rather definite pattern. Similar land-use activities tend to cluster together and make up sections in the city which are devoted to a certain function. This pattern is, of course, changing gradually as the city grows and the kinds of business and industries change. This change is necessary for the good of the city. As it grows it must expand in each part. This may mean a re-shifting of streets and districts. If we are to keep our "house" up-to-date, we must remodel it as our "family" needs change. We may need to add rooms, or change their purpose, as our population and industries shift and change.

USING THE LAND IN A CITY

The buildings, the streets and service facilities, the parks and playgrounds are on *land* and make up *uses of land*. Land is a basic resource for all man's activities—whether it is used as a farm, a building lot, or a city dump. Because the use to which land is put is so important, it is a common resource to all the people concerned. In a metropolitan area, land use affects great numbers of people very directly. What one person or group does with one piece of land affects what other people can do.

As we have seen before, homes are not pleasantly situated in a factory area. Neither is a quiet narrow street with little traffic a likely location for a large department store. These represent uses of land which strongly affect the use of neighboring land. They show how land use affects people—their wants and needs and their activities in a metropolitan area like Atlanta.

Land is owned by people. It is classed as "private property." For a long time we in the United States have believed that a man could do as he pleased with his own property, his land included. We have felt that it is up to the owner to say how his property shall be used.

The founding fathers of our country saw private ownership of land as one of the bulwarks of democracy. They wanted to get away from the feudal system. This system was in force in Europe from the 10th to the 15th centuries and traces of it are still found. It was based on land owned by the feudal lords and worked by serfs and slaves. The serfs in a feudal system were bound to the land, but they did not own

Our Common Wealth

it. They could not move away and had to use the land as directed by their lords who lived in great "manors" or castles.

The great democratic movements in Europe opposed feudalism. So when the first settlers came to America, they wanted a system just the opposite of the feudal type. Here the laws of freedom were made so as to permit and encourage even the poorest people to own land. A man's property was his to do with as he chose. The only exceptions were in some of the colonial towns. Here some land was owned in common or was controlled in the community's interest by other means. You may still find "town commons" or public squares in our older cities.

This system worked very well when there were vast stretches of open land and few people. Land was cheap and if a man did not like the way his neighbors used their land, he could move on to a new place. Some of our pioneers are famous for their desire to live in the wilderness away from other people. When people live so far apart, they do not get in each other's way. Their use of land seldom harms others. This plan also allows ambitious people to develop their property to as high a value as they wish. They are free to make the best possible use of their land resources. This plan has helped make us a nation of people who work hard to gain wealth which is then ours to enjoy as we choose.

However, as towns became cities and small cities became large, our ideas about land changed. Urban land acquired new values. New problems arose. As a result, our thinking about land has changed and may continue to change. The limited supply of land within the city made land valuable. In the 19th century many families were able to acquire fabulous fortunes by holding land bought at low prices. Often its value increased five, ten, twenty, even a hundred times. As cities grew their land values grew. Prices went up and rents increased. Real estate speculation became a highly profitable business. For many, it still is.

Something else happened though. Much city growth was at the expense of many city people. City living became intolerable for them,

Overcrowded slums are poor land use. They are

and their property values, if they had property, went down instead of up. What was good for some landowners and speculators turned out bad for others. High values caused many people and buildings to be squeezed onto small land areas. They had too few trees, too little free space for play, poor light and air, unsanitary conditions, old buildings in disrepair. Many refused to accept such conditions for their residence or business places.

With the coming of the automobile people were free to move away from these areas of blight and slum. The suburban areas began to have their day. People moving away from the central cities spelled lost property values, municipal bankruptcy, transportation and housing problems. At the same time, the suburbs left much to be desired.

So people are gradually learning that there is a public interest in land. We are learning the hard way that what a few people do often affects us all. We see whole communities harmed because of the selfish actions of a few landowners.

...as destructive in their way as erosion of land.

What a man does with his land and the improvements he makes on it are indeed the concern of others because their welfare and their land values are affected. This is especially important in cities where people live and work so close together and depend on one another in so many ways. Group wants become more important than individual wants.

The pioneer woodsman in the remote mountains might burn the woods around his house when he liked. The fire might spread for miles and burn until the rain put it out—and still not reach another man's property. Today a forest fire may spread destruction across several farms in much less space. Many more people are affected and damage is considered greater because we value our forests more today. In the same way the woodsman's log cabin might suit his needs very well. It would be useless and a nuisance in a crowded city business district. Land use must change as our needs change.

Therefore, as time goes on we see more and more clearly that land,

Building Atlanta's Future

and the use made of it, is important to all the people. Forest fires and soil erosion are dramatic examples of poor land use. They are no more destructive than some poor uses of land in the city.

FITTING THE PARTS INTO A CITY

In recognition of the common interest in the use of land, people have developed "devices" for controlling the use of land, especially in and about cities. These practices started in Europe many centuries ago. They are being used more and more. We find some of them right here in Atlanta. By use of these new social resources people can direct the growth of their cities for the good of all the people. They are examples of how a group can get together and work out the means for meeting individual needs by acting as a group. What are these devices?

1. *Public ownership of land* is the most extreme device. The county, the city, the state, or the national government, not private individuals, owns the land. In democratic countries such ownership is always supposed to be in the common interest. Certainly much of it is. And in a very real sense, the people own the land through their duly chosen governments. It is managed through their civil servants, their government officials. Publicly-owned land is often rented to private individuals. Sometimes it is rented or leased for a long time—such as 99 years.

Under public ownership, of course, the land is subject to very direct regulation and control. While our U. S. cities own a great deal of land, it is much less than in some other countries like England. Many people feel public ownership is not in keeping with our way of life. They think it violates our traditional freedom. Others believe there is no way to handle some of our city problems effectively except by public ownership in democratic interest.

2. *The power of eminent domain* is a long recognized power of our governments. By this power a government may acquire land and the property on it when that is necessary for the common good. The courts decide whether this is justified. There must be a fair payment by the government to the landowner. The courts also decide what that pay-

Our Common Wealth

ment shall be. Through this power government may control the use of land.

3. *Subdivision control* is a device used more and more by our cities. It is a device by which the city, or sometimes the county government, controls the dividing and preparation of land for various uses, chiefly residential. Many unscrupulous or unskilled people were buying up large pieces of land, making them into building lots, and putting in streets and other facilities. These were often poorly planned and poorly constructed. People who bought them were sometimes cheated. Most cities now have subdivision ordinances. Minimum lot sizes, street and alley arrangements, and public utility standards are stated in the subdivision control ordinance. Proper enforcement conserves our land and natural resources and protects the individual buyer. It saves money for the investor, the government, and very often for the subdivider as well.

4. *Police power regulations* permit control of various features of land use. Building codes have been adopted by many cities, including Atlanta. These codes enable the city government to see that minimum standards of building construction are met in the interest of public

Atlanta's City Council in session. This body decides on municipal policies in the control of land use.

Building Atlanta's Future

safety and welfare. Health codes, enforced by the city health department, regulate sanitary conditions of land and buildings. Excessive smoke, bad odors, noise, and other "nuisances" are likewise regulated under the police power.

5. *Zoning ordinances* are usually drawn up by the City Planning Commission and passed on by the City Council. They set forth the kinds of buildings, businesses, and other land uses which are permitted in each "zone" of a city. The courts and the police are thus authorized to prevent practices which violate the zoning law.

In most well-ordered cities, the building code requires a person to get a "permit" to erect a building or other structure. When he applies for a permit, the zoning ordinance is checked by the officials to see if such a structure is in keeping with the other buildings in the zone. If it is not, the permit is not granted.

Setting up zoning for a new development is like making a blueprint for a house. We can plan for each room, or part, beforehand and put them together in the most effective way. We would not think of building a house without plans. Why should we expect a city to grow up in the right order without plans? To a degree, that is how Atlanta got the way it is. The bad features are partly the result of haphazard growth.

Zoning ordinances have usually been made *after* the zones were already well-defined by the use of the land. People develop a section of a city as they want it. Then the zoning ordinance is set up to keep it that way. Economic and social factors have really made most of our zones. We now realize it would have been easier and better to plan first than to remodel. We seldom remodel or "redevelop" on a really extensive scale.

POLITICAL BOUNDARIES BLOCK SOUND PLANNING

"City limits" and "county lines" are political boundaries. They are highly artificial as far as using land for the needs of people is concerned.

The neighborhood shopping district prospers because it serves the everyday needs of the people around it.

For example, a zoning restriction may keep anyone from building a stockyard in a residence zone on the edge of a city. However, if the stockyard is built just across the city limits, it is still an unpleasant neighbor. The city limits do not mark the end of the need for good land use. The people themselves and the needs of the community are the real base for deciding on land-use practices.

Suppose the people in a neighborhood want a small local shopping district. The county line may run through the neighborhood. However, this does not keep people from crossing the line to shop. Political boundaries often cause difficulty in planning an area for the needs of the people. The real needs of a metropolitan area are often hard to meet because of such political divisions. People do not follow such boundaries in choosing friends and buying groceries.

Zoning laws, needs and wants of the people, and desire for cooperation cause the types of "improvements" or additions put on land to cluster in groups. That is, stores and business establishments tend to group together. Factories are built close to other factories in order to share water or railroad facilities and the like. Similarly, we build our dwelling houses in areas where there are others like them. This clustering, or concentration, happens because people need other people in meeting their wants. Some activities need other activities. Cooperation

Building Atlanta's Future

is necessary because we are so dependent on one another in our modern economy.

We see that the "common wealth" idea is far-reaching. Everybody in Atlanta has a stake in the welfare of the city. Indeed, people all over the southeastern region, and beyond, have a stake in Atlanta's welfare. As the land, buildings, streets, utilities, and their structure serve Atlanta, they also serve all these people. This great service is the primary function of our city. Individual wants must sometime submit to the greater group wants. One person's wants or whims are of little importance compared to the needs of so many people.

In the long run, there is more over-all individual gain by following group wants. We can make a better Atlanta by guiding our efforts to better serve more people. Orderly development of land-use practices in the city can help us in this.

Atlanta is growing. Growth brings change. Change is good if it rids our city of outmoded structures, habits, and functions. The change, however, should be orderly, not haphazard. It should contribute to meeting group wants. We do not want a horse-and-buggy city in a day of automobiles, fast buses, and airplanes.

LAND USE OUTSIDE ATLANTA

As we have seen in the discussion of Metropolitan Atlanta, the use of land outside the city limits is also important to Atlanta proper. There are the "satellite" communities such as Decatur, the General Motors community, the Bell Bomber Plant, and other smaller communities. They are satellites just as the moon is a satellite of the earth. As the moon is held in place in the universe by the attraction, or "pull," of the earth, so are these communities attracted by Atlanta. They may have their own business establishments and factories and be rather self-contained. But they also are tied in closely with Atlanta's activities.

The kind and location of factories, shopping places, and housing

Our Common Wealth

in these communities affects Atlanta. Some of the industries and stores may compete with those in the larger city. Some people who work or own property in Atlanta may live here. Disease and unsanitary conditions may be transmitted to other near-by areas. Traffic routes and highways must be planned with these communities in mind. All the examples of land use in regard to city and county limits apply to these political boundaries between communities also.

In addition to the communities just mentioned, there are others which are principally bedroom communities for people who work in Atlanta. These include Buckhead, Avondale Estates, East Point, Upper Peachtree, and other neighborhoods in the metropolitan area but outside the city limits. These communities may have neighborhood shopping centers, but the people go to Atlanta for any special shopping they

Surrounding communities and smaller cities like Marietta are affected by land use and overcrowding in Atlanta.

Building Atlanta's Future

want to do. Most of them work in Atlanta, or at least depend on Atlanta business for their livelihood. They are even more closely dependent on Atlanta than those mentioned above.

All these communities must be considered as part of Atlanta. Land-use practices in Atlanta affect them. And land use in these communities affects Atlanta. All must be included if our plans are to be good plans.

ORDERLY DEVELOPMENT TO MEET OUR NEEDS

The kind of buildings people put on their city lots—homes, schools, stores, office buildings, parks, and the street system which connects all these—are the framework within which city life exists. The best city life will not result if we do not develop the best possible land use. The people in a city have so many common interests that they are learning to guide city development for the best interest of all. Often the interests of people all over the region help decide the kind of businesses and industries in Atlanta. This also affects the land-use practices in our city.

Of course not all people think of the "common wealth" principle of land use as important even today. But this kind of thinking is growing because more people see how poor land use helps make a poor city. We realize it in the form of the high taxes, unpleasant living conditions, disease, and poverty which come from poor land-use practices.

The term "common wealth" is not new. The things we have been taking up are now more important because cities are more numerous and the mistakes of former years show us how we can make better and better cities. Many cities, states, and nations have used the term "commonwealth" as one word in their titles and laws. Perhaps we can take the idea and use it toward developing all parts of our city in orderly fashion.

We can hardly tear our city apart and put it together again in short order. But we can plan for orderly rebuilding as we go along—plan so that each "room" fits into our city-house as it should. This will not happen if our city grows in haphazard fashion. It requires a plan

Our Common Wealth

which includes all the rooms. No one of them should crowd out another. Such a plan will help us to develop a well-balanced city.

DISCUSSION QUESTIONS

1. What are some ways, other than those mentioned, in which a city is like a house?
2. How does a main highway through the center of a suburban town affect land use in the town? Give good and bad effects.
3. Does a zoning ordinance express group wants or individual wants? Give examples to illustrate your answer.
4. Does the "common wealth" principle hold true in planning new sections of a city? How can it be used in the plans?
5. How many devices for controlling land uses are used in Atlanta? Have they been effective?
6. Has your family moved from one house to another in or around Atlanta? Can you locate their old residence on the map? Why did they move?
7. What land does the City of Atlanta own in your neighborhood? For what is it used?
8. What was the "common" of our colonial towns? Who owned it? Why?
9. Are there land uses in your neighborhood which are considered "nuisances" by the residents? What are they? How might they be controlled?

HAVE YOU READ?

1. *Report of the Real Property, Land Use, and Low Income Housing Area Survey of Metropolitan Atlanta.* Part I. Atlanta, Georgia: Work Projects Administration of Georgia, 1940.
2. Stonorov, Oscar, and Kahn, Louis I. *You and Your Neighborhood, A Primer for Neighborhood Planning.* New York: Revere Copper and Brass Incorporated, 1944.
3. The Industrial Bureau, Atlanta Chamber of Commerce. *Facts in Figures About Atlanta.* An annual pamphlet. Atlanta, Georgia: Chamber of Commerce, 1944 to 1948.

Part Three

MEETING GROUP NEEDS

8. Communities in Atlanta

SOMETIMES in the hustle of city life it looks as though people are hurrying to get nowhere. We get pushed and shoved as we get on buses. We have to elbow our way along streets. Where are we going? Where have we come from?

A closer look at the problem shows us that after all Atlanta and its people are not aimlessly scurrying around. From all parts of Atlanta people are moving into the heart city to work and trade. From the heart city they return to their homes. But not all this movement of people, this working and shopping, goes into and out of the heart city.

You have watched the buses and trolleys pull up to the safety zones, open their doors, empty a load of humanity, take in the waiting people, and rumble away from the heart city. Have you noticed the names on the front of these street cars and buses? East Point! Buckhead! Druid Hills! These are only a few.

These names are the destinations of the buses and the people on them. More than that, they represent distinct areas of metropolitan Atlanta. These areas in many cases are almost complete little communities. Here the people live. Here they shop, and here some of them work. In these communities there is movement of people, just as there is hurry and bustle in our heart city. But these little communities play a different role in the vast network that is our metropolitan district.

As you walk along the street of downtown Atlanta, you may not meet many people you know. But when you walk around the neighborhood near your home, you see friends. You know something about their problems. They know you. Many of them you have visited, played with, worked with. This relationship among you and your friends is one of the characteristics of a neighborhood. There may be many little neighborhoods in each of Atlanta's major communities.

In these areas, away from the heart city, we do our real social living. Most of our group life takes place in the communities. We belong to family groups, school and play groups, groups for worship, and even work groups, along with many others.

We belong to these groups because we have needs and wants which we can best meet through joint effort with our neighbors. People with common likes—and sometimes common dislikes—get real satisfaction from associating with one another. They like to cooperate with one another or just to be together to talk, to relax, and pass the time of day.

These common likes, wants, and interests are the real "social cement" in city life. They pull people together into group activity. The small communities and neighborhoods away from the heart city provide the physical layout for serving these common wants. Streets, houses, stores, churches, and schools fall into physical patterns. These are shaped by the social cement, or common experiences of the people in the area. Sentiments, mingled with memories of pain and pleasure, surround our feeling about our home and neighborhood.

Here we see that there are two factors which shape the quality of life in our outlying neighborhoods and communities. On the one hand

Communities in Atlanta

there is the matter of "how do the people get along together in their social relationships, or group life." On the other hand, there is the matter of "how well does the physical layout serve the wants and needs of the people." The kinds of group life and the physical structures must meet the wants of people in the neighborhood. It they do not, then we may have a sore spot, or a cancerous growth, within the body of our city.

Those busy buses we see moving in and out of our heart city travel the life lines that connect our many communities. They connect communities with the heart city and with one another. As a super-social resource, Atlanta is a network of connected communities and neighborhoods. The quality of life in each part of this network affects the health and welfare of our entire city.

Atlanta's future must be built keeping the following three points in mind: (1) achieving the best possible life within each of its com-

We work as groups in many of our activities.

munities; (2) creating the heart city as the best possible working and service center for all surrounding communities; and (3) securing the best possible working relationship among all Atlanta communities and their heart city.

Each of these three points involve using our social resources and natural resources. They require attention to human relations and group effort. Likewise, they require attention to space and physical layout relationships among various parts of our city. Let us look first at the problem of human relations.

THE PROBLEM: A PARADOX

In regard to human relations, a city is a paradox. It contradicts itself. The purpose of a city is to bring people together so that they can cooperate. But by bringing together so many people, it may keep them from having the kind of personal and group relations they want.

On the one hand, we know that cities can afford better living conditions in terms of food, clothing, and shelter. In cities, through cooperation and division of labor, we can produce more goods than is otherwise possible. These goods we have because of cooperation—but on a very impersonal level.

On the other hand, we find cities to be blocking the personal side of living and working together. Personal relations between people who have common interests is one of the great forces in happiness. Cities can "de-humanize" people until they look at others as mere cogs in a production machine or as rivals in competition for jobs and prestige. Many thinkers say that this is one of the greatest problems of today. They say that unless people are given greater opportunity to be part of small congenial groups, we will lose much that is good. Then our cities and our civilization will decline. There are several factors which may be classed as parts of the reasons. They are:

1. The very size of the population in a city makes it impersonal. It is hard for people to feel that they belong to such a large group. It is difficult to feel that you are close friends with

someone who has had a totally different background from yours.

2. People move about a great deal—both within the city and in and out. The neighborhoods in a city are thus constantly changing. They are seldom really "neighborhoods" in the way that rural communities are.
3. Competition often may crowd out cooperation. We get so used to competing in urban living that we forget to be friends with our neighbors.
4. Houses are poorly located. The arrangement of streets, schools and hospitals, parks and playgrounds, and public buildings add to the de-humanizing elements. They make people feel "hemmed in" by artificial structures.
5. Our dwellings are poorly adapted to the needs of family life. They should be centers of living instead of mere shelters.
6. Large scale industry—big factories, big businesses, big unions with thousands of workers—make the individual feel very small and insignificant. He may forget his own individual and social responsibilities in this maze of "bigness."

These are some of the things about cities which keep people from being content to live in them. They are the things which make people say that if we do not find ways to make living in cities more pleasant,

Some industries prefer the inconveniences of the suburb to the high rent and overcrowding of the city.

no one will want to live there. People will not stay where they are not happy if they can help themselves. They are not likely to be happy if they do not belong to local groups.

The conditions that we have listed also threaten our government. Democracy thrives on cooperation. Large groups are too impersonal for such cooperation. Group decision about political matters comes from talking with close and respected friends. Small groups can reach a decision in which everyone has shared. Crowds are likely to follow demagogues, to follow a leader in a "mob" spirit.

Our economy also tends to become very complex in large cities. Organized business and organized labor become huge and powerful. Conflicts between the factions may tie up our whole economic system. The very complexity of such large organizations makes them cumbersome. As the taxable wealth moves away from these conditions, municipal finances suffer from the loss of revenue. Cities cannot exist without taxes.

Carefully planned communities and neighborhoods can overcome many of these drawbacks to city life. They allow us to find the right balance between the bigness and impersonal elements and the satisfaction of small group wants and needs. When our neighborhoods do not help find this balance they become centers of dissatisfaction, crime, and disease.

THE SUBURBAN PUSH

What has been the result of the city conditions just mentioned? If people do not like them, what have they done about them? What can they do about them now and in the future? How have these conditions affected the cities of today?

For one thing, many people have moved out to the suburbs to live. Since transportation inventions made it possible, cities have spread out and residential districts moved further from the central city. One of the great reasons people give for moving to suburbs is to get away from the crowding of the city. They want to have some of the advantages of country living—space, air, and sunshine.

The "suburban push" has also taken on a romantic appeal to city dwellers. We find people writing and talking about getting "back to nature." Various groups have been formed on the basis of this romantic interest. Most of them are attempts to get away from the overcrowded and impersonal nature of the city.

People get "fed up" with the rush and routine of their work in such surroundings. They begin to think of their work as detestable. "Living" comes to mean something separate from work, which is done only to be able to live. Some people get to the point where their vacations are the only times at which they feel they are "living." Vacation is the time to get away from the city. It is a time to go to the country, the mountains, the seashore. Here they try to "live" enough to last until the next vacation.

Small wonder that many families want to move to suburbs. Here they can escape the crowded city, the traffic dangers in the street. Here they can have more sunshine and air and more spacious sur-

In the suburbs people have more sunshine, fresh air, and space for children to play.

Building Atlanta's Future

roundings for family life. They can have a larger lot for their home and children's play space. They can have green grass and trees instead of monotonous stone, brick, and pavement.

But, perhaps, more important to many, they can have more permanent friends and neighbors. They can live near, but not crowded against, people who have ideals and interests like their own. In short, they have a better chance to be part of a friendly neighborhood. They can feel that their thoughts and needs and their personalities are respected and are important to other people—people they like. They can feel that they "amount to something" in their community in a way that is difficult if you are lost in such huge groups as the population of a city.

Look at Atlanta! See how the maps show that our city has become fringed with suburbs. Locate the most attractive residential districts. Except for the housing projects and some new developments, most of

Slums and blight mar the central city. Attractive

them are on the outskirts or are outside the city limits. Slum and blight areas mar the central city. These are very real problems. What can we do to improve living conditions and neighborhoods in Atlanta? How can we stop people and businesses from moving to the country and to the suburbs?

But first look thoughtfully at the questions. How much do we want to change these movements? Is it better to get away from large cities? How far can we retreat from our cities and still keep the standard of living made possible by an urban economy? Are we willing to lower our standard of living in order to have the pleasures of country life? Perhaps we cannot "have our cake and eat it too" in regard to keeping both city and country benefits.

Great cities have given us great industries. In them we get high production. Upon these we have built a high standard of living. We have more comforts and luxuries than people have ever had before.

residences are moving outside the city limits.

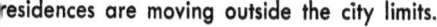

Building Atlanta's Future

We have transportation, communication, sanitation, and other developments which allow us to have large, fairly efficient cities. Are we to do away with these and go back to a simpler, more rural way of living? If we cannot be happy in cities with all these things, perhaps happiness is worth more than they are. Can we improve our cities and correct the conditions which we do not like? This is a problem which Atlanta faces—just as do other cities over the world.

In other parts of America and the world, men have attempted to find a way to rebuild the community life of large cities. They have tried to find a new way of relating physical layout and group wants of people. In a moment we want to study some examples. But first, let us look still closer at the major communities of our own city.

ATLANTA'S NEIGHBORHOOD COMMUNITIES

Can we apply these experiences in other cities to Atlanta? Atlanta already has some neighborhoods in which people feel that they "belong." In several areas we find the community spirit which we have said is basic to happy social life. Such communities as Southside, Bass, Summerhill, West Side, Druid Hills, and many others are known as distinct neighborhoods. The several housing projects have demonstrated how neighborhoods can be improved as places to live.

Why is it that in some parts of Atlanta we find this neighborhood community spirit but not in others? In some areas we find the people working together to improve their communities. Other areas lack this feeling of cooperation almost entirely. Yet they look alike; the same kinds of people live in each. Some spark has been added to give a few of our neighborhoods something others do not have.

This spark might come from several sources. One may be leadership. A few people may start a campaign for improving some community problem. Others may join in as they see the good that can be done. A group of people who live near each other may attend the same church, or school, or buy at the same local stores. As they meet and discuss things at these places, they find they have similar problems. A

146

A common meeting place is a good start toward community group feeling and cooperation.

real community spirit can grow out of their getting together to work at solving everyday problems. The chances are they might never have started if they had not had this central meeting place. They might have continued to be merely casual acquaintances who spoke to each other when they met on the street.

It seems that a community needs a center. There should be some common meeting places at which people come together often. Otherwise they may go on feeling impersonal toward each other. The easier it is for them to gather here the better. That is, neighborhoods which are grouped in clusters of houses are more likely to become organized than those stretched out along a long, straight street. A good community layout then becomes a cluster of houses around a center. The community centers in our housing projects are good examples of how this works. Community centers of some kind nearly always spring up once the people catch the spirit.

Thus Atlanta communities might improve if there were more community centers in them. Perhaps this one move would be enough to start the people cooperating. If we could in some way divide the residential areas into clusters, the chances would be even better. Changing to community high schools had as one of its purposes the use of the schools as community centers. Perhaps they will help add to the several real neighborhood communities we already have.

Building Atlanta's Future

From this we see that Atlanta has a good base upon which to build good neighborhoods. The beginning has been made. It can be extended to take in the metropolitan area. As our city is redeveloped and improved we can plan with neighborhood arrangement in mind. Planning ahead of time will help assure us we will get what we want. As the clearing of slums goes on, and new neighborhoods take their places, Atlanta will begin to become a vastly more pleasant place to live. The changes must take place gradually, but they will not be the changes we want unless we know about and plan for them ahead of time.

Our plans must include all the things which help hold communities together and improve living. We need a street system which not only improves traffic problems, but also marks off and separates neighborhoods and zones. Health centers, parks, and playgrounds should be neighborhood centers as well as health aids. They should be located with this in mind.

Schools, governmental agencies, and churches can also be strong forces for neighborhood unity. Developing these institutions and their facilities should be in our plans. Their locations in central places within the local community area should be carefully worked out.

A community high school can become the center point of active community spirit.

Communities in Atlanta

Having really *good* agencies and services is important. Putting them at the right place can help them be more effective.

The community schools are a great step in the direction we want to go. They should improve in effectiveness as our long-time development progresses. As community centers, the school contributes much to living as well as to education. The effort at slum clearance and good, low-cost housing is another. We have seen how housing is tied in with the worst of our city ills. We can not hope to develop good neighborhoods without good housing. Means and methods of providing it must be improved. These improvements must be aimed at making Atlanta a better place for human relations.

This approach starts with what we have in our city. It means clearance, conservation, and redevelopment. There are some dangers in it. In clearing slums we sometimes must destroy real neighborhoods. People become attached to their homes and neighbors even in slums. Destroying these social groups is at times a big price to pay for new housing. It takes time to rebuild social groups with the bonds of friendship we desire.

These are some things which need attention in our own neighborhood communities. We can see how with much work we can rebuild this part of Atlanta's life. What are some methods that have been tried in other cities and other countries?

THE GARDEN CITY

One scheme for getting away from the problems of large cities is to build small "Garden Cities." Sir Ebenezer Howard, in England, is known as the father of the Garden City movement. He thought that many of the city problems were caused by "too many people living in too little space." He suggested small cities which would be self-contained communities. They were to be planned as a whole before they were built. Spacious residential neighborhoods were to be built within easy walking distance of places of work. The layout of streets, public and private buildings, parks and gardens, sanitation, and recreation facilities were to be in the very best modern design. Several cities have been built along these lines.

In these Garden City communities, people work as well as live. These small cities are not allowed to grow into large ones. Instead, other small cities are built as business and population increases. The communities are thus cooperative affairs. People and industries work together to build the kind of city they want and make sure it stays that way.

Another feature of the Garden Cities is the "green belt" of trees and garden plots which surrounds the city area. No one is allowed to build on this green area. It is kept as a sort of strip of nature to relieve the monotony of city streets and buildings. The living plants, grass, and shrubs make these small cities very attractive and have caused them to be called "Greenbelt" cities and towns. Some of them have been named Greenbelt.

Letchworth and Welwyn are two Garden Cities in England which have been visited by many people. Some communities which are similar in part have been built in the United States. Radburn, New Jersey, and Greenbelt, Maryland, are perhaps the best known. Greenhills, Ohio, and Greendale, Wisconsin, are also good examples of well-planned residential communities with some Garden City features. However, the people who live in these communities in the United States do not usually work there. They are really "dormitory" communities instead of self-contained Garden Cities like Letchworth and Welwyn. If you ever go near any of these places on your vacation travels, you would enjoy seeing them.

Garden Cities have been suggested as ways to keep cities from growing too large. Instead of adding more factories and more people and overcrowding a city, why not build Garden Cities near by? Then the factories and their workers could be put in small self-contained communities. They would be small enough for everyone to know most of his neighbors. By working and living as a social group, they could prevent this part of the big city problem. Spacious, attractive Garden Cities are pleasant places to live and work.

Communities in Atlanta

What would it mean to Atlanta if we were to adopt a garden city plan of development? It might mean that we would make laws preventing new industries from coming into the city. People who wanted to come here to work would not be allowed to move in unless someone moved out to make room for them.

However, these industries and workers would not be sent away. Instead of letting them move into the old city, new garden city suburbs would be built for them. Each of these suburbs would contain only a certain number of industries and enough people to work in them and serve the needs of the local workers.

If this were our plan, our housing and transportation needs would be quite different from those of today. No one would need to ride long distances from suburban homes to work in the central city. In these suburbs growing up around Atlanta, people would work within the community. They could walk to their work. Schools, shopping districts, and recreation centers would also be within a short distance of all residences. Each garden city would be small enough for everybody to know most of his fellow citizens well.

We might even think of tearing down Atlanta and rebuilding it completely as several small garden cities. But this would waste what we now have. In many European cities destroyed by war there is little to save. These cities might be rebuilt following this plan.

Garden Cities are an important part of the British program for rebuilding war-bombed cities and improving others. They emphasize the parks, playgrounds, and open space for group life and health. In the United States, city development emphasizes rebuilding our cities from within. The principle is that we can develop good neighborhoods which in turn will make up better cities.

THE NEIGHBORHOOD APPROACH

We have seen that people like to live in spacious, well-planned suburban neighborhoods. Garden Cities are, in a sense, well-planned neighborhoods. Why can we not have cities which are made up of this

The Atlanta of the future may have "superexpressways" like this.

kind of pleasant neighborhood? Many students of cities think that we can.

In this kind of a city, residential neighborhoods would be scattered about all over the city instead of around the edges. They would be mixed in with the industrial and business sections. People could then get to work without having to travel so far. Many of them could walk to work.

Each residential neighborhood would thus be an attractively laid out unit—something like a tiny Garden City. They would be separated from each other by wide streets such as main traffic arteries, transport lines, expressways, and the like. These thoroughfares would be wide enough so that trees, shrubs, and grassy strips could be planted along them. The green areas could then be used as parks and play areas.

They would shut out the view of the factories and give a feeling of privacy to homes. These neighborhoods would have many of the advantages of suburbs but could be close enough together to cooperate as a city.

Each of these neighborhoods would have its own schools, churches, shopping centers, recreation centers, and other public facilities. People would not have to cross the main traffic streets for ordinary living chores and associations. Yet the special city facilities are near when they need them.

In planning and building these neighborhoods, of course, there is the chance to use all the newest and best practices. Houses can be appropriately planned inside and out. They can be of pleasant and efficient architecture. They can be spaced and arranged in the proper order for neighborly living and privacy. Streets and utilities, parks and playgrounds, schools and recreation facilities can be planned to fit into the scheme. They can be of the newest and best design that we know—because they will be new, and all will be built by a plan instead of helter-skelter.

Every community should have its place to play and relax, away from work and worry.

Building Atlanta's Future

In such neighborhoods as these, people will escape some of the objectionable features which large cities now present. The neighborhood approach seems to be a sound one. By looking at Atlanta as a city made up of many pleasant neighborhoods scattered over and around the business and industrial areas, we can begin to see how much we can improve a city as a place to live. If we can develop our city into a better place to live and work, the economic side is more likely to improve. Improving any part of city life will make it easier to improve the others. By bringing them all up together, we can perhaps raise our city to a quality of which we may be proud.

There are people who say that the problems of large cities are too great to be tolerated. They say that cities do more harm than good. They suggest that we do away with large cities altogether. Then we could all live in small towns or in the country and thus have no more city problems of overcrowding and all the consequences. That is one sure way of solving city problems. But those of us who want to improve our cities and keep the best that is in them can not take this view seriously.

Try to imagine how Atlanta would look if made up of planned neighborhoods and business areas as we have just described. Think of all the improvements you could suggest in housing, streets, recreation, social services, and other phases. The best of everything is what we must plan for. That is what we must work for. Only when enough people know how good a city we can have, and want it badly enough to work for it, will we begin to make faster progress. If you can add your influence to getting others interested, you are doing a real service to Atlanta and all the people who live here.

DISCUSSION QUESTIONS

1. What are some stories or poems which impress you as examples of the desire to belong to a local group?
2. Why do we not find closely-knit local groups in cities to the extent that we do in the country?
3. What are some of the problems

Communities in Atlanta

which the lack of local groups in the city seems to cause?

4. Why do "Garden Cities" have rules which limit the number of people who can live there?

5. What are the advantages of "green belts" and of narrow curving streets in residential areas?

HAVE YOU READ?

1. Hughes, R. O. *Building Citizenship*. Chap. II, "Communities and Community Spirit." Boston, Massachusetts: Allyn and Bacon, 1943.
2. Jarrell, Ira. *Making Americans*, Superintendent's Annual Report to the Board of Education. Atlanta, Georgia: Atlanta Public Schools, 1945-46.
3. Stonorov, Oscar, and Kahn, Louis I. *You and Your Neighborhood, A Primer for Neighborhood Planning*. New York: Revere Copper and Brass Incorporated, 1944.

9. The Houses We Live In

YOUR home is the part of Atlanta you probably know best. It is not only a part of the wealth of Atlanta in terms of real property, it is also the place where you spend a great deal of time. It is the headquarters from which you go about all your activities. It is the place to which you return to be with your family and to eat, sleep, rest, and play among those who are dearest to you. Here you entertain your friends and store your belongings. Your house is indeed your "castle." No person can be happy long without some place to call home.

You can think, no doubt, of many pleasant memories of the house, or houses, in which you have lived. Perhaps you can remember unpleasant ones too. If you have never lived in an undesirable house, you are very lucky. Many people in Atlanta live in houses which do not please them or which endanger their health and their very lives. Often they are ashamed to live there but have no other place to go. No one can be very happy in such a situation. People who must worry about a

The Houses We Live In

good house to live in, along with all their other worries, are that much less happy and efficient as workers and citizens.

Your personal happiness is affected by the house you live in. Do you live in a house which is suitably warm and suitably cool and comfortable? Do you have enough space for your family to live without overcrowding? Are you proud of your house? Do you know other people who are not?

Of course, you think of other things than the building itself in selecting a house to live in. Lawns, open spaces, and surrounding buildings are really part of a home. They make up your local environment for living. A place for children to play outside the house and neighbors to chat with are very important to good housing environment.

People like to be sociable. Very few of us like to live strictly to ourselves. Neighborhoods and neighborly feelings seem to grow up wherever people live near one another. Housing arrangements should be planned to allow this. There must be space enough to give some freedom of action and privacy when we want them. But the plan should allow us to get together with ease also.

Neighborhood and family squabbles may be brought on by poor housing arrangements such as overcrowding. Neighborly living is but one factor which housing affects in our city. It is a way in which land use in the arrangement of housing affects people. It illustrates the fact

Poor houses affect our health and happiness and our whole outlook on life.

that housing is a large part of the common wealth of the people of our city. Good housing is one of the essentials for good citizenship.

HOUSES, PEOPLE, AND CITIES

Since Atlanta's housing is so important to our people, it is of great importance to the city. Our city government has done much to help get better housing. But the problem has not been solved. Many houses in Atlanta are still below the standards of decent living.

There are many reasons housing takes such an important place in a city. We have mentioned the personal happiness and pride which come with living in good homes. This happiness affects the health and efficiency of workers and thus is tied in with the economy of our city. Besides helping workers to produce more, good housing is a product of the economy. Houses are important to us because:

1. People spend so much of their time in their houses:

    A working man —$1/3$ to $2/3$ of his time
    A housewife —$2/3$ to $19/20$
    A pre-school child—$2/3$ to $19/20$
    A school child —$1/2$ to $3/4$

2. Houses are the places for family living. The physical and mental health of children and adults are developed in family life. Pleasant and comfortable houses help make better citizens.

3. More of a city's area is used for housing than for anything else. Streets and alleys are the next largest users of space; then, in order, come industry, commerce, public and institutional buildings, parks, and open space.

4. House building and repair is a large part of the construction work in a city. It gives jobs to many people. Then, of course, as new houses are built, there must be other construction—such as streets, stores, schools—to go along with it. Construction depends a great deal on housebuilding. Since it is one of the largest of employment types, construction is one of the best measures of prosperity. In good times, many new houses are

The Houses We Live In

built. In times of depression, the construction industry is one of the first to slow.

5. Housing provides nearly half the local tax revenues—that is, almost half the money collected by city government is that paid as taxes on dwelling houses. About 60 per cent of total urban real property values are made up of housing.

6. In a normal year, you may expect to spend nearly $3 out of every $10 you earn on your house—whether you rent or own it. If you are an average consumer, you will spend more only on food and tobacco combined. Much attention is being given to lowering the cost of housing, however.

These facts show why visitors measure a city by its houses. No wonder we brag about and show off our attractive residential areas to visitors. For the same reasons we shun the slums even as we go about by ourselves.

In this respect Atlanta contains the two extremes. We have beautiful residential sections which are world famous—picturesque mansions landscaped in natural splendor. But we also have slums which are just as ugly and vicious as any in the world.

SLUMS AND BLIGHT

The fact is that at least 15 per cent of the area within Atlanta city limits can be called slums. A *slum* is an area in which more than half of the houses need major repairs, lack sanitary facilities, and are overcrowded beyond a point of health and decency. Thus if you know of an area where most of the houses have sagging corners, leaking roofs, holes in walls; have no running water, toilets, and baths; and where several families are trying to live in houses meant for only one—that area is a slum. They are not hard to find in Atlanta because nearly ⅕ of Atlanta is slum area.

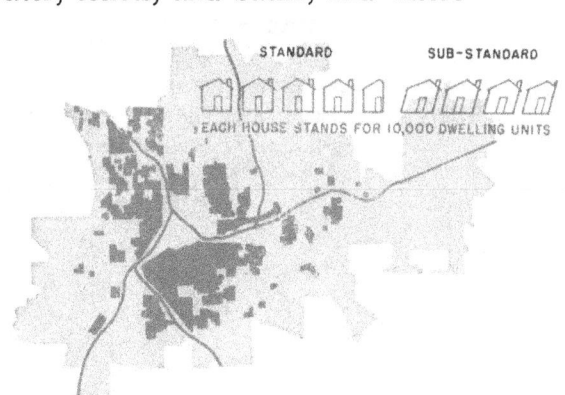

Slums and blight are great blots on the map of Atlanta.

Building Atlanta's Future

In this 15 per cent of the Atlanta area we find:
1. Almost 40 per cent of Atlanta's people
2. 69 per cent of the tuberculosis cases
3. More than 59 per cent of the city's crime
4. 72 per cent of the juvenile delinquency
5. Fire hazards, inflammable as tinder, to endanger the lives of people and adjoining property

Are not these reason enough to call these areas "sore spots," "cancerous growths," "circles of rot," and all the other names which have been given them? We see that crime, disease, and fire hazards are centered in these slums. Would it not seem that to get rid of the slums would rid us of many of these evils?

However, the slum menace is not always so striking and spectacular as are some other ills. The Winecoff Hotel fire was so horrible that the news spread far and fast. Officials hastened to check the safety measures in other hotels to see that such a holocaust would not occur again. But what about the fire hazard of Atlanta's slums? Slum fires can be spectacular too. They can kill people the same as hotel fires.

The terrible Atlanta fire of 1917 spread from a slum to the beautiful Boulevard district and destroyed most of the buildings in that section. The loss was $5,500,000, but only $3,500,000 insurance was carried. Must we wait for another great fire before we take steps toward prevention?

Besides the slums, we have even larger areas of *blight*. Blighted areas are those which are on the way to becoming slums. If they do not get immediate attention they will soon become out and out slums. Blocks in which more than half the houses need major repairs—such as were mentioned for slums—and which lack private baths are classed

Part of the devastated area wherein the great fire of 1917 destroyed 1553 houses in 73 blocks. The loss was over 5 million dollars. This fire started in a slum.

These houses are beginning to show signs of blight. Unless they are repaired, they will soon become slums.

as blighted. Blight has begun in about 60 per cent of the housing area inside Atlanta city limits. Thus much of our city is filled with houses which do not come up to the standards we desire.

WHY WE HAVE SLUMS AND BLIGHT

Atlanta is not the only city which has slums and blight. They occur in almost all cities. In fact there has long been a lack of good housing for low-income groups all over the world. Slums and blight are the result of attempts to provide housing at the lowest possible cost. Keeping down the expense of this housing means poor construction and little repair work. Low rent payments will not support expensive buildings and services. Old buildings have been kept in use long after they should have been torn down. People must live in them because there is often no other place to live that they can afford.

Thus the owners of slum property keep on trying to get as much rent as they can out of their investment. The valuable location and the owners' desire for profit cause high rent for these miserable slum dwellings. This is a good example of poor land use. As with other land-use practices, slums tend to grow and spread at the edges. In most

American cities there have been through the years these spreading circles of rot. They usually begin near the very heart, or older part, of the city and spread outward as the city grows and changes. As the blight and slums creep nearer, the people who can afford it move to newer residential sections in the outskirts. The rot spreads into the areas they vacate.

Neither the people who run from them nor those who live in them are responsible for slums. Slums and blight are the products of the great forces which cause cities to grow and change. In the long run, we can prevent slums only by guiding these forces as they develop. *Slum clearance* is a way to cure the ones we have now. But other slums will develop unless we plan the economic, social, and physical development of our cities as one plan.

HOUSING IN ATLANTA

Atlanta's housing problem has been taking form for years. It will take years to solve it—even if we begin giving it full attention now. The general pattern of slum spread has been at work during all the city's lifetime. The war made the housing problem much worse between 1941 and 1945. As we have seen, the population grew very fast during the development of war industries. As the people poured in, they had

Areas shaded in white are slums and blight in central Atlanta.

Building Atlanta's Future

to have houses. If they couldn't get good houses, they took poor ones. Many moved in with other families. There was also a large increase in the marriage rate during and after the war. This added to the more than usual number of new families to be housed.

During this time, however, building materials were used only for war industry purposes. Housing construction slowed almost to a stop. After the war, materials and labor were so expensive that few people could afford to build new homes. Thus there were many new families and no new houses for them. The housing problem, as you may remember, became very acute. People crowded together as best they could and many lived in almost impossible overcrowding. By 1948 most of the new houses were still being built by those who could own their own homes. The greatest need was for houses for people who wanted to rent.

The census of 1940 showed that there were 84,746 *dwelling units* in the city of Atlanta. A dwelling unit is a house, an apartment, or a room in which a family or person lives. Of these nearly 85,000 dwelling units:

38,653 were substandard—meaning that, among other things:
> 10,000 were without running water
> 22,000 lacked sanitary, inside, flush toilets
> 28,000 were without baths

In these substandard—undesirable—houses live:
> more than 30 per cent of the white families in Atlanta
> more than 70 per cent of the Negro families in Atlanta

A census report for 1947 estimates that 12 per cent of the dwelling units were in need of major repairs as compared with 20 per cent in 1940. This shows that there was some "patching up" improvement

ATLANTA'S PEOPLE AND WHERE THEY LIVE
In standard housing   In substandard housing

○ White
● Negro

Each figure represents 10% of total population

during the war. But there is still room for more. In 1947, three out of ten dwelling units still lacked one or more of: electric lighting and running water; flush toilet; bathtub or shower; private cooking facilities.

You see that housing is one of our greatest problems in Atlanta. A greater proportion of Negroes than whites are badly housed. Estimates of the number of new dwelling units needed in order to give ample shelter to our population range from 3,000 to 14,000. Besides that, many of the houses now in use are slum and blight structures. Many of them are not fit to live in. They must be replaced. This will be a great task with many hindering details.

How can we go about solving the problem of housing in Atlanta? What has been done about it already? It is not a new problem. Some people have been concerned about, and have worked for, better housing for a long time.

During the depression years of the 1930's, there was a great deal done to improve housing conditions. Many cities in the United States had housing problems similar to Atlanta's. There was at the same time much unemployment. Many people had no jobs and no money to pay rent. Something had to be done. So the United States Government stepped in with a housing program. This seemed necessary because the cities did not have money themselves for such a program.

THE FEDERAL HOUSING PROGRAM

The federal housing program set out to do two things. One was to give people jobs by paying them to work at building new houses. The second was to clear some of the worst slums at the same time. This would give new and better houses to people who could not afford to build their own.

This is what they did and how they went about it:

Federal insurance (insurance by the United States Government) for housing loans and mortgages was set up. Banks, savings and loan associations, and other lending agencies could get their loans insured—

1. University Homes
2. John Hope Homes
3. Eagan Homes
4. Herndon Homes
5. Clark Howell Homes
6. Techwood Homes

ATLANTA'S HOUSING PROJECTS

7. Capitol Homes
8. Grady Homes

guaranteed—by Uncle Sam. They could then lend money at a lower rate to families for use in building houses. The loan could be repaid over a 20-year period. These low interest rates and long-time loans made it possible for many families to borrow money and build homes. They could not have done so otherwise.

This loan insurance also helped people pay off old loans on their houses. In this way many saved their homes which would have been lost because they could not pay off the mortgages at the usual rate of interest. They could borrow money on the new plan and pay off the old debt. Then they could pay back the new debt on the same plan as that for new buildings mentioned above.

The housing program also sponsored a slum-clearance drive. The federal government lent up to 90 per cent of the money needed to buy up and clear out slum areas and to rebuild with safe, sanitary, and decent housing for low-income families. The other 10 per cent of the money was provided by local sources. In this plan, slum dwellings equal to the number of new dwellings had to be torn down. This got rid of many areas of unsightly and unhealthful housing.

Construction of this housing had to be kept within certain cost limits. Also, people who could afford to rent or buy

Building Atlanta's Future

houses built without government assistance were not allowed to live here. These projects became known as "public housing" in contrast to "private enterprise" housing built by local businesses. The United States Government paid "subsidies" to these public housing projects so that families with the lowest incomes could have decent houses in which to live. A subsidy is a grant, or gift, of money to aid an enterprise for the public welfare. The government thus helps get rid of slums and gives aid to needy people.

How did this plan work? The slum-clearance job was done by local housing authorities. These were appointed by the city mayors and councils but operated as independent, nonpolitical agencies. The rules were set by the federal government through the United States Housing Authority. The local Housing Authority carried them out.

The Atlanta Housing Authority was one of the first in the country. Atlanta became a pioneer city in slum-clearance. Today it has more public housing than any city its size in this country. People come to Atlanta from other cities in America and as far away as New Zealand just to see our slum clearance projects.

In the shadow of the dome of the State Capitol were these miserable

The Houses We Live In

What did public housing mean to people when it started? Take an example of a family who lived in a tumble-down shack in a slum area. They had no screens, no water toilet, bath, or even an inside lavatory for keeping clean. They were overcrowded and had lost hope of ever making themselves or their house clean and decent.

The depression brought with it loss of jobs, so this family had no money income. The situation looked desperate. At a time like this the temptation to steal is very strong. Starving people will do all they can to get food. In their run-down condition they are easy prey for diseases.

Then the housing and slum-clearance program came along. Perhaps the men in the family got jobs helping wreck and rebuild the slum area where they lived. This brought in money for food and clothing and other necessities.

As the housing projects were finished, families such as this moved into them. Here they had neat, attractive new houses. They had bathing and sanitary facilities. The houses were comfortable. The rent paid was often less than they had paid for the miserable slum housing.

Small wonder that these people changed. They took pride in nice

um dwellings. Many of them have been replaced by Capitol Homes.

People who live under these conditions have two strikes against them to start with.

houses, in neater personal appearance. Small wonder also that their health was better. They felt better and worked harder. With the help of the government, many of them got a new start in life. The city got many new and pleasant residential districts.

Techwood Homes was Atlanta's first public housing project—indeed, it was the first in all the United States. On November 29, 1935, President Roosevelt spoke at the Dedication Ceremonies here in Atlanta. Millions over the radio and fifty thousand in person listened to our President as he said, "Within sight of you today stands a tribute to useful work under government supervision—the first slum clearance and low-rent housing project. Here, at the request of the citizens of Atlanta, we have cleared out nine square blocks of antiquated, squalid dwellings for years a detriment to this community. Today these hopeless dwellings are gone and in their places we see the bright, cheerful buildings of the Techwood Housing Project. Within a very short time people who never before could get a decent roof over their heads will live here in reasonable comfort and healthful, worthwhile surroundings. Others will find similar homes in Atlanta's second slum clearance, the University Project."

The Houses We Live In

Techwood Homes is now taken for granted as an attractive part of Atlanta. Few people remember the slum area which once was there.

Since the first tenants moved into Techwood in September 1936, there have been seven more public housing projects opened in Atlanta. There have been also many instances of slum clearance by private enterprise, but not to re-house slum dwellers. We must remember that the only way thus far found to do that is by subsidy. We must still have public aid to give our poorest people good houses. The amazing change which can be made in slum areas has been seen over and over. By keeping eternally at it we may be able to keep Atlanta in the front as a pioneer for better housing.

President Roosevelt as he spoke at the dedication of Techwood Homes, "the first slum clearance and low-rent housing project."

We still build houses by "handmade" methods.

WHY IS PUBLIC HOUSING NECESSARY?

It is generally agreed that most of the housing in Atlanta should be built by private enterprise. Public housing projects are built for a special purpose. They are financed and partly subsidized by public money—tax money paid by the public. They are built to give decent houses to people who do not make enough income to pay the higher rents or higher prices necessary for private housing. If everyone had a job which paid enough income, we would not need public housing.

Neither would public housing be necessary if private builders could produce houses at lower cost. However, the building industry seems to be slow to take up new methods. Many houses are still being built by outmoded, inefficient, and expensive methods of the last century. It is impossible to build good houses cheap enough for low-income groups by these methods.

We still build houses on a custom-built, handmade basis. This gives good workmanship but great expense. Think of the difference in price of a handmade, custom-built automobile and a standard make. We have developed very efficient new ways of making automobiles. Their prices have been reduced so that many people can own them. The housing industry has not developed nearly such efficient methods.

The Houses We Live In

There are now, and may always be, people who do not make enough money to pay today's normal rent. If they are forced to live in hideous, unhealthy slums, their chances of getting a new start in life are small. Public housing is one way we can help give them a decent environment from which they can work to better their situation.

In fact, when you get right down to it, using money from taxes to clear slums can be more important than using it for schools. A child cannot go to school five hours a day and live in a slum the remaining nineteen hours without the slum undoing much of his schooling. England puts public housing ahead of public schooling although she has both.

The cost of a public housing project seems large. Taxes must be a

Slums are expensive in money and in human suffering.

Building Atlanta's Future

little higher so that we can pay for them. But compare the cost of the project with the cost of the slum it replaces. And remember the $2,000,000 loss those people who owned homes on Boulevard suffered through the fire which started in a slum in 1917.

Tax money must pay for welfare aid, health, police, and fire services in the slums too. The biggest expense for these services in Atlanta comes from the slum and blight areas. Think how much less we would spend for prisons, hospitals, police, and fire departments if we could do away with the 15 per cent of Atlanta which is slum area. Remember that most of the disease, crime, delinquency, and fire hazards in the city occur in this 15 per cent of our area. The slum condition seems to be a great factor in causing them.

Into one slum area of Atlanta, before clearance, we paid for free hospitalization, child delinquency, police and fire protection more than 9½ times the taxes we collected. With the public housing completed, these charges in that area fell to almost nothing.

So, you see, public housing may not be so expensive after all. In addition to the cost, think of the difference between the happiness of the people in the two cases. Living in the wretched, dirty hovels of a slum seems to take the inspiration out of a person.

The records show that a large percentage of the people who move into housing projects in Atlanta soon are able to move out into homes of their own. That has been the hope of the Housing Authority—that

Where these conditions once existed

The Houses We Live In

people will get better jobs and be able to build or rent their own houses. Therefore, as the tenants get higher income jobs, they must move out of the public housing. Then others may move in who have lower incomes or who live in slum areas. The housing projects are meant to be, as much as possible, steppingstones from slum to private ownership.

This does not mean that it is always wise for people to buy houses. For those whose work calls for them to move often to other places, it is best to rent houses. People sometimes saddle themselves with debt to buy a house which they cannot well afford. Then when they move on to better jobs they lose part of their investment through a quick, cheap sale of their property.

The eight public housing projects in Atlanta were completed between 1936 and 1941. In the order of their completion they are: Techwood Homes, University Homes, John Hope Homes, Clark Howell Homes, Capitol Homes, Eagan Homes, Grady Homes, and Herndon Homes. Atlanta now has 4,994 dwelling units of public housing. Less than 5000—a small number compared to our total of 85,000 dwelling units. Some 17,000 people live in these—people in low income groups who would have to live in slum areas otherwise. Here they have comfortable houses, sanitary control and supervision, well-paved streets, and an atmosphere of neatness and beauty. They have nurseries and playgrounds for children and recreation facilities for all ages. What a change from the scene in these areas only ten or fifteen years ago!

Techwood's pleasing scenes greet us today.

PRIVATE ENTERPRISE AND PUBLIC HOUSING

There has been much criticism of this method of public housing. Almost everyone agrees that slum-clearance is necessary. But some say that it should be done only by local business as private enterprise. They point out that this adds to local jobs and businesses and allows us to have a higher economic gain. They do not believe that government should interfere with local business affairs.

The Atlanta Housing Authority takes the stand that private enterprise should provide as much housing as possible. Real estate agencies and construction contractors should build and sell as many houses as they can. However, these businesses must operate for a profit. If they do not make a profit on the sale or rental of a house, they can not stay in business. This sometimes forces them to build poor houses in order to rent at the low rental some people can afford to pay. They must charge high rent for good houses in order to make a profit.

For the people who can afford it, private enterprise housing is doing a good job. It is a thriving business which adds much to our economy. Until now, private enterprise has not been able to produce good houses cheaply enough to be able to rent or sell them at a price our lowest income groups in Atlanta can pay. New construction materials and methods may make this possible in the future.

There is much research being done with new plastic and metal materials and with prefabricated houses. New inventions and techniques are sure to come from this. Private builders may soon be able to provide good housing for the poorest of our people at a price they can afford to pay.

Cities all over the world have slums. These before and after slum clearance scenes are from Naples, Italy. Note the same chimney at the extreme right and the railroad in the foreground, showing the two pictures were made at exactly the same spot.

The Houses We Live In

Until such housing is available, however, some plan for subsidizing may be necessary. As the First Annual Report of the Atlanta Housing Authority puts it, "Our forefathers had a sublime dream—'life, liberty, and the pursuit of happiness.' Certainly, in the slums, life is unsafe; liberty of small account, and to pursue happiness means only frustration. These things must not be—not for anyone, regardless of race or creed. No individual is equal to the task of coping with the slum. Only the people collectively, through government, have the power to establish 'life, liberty, and the pursuit of happiness' on the bed rock of reality."

We must in some way pay the difference between what low income earners can afford and the cost of decent housing. Public housing is one answer. Slums are another. It is up to us to decide which—or to devise another solution. Slums waste our human resources. If private enterprise is to be slow in stopping this waste, then any means at hand may be worth trying.

Housing is one of the great concerns in developing a better city. Surely a city can not reach its highest attainment unless it has comfortable, attractive, and efficient housing. Good housing will not grow up "like Topsy." It takes planning, good planning, to have good housing which is well located in relation to work, play, and community facilities. It must be planned in relation to streets, services, land-use zones—in short, in terms of the whole city.

These are slum clearance houses built for old people in Amsterdam, Holland.

New prefabricated houses are partially built in factories, then hauled to the location and assembled. About one month elapsed between the second and third scenes.

The Houses We Live In

Atlanta has twice missed an opportunity to plan and redevelop a city better suited for its people—all the people: once in 1864, following Sherman's burning the city; and again in 1917 when another great fire occurred. The extensive slums and blight of today offer another challenge. What will happen is up to you in no small measure.

DISCUSSION QUESTIONS

1. In what ways do dwelling houses affect the economy of a city?
2. Why are slums so costly in terms of city expenses?
3. Why do we have public housing? How can we make privately built housing serve these purposes?
4. What have you read in the newspapers recently about Atlanta's housing problems? Do they seem to be improving?
5. What are the latest estimates on the number of new dwelling units needed to house Atlanta's population adequately?
6. Name some streets you know as definitely slum areas. How can you tell they are slums?

HAVE YOU READ?

1. Atlanta Housing Authority. *Annual Reports* for the years 1939 to 1948. Atlanta, Georgia: Atlanta Housing Authority.
2. Atlanta Housing Council. *Proposed Areas for Expansions of Negro Housing in Atlanta, Georgia.* Atlanta, Georgia: Atlanta Housing Council, 1947.
3. Citizens' Fact-Finding Movement of Georgia. *Georgia Facts in Figures, A Source Book.* "Man-made Resources." Athens, Georgia: The University of Georgia Press, 1946. Pp. 45-69.
4. *Community Resources Directory, 1946-47.* "Housing Authority of the City of Atlanta." Atlanta, Georgia: Community Planning Council, 1947.
5. U. S. Bureau of the Census. *Current Population Reports, Housing.* "Housing Characteristics of the Atlanta, Georgia Metropolitan District, April 1947. Series P. 71, No. 6. Washington, D. C., 1947.
6. United States Conference of Mayors. *America Can Not Afford Slums.* "Slums Drain Off Far More Than Their Share of City Revenue." Washington, D. C.: Craftsman Press.

10. Our Streets and Services

BETWEEN the hours of 7:00 and 9:00 in the morning, the central part of Atlanta is the scene of rushing activity. People pour in from all directions. They come in streetcars, buses, trackless trolleys, automobiles, and on foot. All of them seem to be in a hurry to get somewhere. They push and shove and hurry as if they had only one purpose in life—to get to their jobs.

The stream reverses in late afternoon. The same people are in a hurry to get out of this area. Traffic gets into jams. Pedestrians wait to cross streets. The police work hurriedly to keep the streams of traffic moving as smoothly as possible. Expensive traffic signals have been put in to aid the job. People get in one another's way. Tired bodies and taut nerves make people fretful after the long day's work. They want to get home for rest and quiet.

Why do these people rush and fret and hurry like this? Why must they crowd into the small area of stores, shops, and offices and then

Our Streets and Services

hasten out again? Because they must work to make a living, you say? That is the most obvious answer. They do it because many people come to Atlanta to buy goods and services. Workers provide these things. Their work also provides for the needs of people in other places in the region and in the nation.

The same flowing in and flowing out of workers goes on in all modern cities. Cities are built in order that it may happen. In this way people get together to carry on the work of providing the goods and services which we use in living.

The villages of the American Indians and the towns of medieval Europe which we read about in history grew up for some of the same reasons. People built these villages and towns so they could live close together. It was easier to organize hunting parties, to till the fields, and to have social gatherings. They could work together, exchange goods and ideas. A wall around the town provided protection from raids by their enemies. Towns were handy, pleasant, and efficient places to live.

Then these towns became market centers. Traders came and went with goods from other places. Factories grew up to make more goods for trade. Towns grew into cities. Through increased production and trade, people could get more of the things they wanted. Cities helped give these things. They were centers of production and marketing.

The people in this African village can gather and talk together very easily. Transportation and communication are simple and personal.

Building Atlanta's Future

In this way cities tended to grow larger and larger. In them more people could get together to do more complex things—things requiring more cooperation. In order to do this they had to be able to move about and see each other. They had to move people, goods, and ideas from place to place. This had to be done quickly and easily. A cobbler in a medieval town might walk a few hundred yards to the tannery and bring back the leather he needed. He could stroll around and discuss prices with his friends in a few minutes.

Cities are quite different today. Instead of a city within a wall, we now have sprawling metropolitan districts. Metropolitan Atlanta covers

Our street scenes and transportation methods have changed greatly since 1882.

Our Streets and Services

more than 220 square miles. The problems of transportation, communication, and necessary services have increased many fold.

INVENTIONS AND THE GROWTH OF CITIES

In a modern metropolitan district such as Atlanta, people must get from place to place swiftly and easily just as in the medieval or Oriental city—as in all cities. Goods and ideas must be transmitted freely or a city cannot be a center of trade and industry.

To do these jobs, we have developed new ways of transit and communication. New inventions gave us faster and easier movement

when this picture was made. Our street pattern has changed but little.

of people, goods, and ideas. Streets were widened to make room for larger and faster carriages and horse-drawn wagons. Then they were widened again to provide for automobiles and trucks. Street railways, bus, and trolley lines cover our cities. We have changed the cities gradually to include all these things. These very changes, however, do not always fit well into our old cities.

Today, instead of exchanging ideas face to face in conversation, we converse by telephone, telegraph, radio, and postal service. Motor trucks pick up and deliver freight at our doors. Wires deliver electricity for light, heat, and power in our homes and industries. Pipes bring us water and gas, and other pipes take away our sewage. Our cities are wonders of engineering genius. But if any of these services fail for any length of time, life in cities becomes very hard indeed. By tracing the development of the inventions and skills which make these services possible, we can trace the development of the modern city—the metropolitan district.

Ancient cities were usually compact and circular in shape. City dwellers traveled to work on foot or by horse. They had to live close to their work. Then came steam railroads and electric streetcars. Suburban trains and trolleys made transportation much faster. Workers could live near the railways and get to work quickly. Cities took the form of starfish, with arms reaching out along the railways. This influence can still be seen in the form of suburban towns from which people commute to the large center city every day to work.

Then the automobile was invented. In a few years many people were driving their own automobiles to work. They no longer had to live near the railroad or car lines. They could live anywhere within a large radius of the center of the city and still get to work in a reasonable time. Cities took on even more rambling and scattered appearances.

Finding a parking space is often an annoying problem to Atlanta motorists.

Our Streets and Services

At the same time, of course, the interiors of the cities were changing also. Business districts became more concentrated because the workers did not have to live there. The narrow lanes for foot traffic in ancient cities would not admit carriages nor automobiles. Streets had to be made wider and traffic controls installed. A network of rails and then of highways had to be built to take care of the new ways of travel. Where cities were already built, this brought on the need for drastic changes in their patterns. The old sections in the older cities of the world give good examples of how needs have changed.

Traffic congestion in some parts of Atlanta during rush hours is often a nuisance. It shows us that we need changes in our street pattern to fit the needs of automobile commuters and shoppers. Parking space for all the automobiles is another of our problems.

SERVICES WITHIN MODERN CITIES

This freedom of city dwellers to choose their places of residence has changed the pattern of both business and residential districts. Whole cities take on different form. Even the buildings and services have changed to keep pace with the new transportation systems.

With the development of new building techniques and higher city land values came the skyscrapers. They give more sheltered space for offices and shops on the same amount of land. They also bring the need for a new type of transportation—up and down travel. People cannot walk up and down many flights of stairs without undue fatigue. Elevators were developed and improved until some are now automatic. Cities have grown higher as well as larger with the new transit methods.

We have also devised new water supply systems. Ancient Rome had an elaborate system of "aqueducts" and open sewers, as well as lavish baths. Some medieval cities had very poor water and sewage disposal systems. Even after London was a huge metropolis, the people still threw garbage and refuse through their windows onto the unpaved streets. Pigs rooted and wallowed in the mud and filth. Of course there

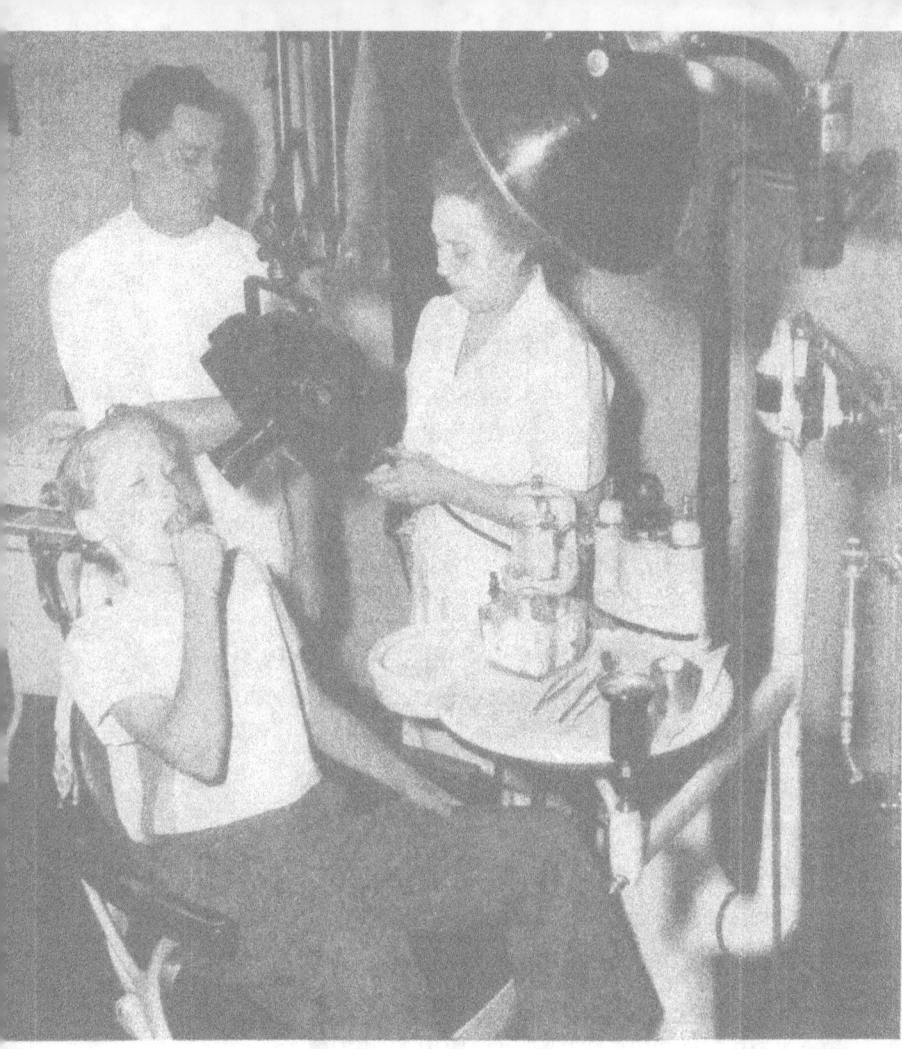

Modern health precautions and medical care make our cities much safer and more pleasant places in which to live.

were foul smells in such a city. People then did not know much about germs, and disease was rampant. History tells of the "plagues" and epidemics which often struck cities. We do not have to wonder long to know why they came and why they spread so rapidly.

This kind of sanitation in one of our modern cities would have even worse consequences. We are more crowded and have fewer open spaces to relieve the crowding. A pure and protected water supply is a necessity. Closed sewers and prompt garbage collection have made cities safer than the open country from the spread of contagious disease. These services we have come to expect and to depend on. They are fairly recent developments in the history of cities. For this matter, Oriental cities still lack many of the health facilities we now take for granted in our cities.

Our Streets and Services

The Bible story of Christ and the woman at the well shows us how people got their water supply twenty centuries ago. Little more than fifty years ago the people in Atlanta had to go to the well, or pump, down the street to get water. Now we get pure water from any of the many faucets we find in most homes.

Inventions in the use of electric power also have made cities better places to live. Besides the many uses of light and heat from electric power, it furnishes energy to turn motors of all sizes which help us to do more work. Electricity is also the basis for telephone, telegraph, radio, and television.

Telephones and telegraph speed up communication so that we can have huge organizations which work as one unit even though the parts may be separated by hundreds of miles. Think how difficult it

Today telephones save us many steps and enable us to work cooperatively when far apart.

Building Atlanta's Future

would be to keep a skyscraper of offices organized if you had to climb ten or twenty flights of stairs to talk to your co-workers. The telephone brings distant places and people right into the same room to talk with you.

All these things help make cities what they are today. They have had their effect on Atlanta. Has Atlanta taken advantage of them? Have we used them to the best advantage toward making our city serve its purpose to the fullest extent?

If we go back to the history of our city we can trace the development of each invention and the effect it had on Atlanta. Since Atlanta grew up in large part as a transportation center, let us look at transportation first. We have a serious problem of traffic congestion in Atlanta. How did this problem arise?

TRANSPORTATION AND THE MAP OF ATLANTA

In Chapter I we saw that Atlanta was but a village before 1850. People traveled over the streets on foot or in wagons and buggies. It did not take long to walk from one end of town to the other. But Atlanta was growing. As it grew, traffic on highways and railroads increased by leaps and bounds. Industries sprang up and trade doubled many times. The need for fast, certain transportation within the city grew also. More streets were paved. People prospered and some had fancy and stylish carriages drawn by spirited teams. The Piedmont Driving Club is a carry-over from those days.

As Atlanta burst its bounds, the city limits were expanded again and again. Distances within the city increased. People who lived on the edges of the city had to spend a great deal of time going to and from their working places. Shopping trips were slow and time consuming. Fast, certain, public transportation was needed very badly.

To fill this need the Atlanta Street Railway Company was incorporated in 1866. This company built the first street railway line in the city. It ran from the railroad crossing on Whitehall Street to Camp Spring, which is now known as West End. The streetcars which

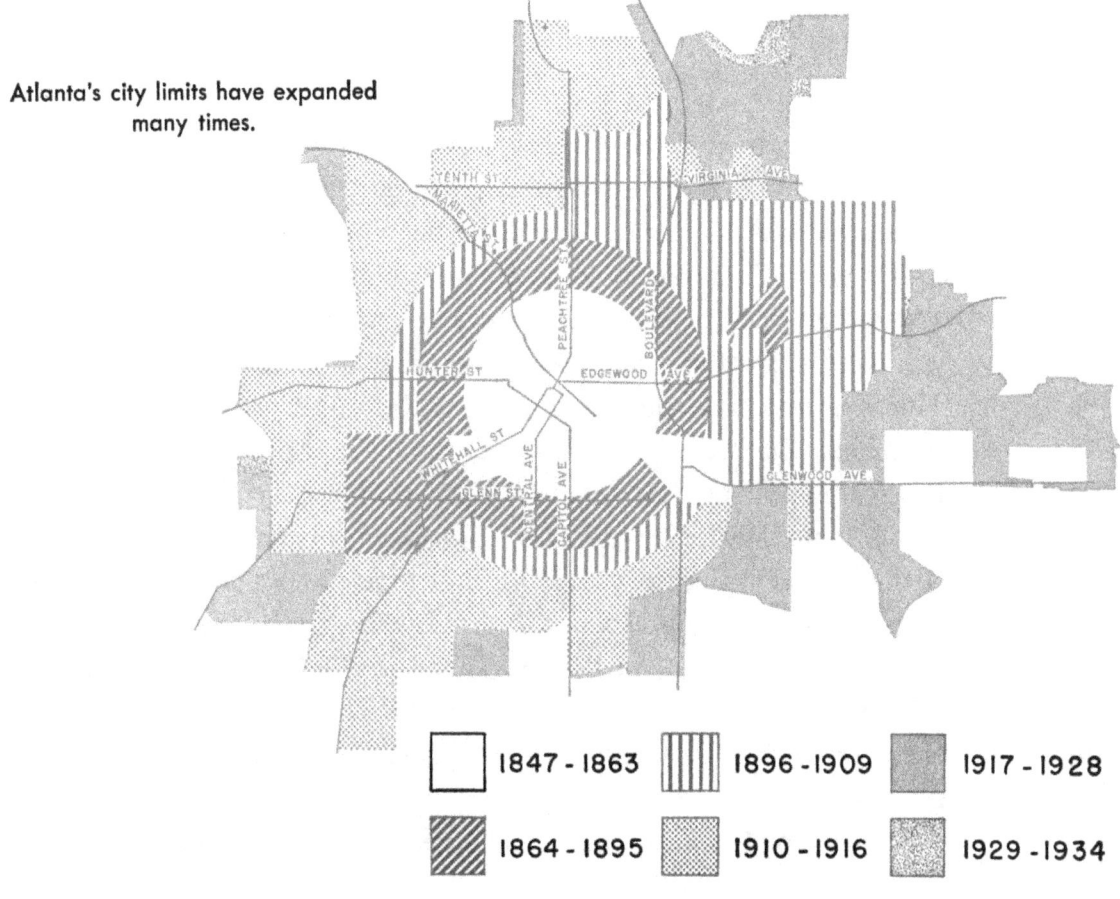

Atlanta's city limits have expanded many times.

ran on this line looked like the "Toonerville Trolley" in the comic cartoon. They were pulled by mules.

People liked the mule cars. They ran on schedule and could be depended upon. Thus workers had a faster, handier, more certain way to get to and from the central city. The line prospered. Another line began operating out Marietta Street in 1872. These lines were soon extended and others added.

These horse-drawn cars were very successful. But new inventions came along. In 1888 two new kinds of transit came to Atlanta. Steam cars, called "dummies," began running on the south side lines. Electric cars were put on the Edgewood-Inman Park run. The dummies were really small trains with the steam engines concealed in the regular streetcar frame. They were novel and entertaining and people rode them for the fun of it. The electric cars were the ancestors of modern streetcars and trackless trolleys.

Building Atlanta's Future

These new cars were improved as time went on. Street transit became faster and more efficient. During the 1890's there was a great expansion in Atlanta's transportation facilities. Electric cars were installed on all lines. Some old companies combined and new ones came along. Car lines reached out in nearly all directions. Within a few years all the small companies were combined into one large company. This was known as the Georgia Street Railway Company. In 1908 it combined with the Georgia Power Company and became the company which we know by that name today.

Atlanta's transportation system grew up in the last twenty years of the nineteenth century. During that time the population increased from 37,400 to 89,800. Before this the city had grown in a circular pattern. The city limits had been extended in the form of circles drawn at a certain distance from a center point. The center of the city was never more than reasonable walking distance from any point inside the city limits.

By 1900, however, fast scheduled streetcars ran out like spokes

The horse-drawn streetcars were a great improvment over walking or driving buggies on mudd

Our Streets and Services

from the central city hub in all directions. People who lived on these car lines could get to any part of the city in a fairly short riding time. The car lines were handy lanes along which to build dwelling houses and neighborhoods. At the end of the car lines there often grew up a suburban residential section.

Instead of expanding in circles as before, Atlanta grew in the form of radial spokes along the transportation lines. The city limits expanded to take in these areas and the city lost its circular shape. It became very irregular because topography and custom made some sides better places to live than others. Most cities in the United States have followed about the same pattern of growth. Established transportation lines have had a great deal to do with this growth. They have helped make the shapes of today's cities.

AUTOMOBILES AND RESIDENTIAL SECTIONS

Then came the automobile. The first automobile in Atlanta was a "horseless carriage" known as a Loco-Steamer. It was bought by

ough streets. The first electric cars were faster and were the ancestors of today's trolley cars.

The coming of automobiles has helped change the shape of Atlanta

Mr. W. J. Alexander in 1897. It was run by a steam motor and was very slow and contrary. To the horses and people of that time it must have been a strange and fearsome contraption.

One day Mr. Alexander set out on a sensational one-day trip to East Point, six miles away. Of course there were plenty of bystanders to see this unusual vehicle get under way. Some said he would never make it. They were right. About half-way there, a stubborn red mule got in the way of the coughing contraption. Neither would budge until the mule opened an attack. He kicked the Loco-Steamer into a ditch and departed winner.

Later automobiles were more dependable. By 1920 they had replaced most of the horse and mule transit. People who owned automobiles did not have to live near a car line to have convenient trans-

—and at the same time has created many new problems.

portation. Residential districts grew up in areas not served by streetcars. The shape of the city limits could change in any direction. Spaces between the starfish-arm car lines filled up because of this new transportation vehicle.

In the early 1920's, a fleet of "jitneys" tried to enter the city transportation system. These were model "T" Fords which picked up people along the routes into the city and took them to and from work. They charged a nickel, or "jitney," for fare, hence the nickname. Not being very dependable, they were abolished by a city law in 1924. Since that time the Georgia Power Company has had a "monopoly" on street transit. That means that it is the only company the city allows to operate transit lines within its limits. The suburban bus lines transport only people going outside the city. Since there is no competition,

Main highways pour many people into and through Atlanta, adding to our business and also to our traffic problems.

Georgia Power Company can plan schedules and routes so as to give efficient, cheap service. It is up to Atlanta's citizens to see that such service is provided, just as they must see that other "public" utilities are provided efficiently and cheaply.

Many people still ride the streetcars and buses in Atlanta. The number of runs keeps increasing. But the number of private automobiles and trucks has increased even more. So many people drive their own cars to work that parking space is often a problem. Those who drive in to shop and to transact business find it hard to park near their destinations. Highway traffic passing through the city adds to the congestion. This through traffic is also delayed by the heavy city traffic.

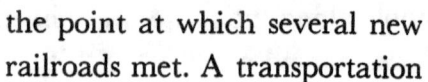

STREET PLANS AND BUSINESS

Stephen H. Long, Chief Engineer for the Western and Atlantic Railroad, selected the site for Atlanta. In 1837 he picked a point from which the ridges made a good location for other railroads to be built to several Georgia cities. Here he drove a stake to mark the end of the Western and Atlantic Railroad. That stake driven in the woods became the point at which several new railroads met. A transportation

Since Stephen Long drove the stake marking the end of the Western and Atlantic Railroad in 1837, railroads have been important lifelines in Atlanta's economy. Our great rail yards are still part of one of our basic industries.

Our Streets and Services

center was born. Since that time the flow of traffic has continued to increase. It is the terminus of many railroads and highways. Much of the traffic on Atlanta's streets today is the result of this flow of goods and people through the city.

Moving goods and people through and about Atlanta efficiently is one of our most necessary functions. This traffic is a large part of our city's life blood. Without it, there would never have been an Atlanta. It is to our interest to keep it moving smoothly. There must be fast and efficient movement in our everyday transactions within the city. We must also arrange for the easy passage of in-and-out and through traffic. Otherwise, our trade and commerce income will suffer.

What has this to do with Atlanta's streets? Streets are the traffic paths in the city. Traffic regulations and parking facilities go along with them to make up our transportation pattern. Each of these should be the very best that we can make it. What have we done toward this important problem?

When you drive to downtown Atlanta from your home, are you delayed by narrow streets, many turns, and heavy traffic? Are there dangerous, blind corners, and unmarked intersections? Does fast through traffic make residential streets safety hazards? Do visitors have trouble finding your street because of offsets and poor markings? Are the streets rough and in need of repair? These are common problems of street design and maintenance. Atlanta has them, as do most cities.

If you were driving a car or truck through Atlanta, would you be delayed by city traffic on your route? Are through routes well marked, or would you lose time in hunting the way? Does through traffic snarl up the city traffic because it must go down the busy

It would be hard for a motorist to watch traffic and find his way at the same time by looking at this cluttered signpost.

main streets? If these problems confront all people who come to Atlanta, they may soon decide to go to other cities to shop. Tourists and truckers may find other routes that do not cause such needless delays. Time is often important to travelers and truckers.

Automobiles have a great deal of freedom of routes. They do not have to follow rails or streams. Trucks can deliver materials and haul goods to and from factories in the country away from railroads and city traffic. For that reason industries and "super-markets" have begun to move out of the congested city districts. The compact city is not nearly so important to business as it was a few years ago. People can drive out to a suburban department store and find much of the same merchandise as in the city. Industries can locate on cheaper land in the open country and also escape city congestion.

Therefore, we must make our city attractive in these respects or we may lose our industries and commerce. Traffic problems are a great factor in keeping these businesses. If fewer people come to the central part of our city, there will be less business. Economic activities will drop off. Land values and rent for business space will be less. Our city will be less important in the economy of the region and nation. In short, Atlanta will dwindle away.

ATLANTA TRAFFIC PROBLEMS

We must make it easy for people to get into and out of Atlanta. We must make it easy for them to go about our city and transact their business. Handy parking places must be provided for shoppers. We must have fast, safe, efficient public transportation for both people and goods.

The great increase in street traffic in recent years has made this problem a big one in many cities. Atlanta has made plans for doing something about it. As we have seen, our street pattern has caused some extra problems. Lack of good planning in the early years has given us a very unusual pattern of streets. Many of our traffic difficulties are caused by this. It will be more expensive to correct them now than it would have been at first. We must now tear out the old and replace with the new. However, it will not grow less expensive to change as time goes by.

Various transportation plans have been proposed for Atlanta. One, called the Lochner Plan, sets forth a system of new arterial streets and highways. Fast traffic would thus take "expressways" through or around the city and only get on the main streets near the destination. The expressways would have no cross traffic to cause delay. This means building expensive viaducts over cross streets. It means new streets and many changes in old ones.

The original plan was to have cost about sixty million dollars when completed. Money was appropriated from the 1946 bond issue to start revising our street system. Whether or not the Lochner Plan is the best we can hope for, it is agreed that some such street plan is necessary. The sooner we make changes to correct our traffic problems, the better off our city will be.

One glaring example of a needed change is shown by travel to and from the airport. It often takes as long to ride from the city to the airline terminal as it does to fly to Birmingham or Savannah. Speed is the main reason for air travel. The bottleneck of ground travel to and from the airport defeats the speed of flight. High speed airport transportation is needed badly.

Proper traffic "arteries" and transportation terminals would help prevent the long lines of trolley cars waiting to load at curbs and safety islands. These lines often block all traffic.

Thus a new street system in Atlanta is one of our most pressing needs. A little patching here and there is not enough. Our outmoded

Compare Atlanta's first water supply plant of 1887 with this only one part of the huge system used today.

street and traffic system must be revised. The Lochner plan has indicated some needed changes. There are also others. The plan must be made in terms of the whole city. It must include the possibilities of new traffic needs in the future as best we can predict them. The well-planned street pattern is the frame within which the city is built. It can add to the beauty as well as to the efficiency of the city. Making our city more beautiful should not be overlooked.

Along with the revised streets, there must be revision of other services. Water and sewer mains usually follow streets. So do telephone, gas, and electric services. Changing streets will also require changes in utilities. It may be that we can modernize and improve them at the same time.

WATER, SEWERS, AND SANITATION

Atlanta has a municipal water supply. Before 1876 the only source of water in the city were wells and street corner pumps. In 1871 the city charter was revised to permit the city to own a water works. A board of water commissioners was elected and the next year a contract was let. The South River Reservoir (Lakewood Park) began operating in 1876.

The present water supply comes from the Chattahoochee River.

About 45 million gallons are used each day, though the system can deliver about 65 gallons if necessary. The two reservoirs at Hemphill Station have a storage capacity of 400 million gallons. There the water is filtered and flows into a clear water well and underground reservoir. Then it is distributed to the water mains. Hundreds of miles of underground pipes deliver water to all parts of the city.

Good tasting, pure, safe water comes to our homes and businesses. Getting it there requires intricate, expensive equipment. More than 4.5 cents of each dollar of city taxes goes to the Water Department, which is supervised by a committee of the city council appointed by the mayor.

Eight per cent of the dwelling units in the city lacked running

Atlanta's sewage disposal plants conserve by-products which once were wasted. Instead of being a great expense, sewage pays for its own disposal.

water in 1940. By 1947 it was estimated that about 5 per cent still had no running water. Many others lacked water toilets or other plumbing equipment. The percentage of houses without running water is much higher in parts of the metropolitan area outside the city limits. So while some progress is being made in furnishing water to all our people, there is still room for improvement.

Atlanta's sewerage system is also owned by the city. It is a double system. One set of pipes removes rain water. The other is for sewage. The sewage is disposed of at three disposal plants, located separately.

Our Streets and Services

These plants dry and burn the sewage, thus generating power and by-products. The sale of by-products pays for the operation of the disposal plants. The Department of Sewers receives about 3.8 per cent of the city revenues for other expenses.

The Department of Sanitation is separate from the Department of Sewers. Sanitation includes garbage collection and street cleaning. The refuse collected by the sanitary workers is disposed of in an incinerating plant. This plant also pays for its operation through the sale of scrap and ash. Modern methods thus make what once were expensive tasks pay for themselves through conserving waste materials. This is an example of using resources that might easily be wasted.

Water, sewer, and sanitary services are so important to the health and welfare of the city that they are made a part of city government. As a rule, such vital services are more dependable if they are operated by government. Some other very important services are provided by private companies which have monopolies. This, however, leaves the people little power for bargaining if the service is not efficient. The Public Service Commission has been set up to regulate utilities by law.

GAS AND ELECTRICITY

Natural gas is furnished to the metropolitan area by the Atlanta Gas Light Company. This is the oldest corporation in Atlanta, the second oldest in Georgia. It was chartered in 1856 and has since spread

Collecting garbage is essential for city sanitation. This service also helps pay for itself through conserved scrap and ashes.

its operation over the state. The change from manufactured to natural gas was made in 1930, though emergency tanks of manufactured gas are still held in reserve. The natural gas is furnished by the Southern Natural Gas Company through pipe lines.

Despite the name of the company, gas is now used as heating rather than lighting fuel. It is used a great deal by industries as well as for heating homes and cooking. Over 20 billion cubic feet of natural gas were used in 1945. The kind of street lighting Atlanta had before the Civil War can be seen from the "perpetual light" which burns at the corner of Whitehall and Alabama Streets.

This old lamp post was first lighted with gas on Christmas day, 1855. The holes in the post were made by the first shell that exploded in the business section of the city during the siege of Atlanta in 1864. The shaft was broken in three pieces but later repaired. For the world *première* of *Gone With the Wind* in December, 1939, the gas was again connected and the lamp burns with a perpetual flame as a memorial to the traditions of the South.

Electricity has now taken the place of gas as a lighting fuel. Natural gas is, of course, an exhaustible resource. Much of it, however, would escape into the air from oil wells if it were not captured and used. It is wise resource-use to conserve that part which would otherwise be wasted.

Electric power in Atlanta is furnished by the Georgia Power Company. This large corporation has a network of power lines throughout the state. The power is generated in both hydroelectric and steam generating plants. The power system is also tied in with those of the

This old lamppost at Whitehall and Alabama streets with its perpetual gas light is a reminder of days gone by.

Our Streets and Services

neighboring states and the Tennessee Valley Authority (TVA). If one generating plant fails, the others furnish power throughout the system. Since electricity has become so common a source of light, heat, power for refrigeration, and other uses, such a system is necessary to assure uninterrupted service.

Coal, an exhaustible resource, must be burned in steam plants. It seems wise to make full use of our hydroelectric power resources, of which the streams of Georgia can afford an abundance. Steam plants would then be an emergency source of power in times of long drouth or power-line trouble.

More and more homes in the Atlanta area are being given electricity each year. But there are still many of the houses in low rent sections that do not have electricity. Modern electrification is now so cheap that it should become a standard part of all housing.

COMMUNICATION SERVICES

As a regional center, Atlanta is a great user of telephones and telegraph. The Southern Bell Telephone Company makes Atlanta its headquarters. More than 20,000 long distance calls a day are handled by this, the largest telephone center in the South, and the third largest in the world.

This volume of communication shows the importance of exchanging ideas in our business transactions. Without this service, we could not remain the headquarters and regional center that we are.

The great volumes of mail and express which the post office and Railway Express agency handle are other communication services. Our many radio stations give immediate and wide scattering of ideas. News, advertising, education, and recreation are given through radio programs. The newspapers also serve an important function in keeping the people informed of news and various programs in the city and in the world. Many agencies help us in living the kind of lives we want in the kind of city we want. A good city includes the best of such services that we can get.

Telegraph service, telephones, and radios are now taken for granted as necessary means of communication.

Most services of this kind in Atlanta are good—compared to those in other cities and in other times. But they may not be the best that modern "know how" can afford. Many of them can be made better as new inventions and new knowledge are discovered.

Our streets and services are parts of our city. Some are furnished by government, others by private monopolies. Since private monopolies have no competition encouraging them to give the best and cheapest services possible, they are controlled by law. Both municipal and private services are set by the laws. We must see that we have the laws and law enforcement which will give us the best services.

The voters elect the city councilmen and the mayor, who make the laws. By our votes we can elect people we know will make and enforce the laws needed. If our streets and services are allowed to become antiquated and inefficient, our city will be less attractive. By offering efficient services we can attract and keep businesses to support our economy. We can also develop streets and services which will contribute to better all-round personal and social enjoyment.

DISCUSSION QUESTIONS

1. What are some ways in which streets and transportation systems affect a city?
2. Name some inventions and discoveries which have changed the shape of cities. How did they affect changes?
3. Why are "utilities" and other city-wide services usually given a monopoly right? How can citizens be sure that these monopolies are giving good services at a fair price?
4. What are some examples of wise and poor use of resources in Atlanta's streets and services systems? How could they be improved?
5. Plan a campaign to make improvements in a utility which you believe to be inefficient. What are the ways and the steps you would take to get a new law, or to change the old law, affecting the service?

HAVE YOU READ?

1. *Atlanta, A City of the Modern South.* America Guide Series. New York: Smith Durrell, 1942.
2. *Atlanta City Government.* Atlanta, Georgia: Atlanta Public Schools, 1945.
3. *Highway and Transportation Plan for Atlanta, Georgia.* Chicago, Illinois: H. W. Lochner Company and DeLeuw, Cather and Company, 1946.
4. Hughes, R. O. *Building Citizenship.* Chap. VI, "Providing Pure Water," "Disposing of Wastes." Boston, Massachusetts: Allyn and Bacon, 1943.
5. Reed, Thomas H. (dir.) *The Governments of Atlanta and Fulton County, Georgia.* Vol. II, "Water Supply," "Department of Electricity," "Sewerage," "Sanitary Department," "Department of Public Works." Atlanta, Georgia: The Atlanta Chamber of Commerce, 1938.

11. Using Social Resources

THERE is seldom a time when some part of the world is not in a turmoil. Wars, famines, epidemics, hurricanes, and extreme poverty are ever present to cause suffering among some of the world's people. At such times people have to depend on those who are more fortunate to give assistance. It is part of our American tradition to help people who are down and out. But people on the other side of the world seem far away. We are not so conscious of their needs if we cannot see their suffering with our own eyes. Yet most of us are willing to help them as much as we can.

Sometimes we do not notice the suffering which is to be found in Atlanta. In looking at the splendor and prosperity of our city, we often overlook the other side. There are those among us who seem to have more than their share of troubles and ill fate. Many people in Atlanta are slowly starving for lack of proper food, suffering from disease or handicap, or are in need of advice and help with personal problems.

Using Social Resources

To whom can they turn in their distress? What community services do we offer to those who need help?

SOCIAL SERVICES

Have you ever had a great misfortune? Did you ever feel that your troubles were so great that you just couldn't go on? Almost all people sometimes face problems that they cannot solve alone. Perhaps you have felt that trying was no use—that you might as well quit and sit down and cry.

That will not solve your problems. It is true that your own efforts may not be enough when you are sick and have no way to get money to pay for a needed operation. You cannot do anything about a fire after it has already burned all your belongings. Hurricanes, floods, and some kinds of illness are beyond our control.

In order to take care of such disasters and emergencies, people have set up organizations, or agencies, so they are ready when they are needed. The assistance given by these organizations is known as "social services" or "welfare services." They serve by helping people with their

Social workers from many agencies of assistance in Atlanta are ready to help people who are in need.

personal problems. Social services are social resources. They help people become healthy, happy citizens again after they have had trying circumstances.

In any society we find at least a few people who fail to find successful places. Others, for many reasons, become dependent on society. For instance, there are children whose parents die or leave them; old people who cannot care for themselves; victims of disease and accident; mentally ill persons; healthy persons who are unemployed; people who have made legal mistakes; and many others. We must have agencies to help them help themselves.

There are two kinds of agencies of social service: public agencies and private agencies. Public agencies are set up by law. They are supported by tax funds in the same manner as other governmental agencies. The private agencies are set up by individuals or by private organizations such as firms, foundations, and churches. Private agencies are supported by donations and grants. Many are financed in one great drive each year through the Community Chest. There are many agencies of each kind in the Atlanta area.

In early rural societies, families were usually large and were grouped in close neighborhoods or villages. Each family was able to look after its sick and unfortunate members. The neighbors could drop in to help in an emergency. But in a large city, families tend to be smaller. Relatives do not so often live near one another. People move around more and do not know their neighbors so well. Then, too, in a money economy people have to work certain hours on schedule. It is easier for city dwellers to pay a small fee and assign specialists to the job of caring for dependent persons. By scattering the cost so widely, one person pays very little. The service also is usually better.

Our money economy in cities makes us very dependent on our cash income. If we lose that income we cannot pay for the things we need. We cannot raise our own food—few of us have even small gardens. This gives rise to one of the great causes of the need for social services: extreme poverty.

Employment service agencies help workers find jobs in the effort to prevent unemployment and raise production.

Unemployment is one great cause of poverty. It matters little whether unemployment is caused by sickness or by being unable to find a job. Whatever the cause, people must have food to eat and a place to live or they starve or die of exposure. We must have agencies to see that they get money or the necessities of life before it is too late. Then there must be agencies to help them get jobs again or to take care of them if they are disabled.

We have agencies which give temporary emergency relief to those who need help. There are also several kinds of agencies which attempt to correct the conditions which brought on the emergency. One of these is the employment service. Local, state, and federal employment agencies help people find work. We have schools which teach new trades and vocations. Emergency relief, old age pensions, county homes, Social Security, unemployment benefits, and other similar agencies and programs help the financially dependent.

HEALTH SERVICES IN ATLANTA

Sickness seems to go hand-in-hand with poverty. Slum dwellings and unemployment result in poor living conditions, poor food, and poor health. Run-down, poorly fed bodies are apt to contract disease. We often find that many people who need medical care most are least able to pay for it.

A great many diseases are contagious. Wherever they start, they may spread to other areas. Many agencies in Atlanta are concerned with the physical health of all the people. Remember that health is one of the prime factors in the efficiency of the people and thus of the city.

There are three points of attack in the war against disease and poor health in Atlanta. We must cure those who are sick, we must prevent illness, and we must promote good health.

The Health Departments of the City of Atlanta and of Fulton and DeKalb counties are the backbone of the health services in the metropolitan area. The Georgia Health Department serves the area through these local units. There are also some fifty-eight other agencies in this area which are tending our health needs. Many of these try to improve health conditions by programs which teach people good health practices. Others concentrate on fighting one particular disease or promoting a certain kind of health program. Even with all these groups working at it, there is much to be done to bring the health of our people up to the standards we desire.

Public funds provide Grady Hospital for Atlanta and Fulton County patients who cannot afford to pay for medical care. DeKalb County patients are admitted under a plan whereby the county bears

"Shots" take only a moment but protect us from some of the serious diseases for many months.

the cost. For those who can afford to pay, there are numerous private hospitals, sanitariums, and clinics.

These institutions cost a great deal of both public and private money to build and to operate. They represent an interest in the health of *all* the people of our city. But they are often overcrowded. They cannot give the type of attention needed by many of those who should have medical care. We especially need more hospital space for tubercular cases, maternity cases, and for those who are recuperating or are permanently disabled.

In a good health program we need to know what diseases are most common. Which are most often causes of death? The first ten causes of death in Atlanta, in the order of their importance, in 1941 were:

1. Heart disease
2. Nephritis
3. Brain hemorrhage
4. Cancer
5. Tuberculosis
6. Accidents
7. Pneumonia
8. Premature birth
9. Influenza
10. Diabetes

These ten "killers" are given the credit for a large part of the deaths. But behind them are other diseases and conditions which set the stage so that the killers can step in. Heart diseases and nervous disorders are said to be caused, in large part, by the strain of modern living and the lack of proper and early attention. The common cold and a run-down condition leave one weakened so that pneumonia and influenza may be contracted more easily.

Not so many years ago contagious diseases, such as typhoid and smallpox, were listed in the first ten causes of death. Inoculation and vaccination, along with a great public health program, have almost done away with these killers. People have learned how to prevent them. Now the great drives to find and cure early cases of tuberculosis and cancer are doing much to rid us of these dread diseases. Work goes on to find new cures for all diseases.

GOOD HEALTH PROGRAMS

In addition to research to find new ways to cure diseases, we need a vast program of public education. People must know how to recognize the early symptoms of cancer, tuberculosis, and venereal diseases. Then they must realize the importance of prompt medical treatment. They must know where and how to get it. Public funds must pay for treatment of those who cannot afford to pay for themselves. Otherwise we will be slow to get the killers under control.

Recognizing and curing disease is but a part of a good health program for our city, however. As we have seen, the physical city has a great effect on health. Sewers, sanitation, land drainage, insect con-

Poor sanitary conditions like these outdoor toilets in slum areas of Atlanta are one reason health services are no more effective in stamping out disease.

trol, and safety measures are city-wide and county-wide projects. Comfortable, clean dwelling houses with adequate bathing and toilet facilities are a great factor in health. People must be educated in how to care for themselves and prevent illness—more than that, they must know how to keep in the best of health. Just preventing disease is not enough. We must develop ourselves to the point of the best physical and mental health.

The problem of mental disease is a sly, elusive factor in the health of the community. It is not only a health problem, it is a social problem. We have not yet come to look on mental illness as we do physical illness. A person who cannot control his actions toward other people is mentally ill. His behavior may be in the form of brooding, tantrums, unusual aggressiveness or withdrawal from other people, distrustfulness, and fears. In mild forms it is often passed up as mere unpleasantness or "meanness."

These mild forms of mental disease, called "neuroses," lie at the roots of many family and community problems. They are often tied up with divorce and crime and the inability to work or play satisfactorily. The antisocial behavior of even one person can make much unpleasantness. The extreme form of mental disease is insanity, or "psychosis" in more technical language. It is not hard to recognize and we have agencies to care for insane people. Modern medical care

Building Atlanta's Future

can often prevent insanity. Most mild cases can be returned to healthy normal citizenship if properly treated in the early stages.

"Psychiatry" is the name given to the field of medicine which deals with mental disorders. Psychiatrists are learning much about the treatment of mental illness. This field has great promise of becoming a boon to better social living with each other—to create better citizens of community and city. Perhaps we can find new ways to help people fit into their places in society. If so, we can do much to prevent crime and make the world a happier place to live.

CRIME AND DELINQUENCY

Think what it would mean if we could do away with crime. No one is a "born criminal." Criminals are people who have not adjusted to other people in an acceptable manner and who act in a way that the law defines as criminal. That is, they fail to abide by the legal rules of society. Of course there are many reasons why people commit crimes. We cannot name them all. But a great many crimes are the result of ignorance and a series of unfortunate social situations. If all people from birth could be taught in the right way, and if their activities could

The Criminal Court tries persons who have broken certain legal rules of society. This is a service we would be proud not to need.

The Juvenile Court is more interested in preventing delinquency than in punishing offenders. Through education we strive to remove the need for this service.

be steered in the direction of constructive things instead of antisocial activities, there would be few criminals.

The same causes account for juvenile delinquency. Juvenile delinquents are those youths under 16 years of age who break the laws. These include such actions as: stealing, acts of carelessness or mischief, traffic violation, truancy, injury to person, and running away. Fulton and DeKalb counties have juvenile courts for young offenders. Very frequently they work closely with the departments of public welfare.

Building Atlanta's Future

Punishment is not their major purpose. It is much more effective to find the causes of the misdemeanor and do away with it. If we know why people are caused to break laws we can help prevent others from doing these things. Finding these causes is an important phase of the work of welfare agencies.

There must be a system of punishment for those who refuse to obey the rules of our society. For that purpose we have courts, law enforcement officers, and prisons. But these are expensive. Punishment does not undo the crime. It is much better to spend the money on preventing crime. What can be done to help prevent crime and delinquency?

You will recall that most of the disease, crime, and delinquency in Atlanta occurs in slum and blight areas. In these areas we find low income, poverty, poor housing, overcrowding, and people who have had very little education. By clearing out the slums we clear out many of the things which create criminals and invite disease. The people move to neat, attractive houses with good sanitary facilities. They take more interest in making their community a safe and pleasant place to live.

Healthful recreation is as necessary as work and study for making healthy, useful citizens.

Along with the new surroundings, however, must go services to help them with their problems. Money, food, care of old people and dependent children, and other emergency relief must be available in time of need. Stealing and shady dealings are often born of desperate need. Employment services and a sound economy help prevent poverty and the need for crime.

Housing, the physical structure and services, and economic security are part of a better city. But there are many other factors affecting the health and welfare of our people. We must learn the principles of nutrition, physical development, and recreation. Health is not guaranteed to us unless we care for it. Recreation is a necessary part of both physical and mental health. Our minds and bodies need relaxation and change from the routine of work.

RECREATION

People get recreation in various ways. It may be through conscious or unconscious effort. There are poor ways to play that may lead into activities which are bad instead of good. Loafing and idling serve as change from routine. If done in the wrong surroundings, they may invite unconstructive acts. The old adage that "idle hands find mischief to do" is no less true today than when it was first said. Good recreation should be both pleasant and beneficial. It should build up our bodies and character together.

A good recreation program must, therefore, be planned as part of our city services. It cannot be left to chance any more than can the water supply. It must include parks, playgrounds, gymnasiums, swimming pools, auditoriums—play space and equipment for both quiet and active games for young and old. It must include physical instruction and supervision. Since everybody needs recreation, it should be organized on a community basis.

A community center with recreation facilities should be in easy walking distance of all residential districts. Some recreation centers are special buildings with playgrounds built for that purpose alone.

These camping scenes suggest an environment for learning many things we seldom learn in school, at home, or in the city.

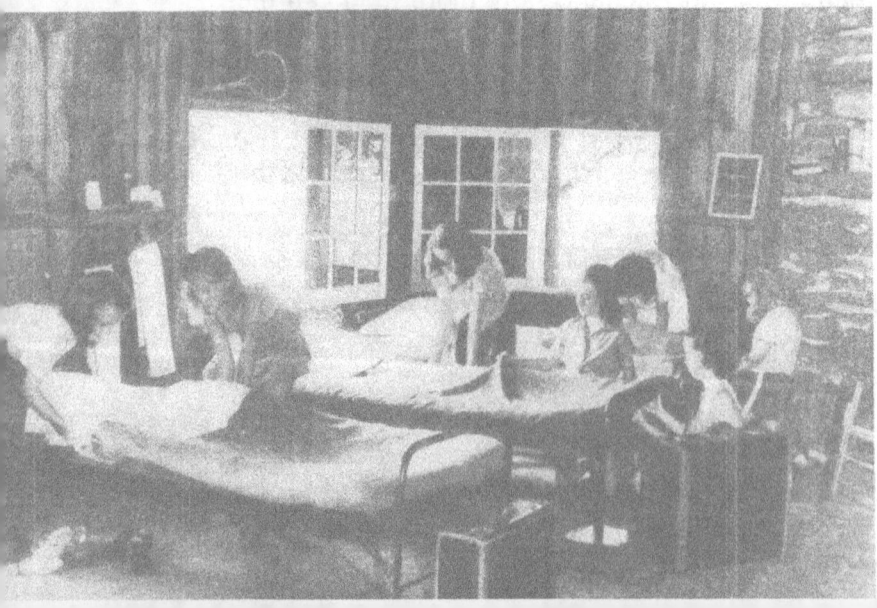

Other programs are centered at the school or other public buildings. The main thing is to be sure that the facilities are there and that people feel free to use them. A meeting place for clubs, picnics, and dramatics programs is as important as softball diamonds and tennis courts.

People often have to learn to play like this. There must be a program to get them started. It is much easier for most of us to loaf than to play in a beneficial way. A program of healthful recreation must include some means of getting people to start using the facilities. This is part of the program of education we have mentioned.

EDUCATION

What do we mean by "education" in this sense? It is much more than learning "reading, writing, and arithmetic" in formal schooling. To be sure, schools are a very necessary part of education. But we must also think of education as learning to talk when we are small children, as learning to get along with other people, to make a living, and to live healthy, happy, and useful lives. Education includes learning what is right and wrong and how to lead people to do the right things. All your experience is educative—whether it happens at home, at school, on the street, or on a camping trip. Anything you learn is part of your larger education. It may contribute to your good or it may be a detriment.

Guiding the education of young people is, therefore, of great importance. Schools are set up to make sure that children learn many things which are necessary to their well-being. The school is a leader in education, but it is not the only agency of education. What you learn outside of school may be just as important. It may help or hinder you from being a well-balanced, happy, useful person in your community and in society.

The public schools are a social resource to assist in developing our minds and bodies. The citizens of the Atlanta area have invested millions of dollars to provide you this opportunity. In 1946 they voted a bond issue allotting nine million dollars to improve education. This

Almost everyone had to ride long distances to the old central high schools. Many pupils now walk t[o]

money was to be spent to revise the school system so that it would better serve the needs of the people in the area.

Committees were appointed to study the needs of the people in regard to the schools. They were to make recommendations as to how the money could best be spent to improve education. The committees found that the old school system had been outgrown. It worked a hardship on most of the pupils and on their parents. For one thing, many high school pupils rode long distances to get to school. This took time which could better be spent in work, study, and recreation. The schools were also far removed from home and did not enter into local problems and needs.

Another difficulty discovered was that of crossing county and city lines to attend a school. This created much "red tape" and kept some pupils from attending school. They had to travel to a school farther away rather than cross a political boundary to a near-by school. Then, too, there were differences in requirements and in courses which made

...mmunity high schools which are centers of community affairs as well as training centers for pupils.

it difficult to transfer credits from one school to another. The separation of boys and girls, and of technical and vocational high schools, made for even further lack of uniformity.

COMMUNITY SCHOOLS

In place of this outgrown mixup of schools, a uniform system was recommended. The junior high schools were omitted. Instead a "K–7–5–V" plan (kindergarten, seven-year elementary, five-year high school, and area vocational schools) was installed. The huge central high schools were done away with and "community" high schools took their places. As the map shows, these were placed in different parts of the area so that they would be near the pupils' homes. The program in each was the same so that there would be little trouble in transferring. This program was varied instead of specialized. It was designed to teach the things which the pupils needed and wanted.

You know about the varied program that is offered in your school. You can get instruction which will fit you to go to college. You can

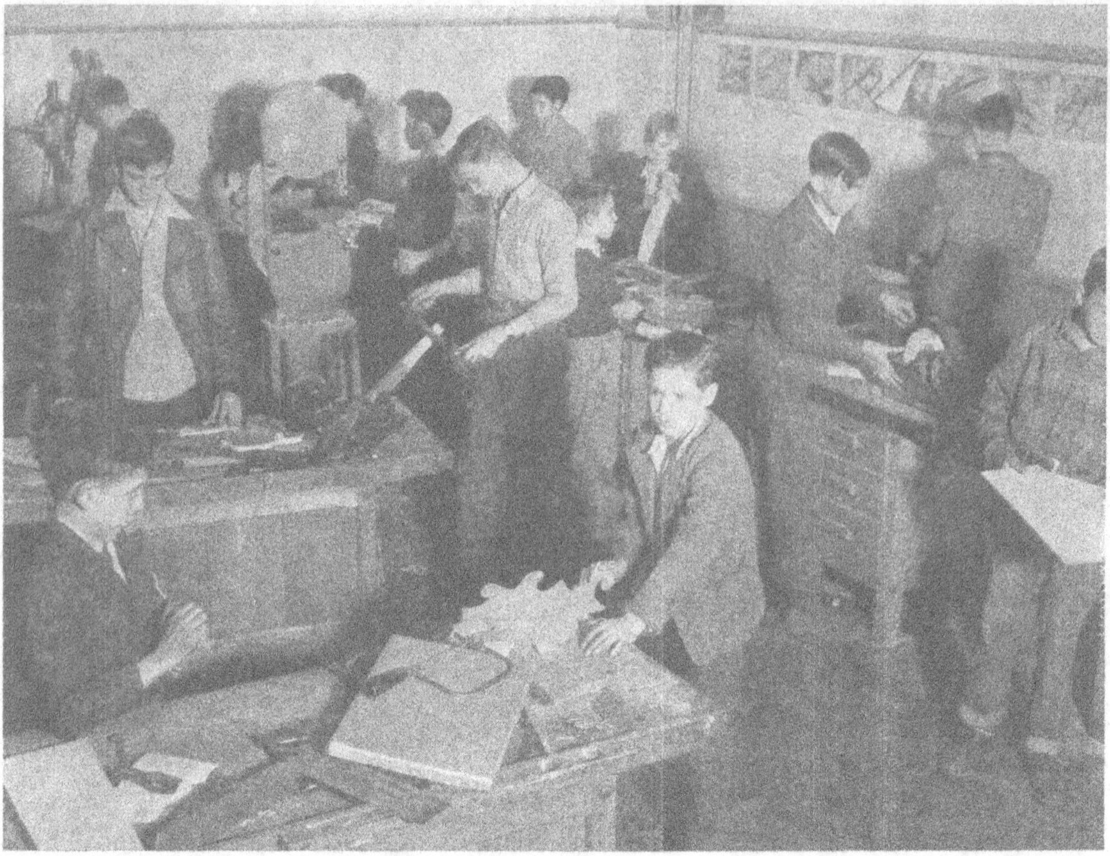

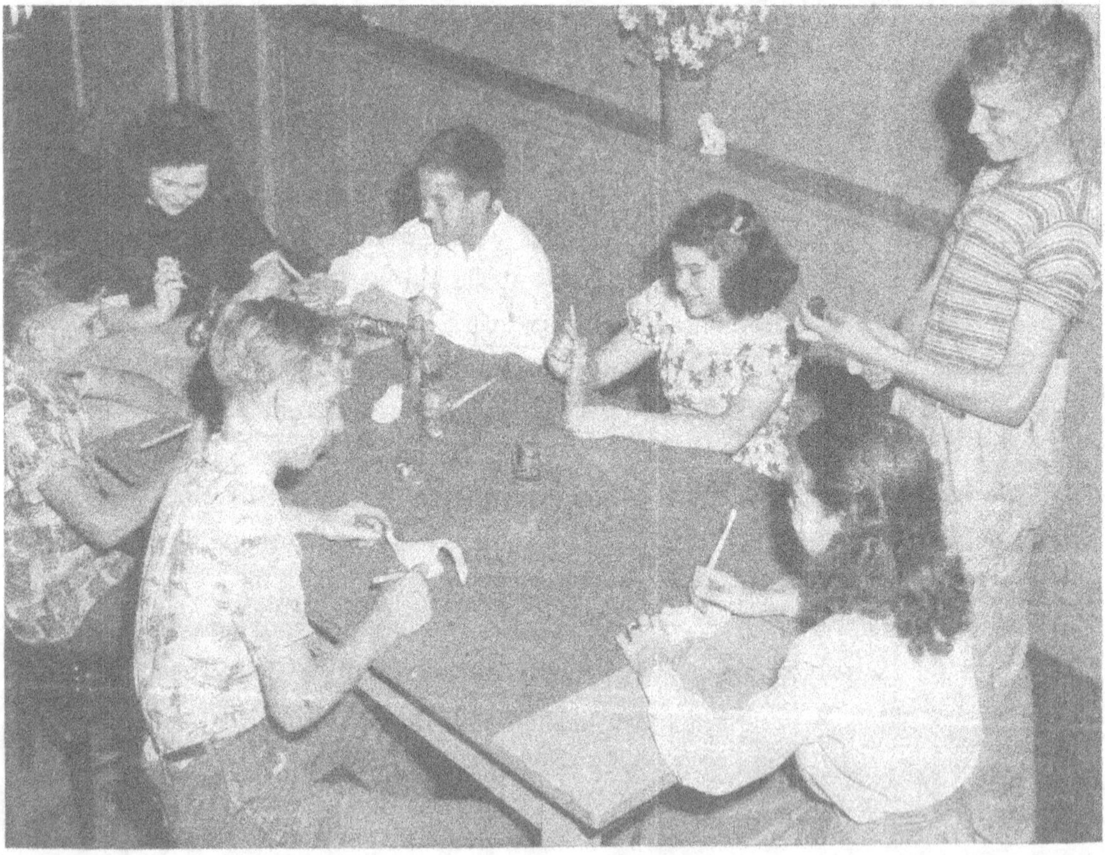

You may choose from a wide variety of courses according to your needs in your school.

learn technical and vocational subjects. Physical and health education are varied and extensive. You can get training and guidance in many fields of interest. The high school program in the old system was much more set and unchanging.

It was also hoped that the community high schools would become more and more a center of community life. No matter how well-educated and energetic one person is, he cannot accomplish much by himself. If most of the people in a community get together, however, they have a great power to do things. The school is a natural place for a community center. It belongs to all the people in the community. Where can we find a better place to gather for recreation and for neighborly discussion?

A community school near our homes and close to the interests we

Building Atlanta's Future

have in common can be a center of action. All the people may gather here for a school program, an athletic contest, a club meeting, for recreation, or just to chat. They get to know one another better. They find that all have many of the same problems. Finding the problems and needs of the community is the first step. Then they can plan ways to solve the problems. They can develop programs to meet the needs. The combined abilities and energy of all the people in a community can do almost anything they set out to do.

For instance, suppose a community has become lax in taking care of lawns and sidewalks. A beautification program is needed. If a few people try to rake leaves and cut grass along the walks and curbs it is a big job. Debris will soon blow and scatter again. But if everybody agrees to cooperate, each can look after a small section and the entire community is soon clean. It is much more likely to stay that way if everybody has had a part in the planning and cleaning up.

The same is true if they need a swimming pool, a nursery school, a zoning ordinance, or a new traffic control system. If all the people see the need and work to fill it, it is an easy task. People are usually willing to help if they know others are willing to work also. It is sur-

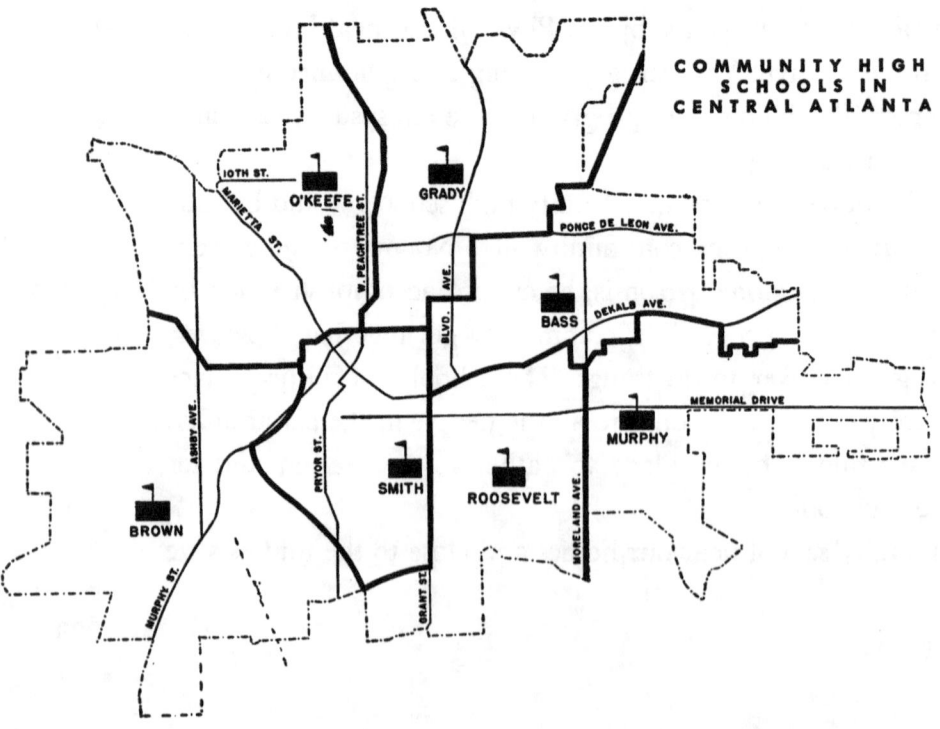

COMMUNITY HIGH SCHOOLS IN CENTRAL ATLANTA

Carnegie Library and its branches offer many educational services to the people of Atlanta.

prising that we are slow to realize this. You in your school groups can do much to bring parents and school programs together to make your community and city a better place to live. There are always problems to be solved. The energy and intelligence with which we attack them determines how many of them we can solve.

The school can be a center and a power in the community. But if it is to be such, it must be built and run for that purpose. The buildings must be located in a central place. They must contain recreation facilities. Without these adequate physical facilities, a good community program is at least severely hampered. The school program must also be geared to the needs of the people in the community. Pupils, teachers, and parents must be on the lookout for community needs. They must all work together in planning and executing programs to make a better community.

The first responsibility of schools is to teach young people the skills and knowledge which are so necessary to successful living. We are coming to realize that these things can best be learned if they are related to life in the community. Usable facts are easier to learn and remember. If we can help make the community a better place to live while we learn, we are being educated in the highest sense. Community schools are designed to afford this kind of education.

OTHER AGENCIES OF EDUCATION

There are other educational agencies in Atlanta besides the public schools. We have business schools, night schools, and informal study groups for those who want to learn special things. We have several

Building Atlanta's Future

colleges and universities for those who want higher education. Atlanta University serves as a hub and regional center for Negro education in the Southeast. Since education is so important in our specialized economy, we must continue to provide the best that is available.

Libraries are a vital part of any educational system. They are not only a source of information for students, but serve the public as a means of information and recreation. The Carnegie Library operates a wide service in Atlanta. The bond issue of 1946 allotted more than one and a half million dollars to expanding library buildings and services in Atlanta.

Education must include opportunity for both children and adults to learn needed skills and information.

It is because of the vast knowledge and experience that man has gained through the ages that we are civilized. If you had been brought up among animals, you would act like an animal. You could not talk and would know nothing of civilized ways. It is through language and the ability to pass knowledge on to others that man has made his progress. Each generation learns more to pass on to the next. That is the process of social education. Through it we may be able to learn ways to cure and to prevent today's problems. The cave men made progress. The American pioneers made progress. Who knows how far we can go if we apply our energies to our much greater store of knowledge?

OUR SOCIAL WELFARE

The people of the world have always had to contend with ignorance, crime, disease, poverty, and a "don't care" attitude. Atlanta people have developed agencies of service to fight these evils. Some are for the purpose of treating and curing the ills—of helping people who need immediate aid. Other services aim at helping prevent the problems and the conditions which cause them. Still others are to teach people how to improve themselves physically and mentally. We must not be content just to stay out of the hospital or to get along "fairly well." We must develop all our resources to the highest degree possible.

Therefore, if we are to have healthy, happy, and prosperous people, we must have the best physical city possible. Our houses must not be a cause of disease and human despair. Our city-wide utility services must be efficient in meeting the needs of health and industry. Streets must be planned to give safe, economical paths for traffic. Land must be used for the best interest of living, working, and serving both workers and industry. Our economy should afford ample incomes and security from want. We have seen how buildings, streets, laws, and initiative work together to give us the economic base for our city. They at the same time affect the social needs of the people.

There is little use to teach children the value of cleanliness if they have no bathing facilities—not even running water in their homes. Mothers can not use training in the nutrition of children if they have no money to buy food. A criminal may be led to steal again if he can find no job. A person cured of disease may catch it again if the water or sewer service is faulty. Money spent on such treatment is wasted.

In the same way the school can not be a community center unless it has the right kinds of buildings. They must be near the center of the community. The importance of this spacing is seen in the old system of large central high schools in Atlanta. On the long ride home the pupils added to traffic congestion. They often stopped off on the way. Sometimes they loitered on street corners and got into mischief. They

Social resources are developed by people themselves. Community groups such as this can do much to make better use of our social resources for better living in a better city.

helped create several problems: traffic disruption, juvenile delinquency, wasted time, and health problems from the long tiresome rides twice a day. Placing the schools in the communities has helped relieve these problems.

A better physical city relieves the pressure on social welfare services. It allows them to do things they otherwise could not do. As both are improved, we arrive at a better city.

Several years ago the social agencies in Atlanta organized a

"Council of Social Agencies." This organization brought together all these agencies so they could plan their work better. They could exchange information about people who need help and divide the cases among the agencies best fitted for each type of problem. The organization has been very successful and is now known as the "Community Planning Council of Metropolitan Atlanta." All the agencies of health, welfare, and social service belong to the council. In cooperation with the Community Chest they are doing a fine job of helping people in need—though they often do not have enough money to do all they would like to do.

The council and its members have learned that their work is affected by the physical city. They know that most of the people who need help are those living in slum areas. They see that much of their time and money are wasted because these people must continue to live in such surroundings. They soon slip back into the same conditions which caused them to need help at first. Our economic system, our streets and utilities, our housing, zoning, and other laws are tied in with the personal problems of the people.

While the social workers of our assisting agencies go about doing their jobs, they see how the whole city is the cause of much of the poverty, crime, and disease that bring on the suffering. They realize that their work is only a stopgap for the real solution—that we must start at the source rather than scratch at the surface with "cures." Our whole city with all its resources must be developed in such a way that it will not be a cause of human suffering but a means of human happiness and well-being.

We need accept none but the best. We do not have to be content with "well enough." If we go at the problem in our own local community with a will, we can soon have a group of good communities making up a better city.

Our social services are some of our most necessary social resources. They assist people in many ways, but they are powerless to help in others. One reason they are not serving to their highest purposes is

Using Social Resources

because our physical city is undoing some of their work. Perhaps another reason is that we have not learned to use and develop methods which would make them most effective.

We have seen how mechanical inventions have changed our ways of living until our world is quite different from that of a few decades ago. We have also improved our social living in that time. But our social growth has not kept up with the mechanical and physical. There is a great need for "social inventions" which would make our new knowledge more useful. New methods of farming and manufacture are hailed with much gusto. New methods of helping people solve their personal and social problems are needed even more. Perhaps if we work at it hard enough, we can find ways to prevent much of human want and suffering.

DISCUSSION QUESTIONS

1. What are some social agencies which have helped unfortunate people you know or have heard of? Are they public or private agencies?
2. Why are poverty, poor health, lack of education, and crime likely to be found in the same general area? Discuss a program for correcting these evils.
3. Why are agencies of health, welfare, recreation, and education called "social resources"? Do they use any natural resources in their work?
4. How does the arrangement of streets and buildings in a city affect the organization of the people into communities?
5. What are the benefits you see in community high schools? Does education stop when you leave school? What is education?
6. Which is the less expensive in the long run, preventing or curing social problems such as disease and crime? Why?

HAVE YOU READ?

1. *A Report on Health and Welfare in DeKalb and Fulton Counties.* Part I, "Public Recreation." Part II, "Juvenile Delinquency." Atlanta, Georgia: Social Planning Council, 1943.

2. *A Report of Public School Facilities for Negroes.* Atlanta, Georgia: The Atlanta Urban League, 1944.
3. Citizens' Fact-Finding Movement of Georgia. *Georgia Facts in Figures, A Source Book.* "Education." Athens, Georgia: The University of Georgia Press, 1946.
4. *Community Resources Directory, 1946-47.* Atlanta, Georgia: Community Planning Council, 1947.
5. Jarrell, Ira. *Making Americans.* Superintendent's Annual Report to the Board of Education. Atlanta, Georgia: Atlanta Public Schools. 1945-46 and 1946-47.
6. Reed, Thomas H. (dir.) *The Governments of Atlanta and Fulton County, Georgia.* Vol. I, "The Need for Recreation." Vol. II, "Public Health," "Hospitals," "Public Welfare," "Library," "Schools." Atlanta, Georgia: The Atlanta Chamber of Commerce, 1938.
7. *The Atlanta Letter.* Atlanta, Georgia: Community Planning Council.

Part Four

GUIDING CITY GROWTH

12. How People Build Cities

IF you were flying high over Atlanta in an airplane, you could see all of the sprawling city. It would appear as great buildings crowded closely together near the center. At other places the buildings would be smaller and some trees and open spaces appear. Perhaps you could pick out the business and industrial districts—skyscrapers and factory smokestacks. You could tell which are residential and park areas. Through and between these areas, you could see the network of streets, communication, and power lines. You would know that underneath the streets there were other pipes and cables which furnish necessary utility services.

This is the visible Atlanta. Since it is made of stone, steel, wood, brick, and pavement, it is there to see and feel. It is the *physical structure* of Atlanta, built on land, the geographic base. Into and out of it run the ribbons of railroad and highway connecting it with other places. Over these lanes travel the people and goods which enable our city to exist.

Building Atlanta's Future

However impressive this physical city is, we know that it is merely the shell within which the real city activities take place. The buildings, streets, and other man-made structures are built so that people can work together to produce goods and services. The actual basis for any city is its people and their working together. We may call this working and living together *social relations*. How well the people work together and the satisfaction they get from life among other people are the basically important features of a city. The physical structure is important only as it contributes to the social relations within the city. It should be built to best serve people's needs.

How do people make sure that their social relations will be the kind they want? Do people "just naturally" do the things that will be best for their welfare and the welfare of others in the group? We know that they do not. Therefore, we must have some rules and regulations. We must have organization—must develop social resources which will allow us to work together in achieving things we cannot do as individuals.

The physical city of Atlanta, then, has been built as a result of the social relations among the people. Through their working and living together, they have found ways to regulate their cooperation. They have built the physical city to "house" their activities as well as themselves. As their activities and social relations increased, the physical structure expanded also. The quality of this physical structure greatly affects the quality of social relations.

Now this great city we look down upon is a vastly complex organization. Yet it functions remarkably well to contain so many and so diverse peoples. How do people keep their social relations and physical structures in harmony? What ways have the people of Atlanta developed to regulate and direct their efforts? And what means do we use to keep the social and physical features of our city in harmony with each other? In other words, what are some of the social resources we have developed to make sure that our human and physical resources are used to good advantage?

THE ORGANIZATION OF A CITY

How did people develop the organization which makes Atlanta tick? Perhaps a short review of the growth of our city will help us to see. You will remember that the little village of Terminus had very few people except railroad workers. There was little organization because none was needed for such a small group. They could talk over their plans and desires with one another and come to face-to-face agreements. Since this was a frontier town filled for the most part with rough men, those who disagreed often "fought out" their troubles. But unlike today's "western" movies of frontier towns, there was not always a hero to see that right came out the winner. "Might" is by no means always "right."

Then, during the 1840's, Terminus became Marthasville and later Atlanta. The population increased rapidly. As trade and commerce grew, the needs of the people changed. Permanent businesses were set up. Local businessmen wanted to attract people to come to Atlanta to buy and sell. But the "rowdy" frontier element was still there. Early Atlanta was known for its gambling, drinking, fighting, and lawlessness.

Also, since the town had grown up in haphazard fashion, the streets were narrow and winding. They were unpaved, and mud and deep ruts made travel difficult. Perhaps this did not bother the rowdies much, but it did bother those who wanted to have permanent homes and businesses there. Atlanta was an unattractive place in those days.

When the first locomotive for the Western and Atlantic Railroad arrived in 1842, drawn by mules, Marthasville was but a small frontier village. The people needed little organization to meet their common needs.

As Atlanta grew into a large city, more and more rules and regulations were necessary. As our needs change, our regulations must change.

Sanitation facilities were very poor. Civic-minded citizens realized that conditions must be improved if the city was to prosper.

Thus we can see that early Atlantans had some pressing problems. Some people were doing things which harmed other people. Social relations were at a low level. Atlanta as an organized town could not make progress because some few "rowdies" and selfish individuals were preventing the group from working as a whole. Small groups trying to correct the situation often pulled against one another. They had little cooperative group action. What could they do to get themselves organized for working toward desirable goals? What methods could they use to get some public improvements? Their public needs, or "group needs," were very great.

So we find that in 1848, before Atlanta was a year old, a Health Department was established. Churches were built and newspapers

How People Build Cities

tried to inform the people of ways to improve their city. Soon public schools were opened in the attempt to educate young people. But these agencies made slow progress against the "rowdies" and the unhealthful practices of so many people. The Health Department might cure some diseases. But the filth and bad conditions spread disease faster than they were cured. Churches, schools, and other small groups cannot stop lawlessness at once. Neither do they have power nor money to pave and straighten streets.

These conditions frightened away many settlers who might have moved into Atlanta. Many others who came threatened to move away unless drastic changes were made. The life of the city was in danger unless a strong central authority was organized. Instead of working together in small groups, Atlanta people had to be organized to operate as a *city*. The welfare of everyone—the *public welfare*—depended on correcting some of these public problems which affected everyone.

For such a large group as lived in Atlanta during the 1850's to work as a unit, they needed to invent some form of *social machinery* to guide their relations with one another. This social machinery should set forth rules and delegate responsibility for getting each task done. Otherwise, people would go on pulling in all directions as individuals or small groups and getting little done. The social machinery, made up of social resources, is the element which makes a city "tick."

The old Fulton County Court House in 1890. Government has long been our way of regulating public affairs and doing public business.

ATLANTA'S MUNICIPAL GOVERNMENT

An efficient city must have an organized method for doing public business. In our American tradition the machinery for the efficient operation of cities has been municipal government. In American democracy we believe that the best method for doing public business is one in which all the people have a strong voice. We believe that all the people should take part in making the decisions. At the same time they must share in the responsibility for setting up programs of action that get things done. This is a basic principle of the *democratic process*. Remember that to share in the rewards we must also share in the duties and responsibilities.

One of the most democratic and perhaps best-known types of city government has been the "New England Town Meeting." Early New England towns were small. Most of the people could attend the town meetings held in the town hall or square. Here they could discuss public issues. Everyone could have his say and debate his views. From these they could reach group or majority decisions. Each knew about the public problems and knew the people with whom he had to work. This was democracy at its best, working in a small, closely-knit, slow-moving community.

The town meeting kind of community government might have been possible in Atlanta in 1847. Then the entire city was in an area with a one-mile radius. But today, the hundreds of thousands of people in Atlanta cannot possibly gather in one place to discuss public issues. Our city government has become a complex business.

Atlanta's City Hall rises fourteen floors toward the sky. It houses many departments and bureaus of city government and is a symbol of how large the public business of Atlanta has grown. Today the city of Atlanta has a government, by representation, of the mayor-council type. The mayor, six aldermen, and twelve councilmen are elected by the people of the entire city. The people vote for the men they think will best represent their views on public matters. Then these men get

This picture of Five Points in 1892 shows street railway construction and a water tank—both are for the purpose of providing needed services. We need transportation and water today but this scene is now greatly changed.

together to decide on and plan the programs of action for the city.

The aldermen and councilmen together make up the General Council, or legislative body of the city government. This body has the power to decide on laws and ordinances for regulating our actions. One alderman and two councilmen are elected for each of the six districts of the city. However, all the people in the city can vote for each candi-

Building Atlanta's Future

date for these offices. This helps keep small groups in an area from dominating the council through their representatives.

As Atlanta has grown in area and in population, there have come other types of growth. There has been an increase in the number of functions of city government. With growth has come greater public need for safety, law enforcement, sanitation, health, recreation, and other regulations. To meet these needs we must hire a large corps of professional public servants. Each is a specialist in the skills of his particular task. The City Council is the central authority which makes the policies and coordinates the work of the departments. Each department then administers the details of its duties in accordance with the policies made up by the representatives of the people—the City Council.

Today Atlanta is a great corporation. It collects and spends about 15 million dollars each year in meeting public needs. This means that the citizens of Atlanta pay more than $15,000,000 in taxes each year to operate their public corporation. That is a great deal of money. In return, the city government furnishes public services to meet the needs of the people.

PUBLIC NEEDS: PRESENT AND FUTURE

Now stop for a moment. Think back over these ideas: Here is our city—a tremendous organization of physical layout and social relations. Like any other organization, Atlanta must keep its sights on where it

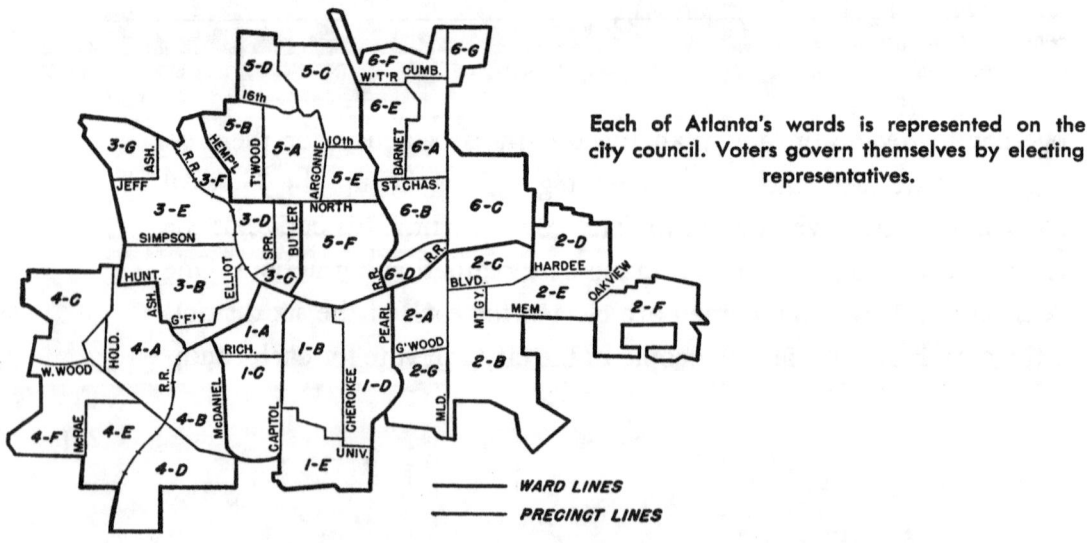

Each of Atlanta's wards is represented on the city council. Voters govern themselves by electing representatives.

WARD LINES
PRECINCT LINES

How People Build Cities

is going. Government as the paid servant of the people must keep the city operating efficiently as a place to live and work. As the paid servant, it is also responsible for looking beyond the *present* needs to the *future* needs of the city. The future organization of physical layout and social relations in Atlanta must be geared to changing needs and methods of meeting needs.

Atlanta did not become the city it is today by mere haphazard chance. A flashback to the days of Marthasville shows us that even in those days the people had some plans for working together. But they were more or less informal. As the population increased, people could not work together so informally. There were some who would not abide by informal rules and customs. The city government had to be improved and strengthened. Courts and jails were provided to elimi-

Our government is responsible for enforcing laws and protecting property and also for looking toward the future welfare of the city.

nate the worst offenders. But government also provided an active social machine for getting improvements as well as for doing away with the bad influences.

City government supported by all the people is a corporation which can raise money to make public improvements. It can pave streets, build sewers, schools, public buildings, and regulate the kinds of buildings and other improvements people can build in various zones. It can also make laws controlling the kinds of businesses and other activities in which people can engage. The governments of Marthasville and of early Atlanta began doing some of these things. If this had not been done the city would very probably have died out.

As Atlanta grew, the government had to be improved and take over more public duties. If it has not been improved, we would not have a good city today. People not only considered their own pressing problems, but they looked to the future and made plans. We can see today that they did not plan well in some respects. Some of our problems are caused by their poor planning or failure to plan. However, they developed methods of doing public business which have served well to meet the needs for which they were designed.

Today we still have many pressing problems in Atlanta. Future generations may look back and say we did not plan well for them. But perhaps we can profit by the mistakes of those who came before us. We can make use of the good methods they have developed for us. We may be able to improve the government and solve some of our problems through it. Other agencies may be able to care for other problems. Someone had to devise the methods we now have. They were new at that time. If we can find better methods, there is no use in keeping old ones. With new inventions and discoveries coming along all the time to change our needs and problems, we cannot expect old methods of social machinery to be always best for meeting our needs. In the next chapters we will take up some of our problems and some methods we may use in attacking them.

City government is one major social resource for maintaining

How People Build Cities

efficient physical structure and social relations in Atlanta. Governmental services have grown up as the need for them arose. New and revised services will continue to be necessary as needs change. One of the duties of government is to take note of the changing needs and serve them with as little delay as possible. Unless public needs are met efficiently, people will not want to maintain businesses and homes in our city. Governmental services do much toward making a city a pleasant and desirable place in which to live and work.

Many private agencies in Atlanta are also social resources for public well-being. Some of them have taken the responsibility of improving the welfare of the people. They see that the welfare of the people is really the base of the welfare of the city and its business. They also put forth every effort to strengthen and maintain the efficiency of their chief instrument of public service—city government.

We have come a long way toward a better "physical structure" for Atlanta since streetcars like this ran down muddy, rough streets. Perhaps we can go much further with improvements in the years to come.

ATLANTA'S CITY PLANNING COMMISSION

In order to keep an eye on possible future development, Atlanta established a City Planning Commission in 1932. The purpose of the Planning Commission is to make studies and recommendations for the orderly development of the city. It is composed of nine members—six citizens and a member of the City Council appointed by the mayor, the mayor himself, and the Chief of Construction. The City Council elects the Secretary-Engineer, who is head of the department. Some of these members are also members of the Zoning Commission. The Zoning Commission makes recommendations regarding the proper areas for residence, business, and other uses of land.

The Planning Commission employs a technical staff to do research and actually draw up the detailed plans. City planning does not mean merely widening streets and locating parks as many people suppose. Planning includes all phases of city development which affect the public welfare. It is concerned with developing our physical city to best serve our social needs.

Therefore, planning means widening streets and locating parks, because they are important to our living and working. But it means making good housing regulations too. It means putting good housing into good neighborhood organization layout—both of which, as we have seen, are essential to human welfare and happiness. Planning means good zoning laws, well-enforced; community beautification; getting rid of dirt and noise; supplying water, gas, electricity, and other utilities. It includes transportation systems and traffic control, as well as the convenient location of schools and playgrounds. Most of the ways we can improve our city come under the heading of planning for orderly development.

You can see that *planning* means guiding all changes in our city so that these changes make a better city instead of a worse one. We have seen that the problem areas in Atlanta, such as the slums, show the results of poor planning.

Sometimes the best use of valuable land is for parks, open space, and green plants to give relief to crowded city environment.

Planning like this must take in the whole community. It cannot be effective if done only in spots. Therefore we must have a *master plan* for the city which takes all the factors into consideration. Planning for the development of housing, streets, schools, neighborhoods, and all the other phases must be included in the master plan. Detailed plans for each of the parts must fit into this master plan. You can see that the professional staff of a planning department must have had years of study in order to make a master plan which will cover all these desirable points. Good planning is a task requiring great skill and wisdom.

What is the social machinery through which Atlanta's Planning Commission can carry out its plans? We have seen that it is a department of city government; therefore, it operates through our government. Its purpose is to "make studies and recommendations for the orderly development of the city." The commission, and its staff, recommends plans to the city council. Then the council must pass laws

Building Atlanta's Future

and furnish money for carrying out these plans. The planning commission cannot enforce its plans. It can only recommend them. If the city council does not agree, the plans are never carried out. This system may allow political groups to control the city council and thus defeat the good planning recommendations—unless citizen groups organize themselves to support the Planning Commission.

Thus the kind of planning done in a city with this system often depends on the kind of government the city has. How well has the government of Atlanta fostered its planning function?

HOW GOOD IS OUR GOVERNMENT?

In 1938 a study of the governments of Atlanta and Fulton County was made by the Consultant Service of the National Municipal League. The National Municipal League is an organization to which many of the cities of the United States belong. The League maintains a consultant service from which specialists go out to study the various city governments. These specialists try to find out the best ways to govern cities by studying all kinds of city governments. They have seen many kinds tried and know which have proved most effective. Through their experience they may help cities improve their government.

Atlanta and Fulton County requested that their governments be studied and criticized by these specialists. They hoped to find in what ways their governments were good and in what ways they could be improved and made to work together better. The report of this study is called the *Reed Report* because it was directed by a man named Thomas H. Reed. Its full name is *The Governments of Atlanta and Fulton County, Georgia.*

This report was very critical of some phases of our government. We will discuss some of the good and bad findings in later chapters. Some of the poor practices have been corrected since the study was made in 1938. Some others are still with us.

Of the Planning Commission, the report states, "The city has no

We have changed our governmental machinery but little since this picture of the Old House of Representatives Chamber, Georgia State Capitol, was made in 1890.

plans and the City Planning Commission does no planning worthy of that name." In the light of our definition of "planning" that seems to be a deplorable criticism, does it not? Between 1938 and 1948 the money spent by the Planning Commission has increased five times. But in 1948 we still had no "master plan" to guide the orderly development of Atlanta.

The Planning Commission has attended to routine zoning matters and planned the extension of utilities services. The staff have been busy with various jobs regarding engineering problems in Atlanta. But they have not been able to achieve the "community planning" ideals which we have just discussed. Why have they not done this? Is it the fault of the commission, of the city council, or is it that we have not set up the proper social machinery for doing this kind of planning? The chances are that we will not be able to lay the blame on anyone. Nor would this correct the situation. Perhaps it would be better to see how we can go about getting some good planning done.

The *Reed Report* recommended new machinery for planning in the Atlanta area. It suggested that instead of a city planning commission for the city of Atlanta, we have a planning commission for the entire metropolitan area. Many citizens and officials have agreed with this suggestion, and we now have a Metropolitan Planning Commission.

Building Atlanta's Future

We have seen that Atlanta, as a metropolitan area, contains several communities. Some of these lie outside the city limits of Atlanta proper and have their own units of local government. Metropolitan Atlanta also extends into four different counties. The state and federal governments also have agencies operating in the metropolitan area.

GOVERNMENT AND PLANNING FOR ORDERLY DEVELOPMENT

Since government is the organization which people have set up to direct the efforts for their common good, planning must be done through the medium of government. The government is the representative of all the people and as such should be responsible for meeting their needs.

We might say that planning in Atlanta takes place through several "layers" of government. Within the metropolitan area we find: city government, county government in the four counties included in the metropolitan area, the Georgia state government, and the United States Government. All these levels of government are interested in the welfare of the area. They must all cooperate if we are to have the best and most effective planning for the metropolitan area.

It is not always easy to get several governments to cooperate. The county governments have for years had their traditional ways of doing things. So have the city governments. Each of these may have different ways of working with state and federal agencies. Counties are created by the state constitution. Cities are created through petition to the state legislature. The states cooperate through the federal government of the United States. Each level or "layer" of government must coordinate in some way with the higher and lower levels.

Each government also has different powers and responsibilities. The duties of Atlanta and Fulton County, for example, are often divided. The city police are responsible for certain law enforcement; the county police take care of other cases. Sometimes it is difficult for them to decide which is to be responsible for unusual cases.

Our city government must operate within the laws set up by state and national governments. These laws are very important to Atlanta's welfare.

Remembering that in a democracy the government is set up so as to be stable and reflect the desires of the majority of people, we see that it must often be slow-moving. This keeps it from going off at a tangent when a new "fad" comes along. It also at times makes it slow to change to meet new needs. These differences in duties and traditional ways of doing things make it difficult to get governments to work together on changing their activities in planning for new and changing needs of the area. The government of East Point, for example, may not become concerned with bad housing conditions in Atlanta or Decatur until they begin to affect its own area.

Building Atlanta's Future

This problem has been faced in cities like New York, Cleveland, and Chicago by creating metropolitan governments. These may be created by four methods. The first is the process of "annexation." That is, the entire metropolitan area is "annexed" or taken into the city limits of the central city. Thus the one city government serves the whole

Our modern fire fighters may give better service than this one because of better equipment. Such necessary services should be organized to be most efficient, not just to serve one political unit.

area. All smaller governmental units are combined into the large one and disappear.

A second process gives the city "extra territorial" powers. The state gives the city power to go outside the territory in the city limits for purposes which benefit the people of the city. In this way water supply reservoirs may be built long distances from the city. Sewage systems, parks, hospitals, cemeteries, and the like may extend and serve beyond the city limits. Zoning and land-use controls may extend to the surrounding fringe area.

A third way is to combine city and county governments. The city limits are extended to take in the entire counties which contain parts of the city. A large city may cover all or parts of one or more counties. This often causes the city and county governments to overlap in authority. Since both of them collect taxes to pay for their operation, this is a wasteful duplication. There is no need for two agencies doing nearly the same job in the same place. Atlanta is in this situation in many respects with regard to Fulton County. Under this plan, the city limits are made the same as the county limits and the two governments combine into one. This was done in Philadelphia as early as 1854 and in New Orleans in 1874.

A fourth solution to the metropolitan problem is a combination of the above. It is called "municipal federalism" and is a teamwork arrangement of the small units within the area. The metropolitan region becomes a political unit, but the smaller units remain within it. The central city government takes over all the duties which affect the area as a whole. The smaller communities continue to control their purely local affairs. This federation is similar to that by which the forty-eight states make up the United States.

This federation of local city and county governments within a metropolitan area is a complicated organization. But it has many advantages. The metropolitan government can make and carry out plans which affect the entire area. The smaller units do not have to bother with these tasks. Such things as water supply, sewage systems, streets and highway systems, and zoning ordinances are in this way done better and more economically. Yet suburban communities may enjoy their own vigorous control of local life. Such local units may cooperate closely without a federation. But a metropolitan federation as a political unit makes the system work more smoothly.

PLANNING FOR OUR METROPOLITAN COMMUNITY

Atlanta has begun to plan for our metropolitan district. The local governments in the area have always cooperated to some extent. But to make the cooperation more secure and effective a "Metropolitan Planning Commission" has been set up. It is similar in some respects to that recommended in the *Reed Report*.

The Georgia Legislature in 1947 passed an act establishing a metropolitan planning district for Fulton and DeKalb counties. (Only very small parts of the metropolitan area are in Cobb and Clayton counties.) The Metropolitan Planning Commission was established in the same act. It provides an authority to make an over-all plan for the orderly development of the district. Perhaps you would like to read a copy of the act to find out how the State Legislature grants powers to political units.

The Metropolitan Planning Commission is composed of fourteen members as follows:

4 Citizens from the city of Atlanta (2 from Atlanta in Fulton County and 2 from Atlanta in DeKalb County) appointed by the Mayor
3 Citizens of Fulton County, appointed by the Board of Commissioners of Roads and Revenues
3 Citizens of DeKalb County, appointed by the Commissioner of Roads and Revenues
1 Chairman of the Board of Commissioners of Fulton County
1 Commissioner of Roads and Revenues of DeKalb County
2 Mayors of county seat municipalities of Fulton and DeKalb counties

The citizen members are appointed for terms of three years. The officials are members as long as they hold their offices.

You see that we have both citizens and governmental officials from both counties and the city of Atlanta represented on the Commission. They have the power to employ a manager and technical and engineering assistants to do the actual work of planning. The money to pay these people is supplied by the city and county tax revenues—in proportion to their revenues. The commissioners do not do the actual work of planning. They set the policies and hire specialists, who are trained for the job, to do the detailed plans.

The members of the Commission and their staff can work together to make plans which will meet the public needs of the people in every part of the district. But as is the case with the Atlanta Planning Commission, they can only advise the governments and recommend desirable changes. The act creating the Commission does not give them power to enforce their plans. You can readily see that this may be a disadvantage. A master plan for the whole district has to be approved by all the local governments. If one or two of them do not agree with the others, the entire plan may bog down. Nothing can be done. There is little chance in such a system to do things for the public good when they are opposed by powerful political interests. It has been said that the Commission has no "teeth" with which to "nip" the several governments into action.

We have made great progress in that we have a Metropolitan Planning District with a Planning Commission. It is very helpful for the members to work together and make plans for orderly development of the area. But a basic problem still remains. Regardless of the good decisions made by the Planning Commission, the various governments must accept them and carry them out. We still have no central authority for carrying out their plans. The problem of getting all the units and levels of government to agree is still with us.

PLANNING AND CITIZENSHIP

It is possible that the Metropolitan Planning Commission would be more immediately effective if it had more power to enforce its recommendations. Or perhaps it has power enough if our governments are run by efficient and forward-looking officials. One solution is for

How we get something done through our government. Learn about it—discuss it—organize a program—vote for it—success.

more of our citizens to take interest in public matters and vote for capable officials and representatives who have the public interest in mind. Then our legislative bodies will accept good recommendations and carry them out without delay.

Unfortunately, however, many of our citizens do not take interest in promoting and supporting good government. They consider it as mere "politics." As a result, the politicians sometimes run the government to please themselves. Powerful "vested interests" apply pressure to the politicians whom they have helped elect to office. The politicians do what they are asked in order to stay in office. The majority of citizens do not get what they would like because they have not used the rights and privileges of sending officials to represent them.

Thus we often find that a few individuals largely control our local governments. These people may be those who are civic-minded and interested in public welfare. On the other hand, they may be those who want personal gain without regard for others. The majority of our citizens tend to stay at home on election days and to not even know what the government is doing. Doubtless, there are many people in Atlanta who have not bothered to find out about the purposes of the Metropolitan Planning Commission and other public issues. Democratic government cannot work to best advantage so long as this is true.

The *Reed Report* has shown that perhaps our governmental machinery is not the best that we could wish. But we can see that we do not make the best use of what we have. No democratic style of government is better than the citizens who make it. One of the best ways to improve our social machinery for making a better city is to learn what is better. After a majority of our citizens know what they want, they must work to get it. We have social machinery. We must learn to use and improve it. The machinery for doing this is that of getting a majority of all the people to vote. They can direct their government the way they want it to go through their votes.

PRIVATE AGENCIES

But not all social machinery is found in government. There are many organizations through which people work for the common good. Civic clubs such as Rotary, Kiwanis, Civitan, Lions, and many others have the public welfare as their purpose. Private schools, philanthropic foundations, professional organizations of doctors, lawyers, teachers, and others do much to help all the people. So do such groups as the League of Women Voters and the Urban League.

Perhaps the largest group of nongovernmental agencies with public interests are those concerned with health, welfare, and social problems. You will recall that we discussed them in Chapter 11. In Atlanta these agencies have organized themselves into the Community Planning Council of Metropolitan Atlanta. The "planning" done by this organization is, of course, not done directly through government as in the case of a city or metropolitan planning commission. However, some governmental social agencies are members and cooperate with them.

The social problems of Atlanta cannot be solved unless we improve the physical problems which help cause them. On the other hand, there is no need to change the city unless we make it serve better the needs of the people. Social and physical planning are too closely related to be separated.

We find in Atlanta, as in all cities, that social and physical planning have the same purposes. By its nature, physical planning must be done largely through governmental action. The Community Planning

Building Atlanta's Future

Council acts through educating people to know what is desirable and to work for such action. It adds its weight to getting changes in the physical city which will be for the public welfare. In that way it achieves its purpose of reducing human suffering and disease.

This should lead us to see again that most of our group effort for improving our living is done through our social resources. Through our governmental and other social machinery we can act to improve our city. Perhaps we have enough *quantity* of city now. Our efforts can best be turned to developing and using new social machinery toward better *quality* of living in Atlanta.

DISCUSSION QUESTIONS

1. Why is the "New England Town Meeting" considered an example of democracy at its best?
2. What kind of "social machinery" does Atlanta have for doing public business? How does it differ from the town meeting?
3. Why is the quality of our "physical city" so important to the social relations of our people? Can you use housing as an example of this?
4. What department of city government is responsible for guiding the orderly development of our city? What criticisms have been made of its work by the Reed Report and others?
5. Describe the social machinery set up for guiding the orderly development of our metropolitan area.
6. What recent progress toward developing and carrying out a "master plan" for Metropolitan Atlanta have you found in newspapers?

HAVE YOU READ?

1. *Atlanta City Government*. Atlanta, Georgia: Atlanta Public Schools, 1945.
2. *Building America, Illustrated Studies of Modern Problems*. Vol. V, "Community Planning." Building America Illustrated Studies. New York: American Corporation, 1940.

3. Chapin, F. Stuart, Jr. *Communities for Living.* Prepared for the Advisory Panel on Regional Materials of Instruction for the Tennessee Valley. Athens, Georgia: The University of Georgia Press, 1941.
4. *Community Resources Directory, 1946–47.* "City Planning Commission." Atlanta, Georgia: Community Planning Council, 1947.
5. Reed, Thomas H. (dir.) *The Governments of Atlanta and Fulton County, Georgia.* Vol. I, "The Government of Atlanta," "Consolidation in the Metropolitan Area." Vol. II, "Planning." Atlanta, Georgia: The Atlanta Chamber of Commerce, 1938.
6. *Your Part in Georgia's Politics.* Atlanta, Georgia: Committee for Georgia, 1945.

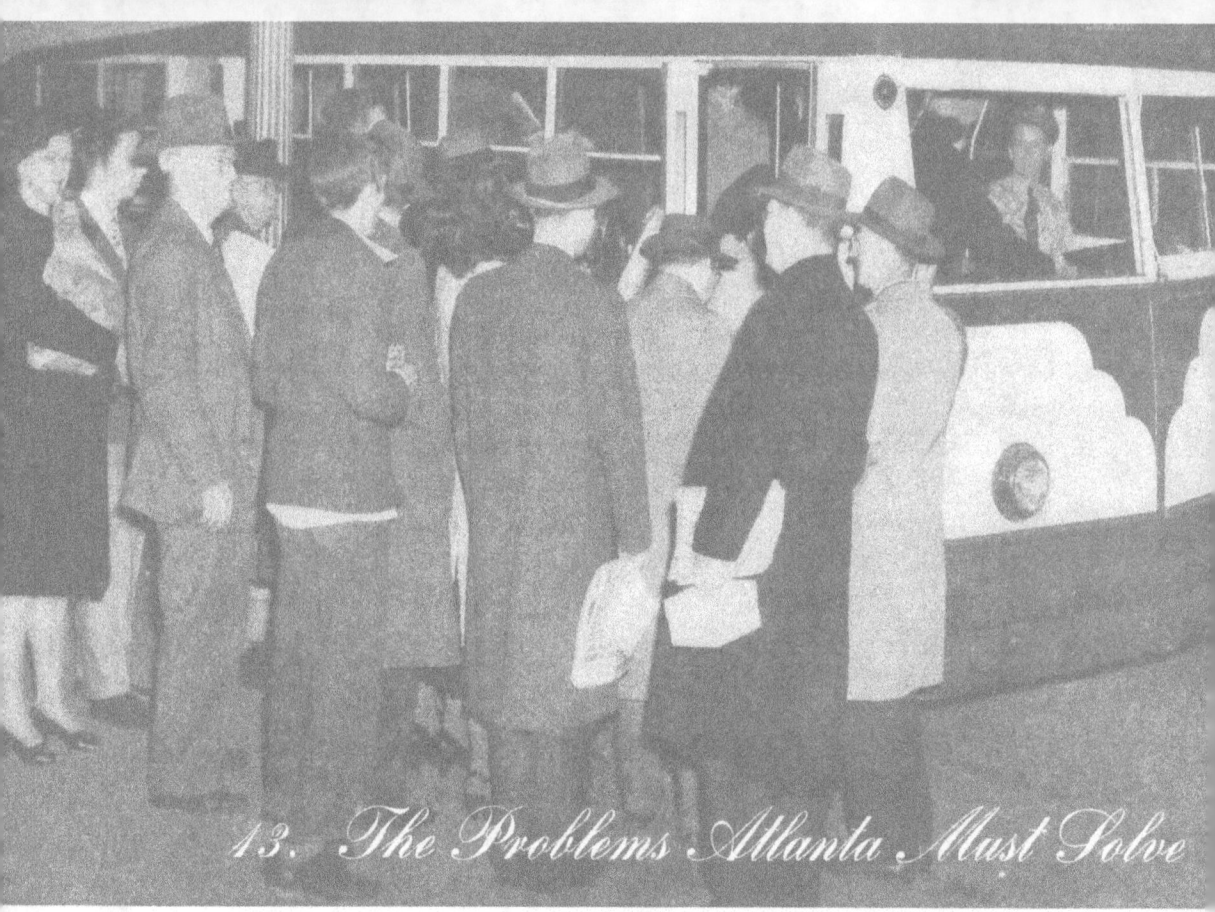

13. The Problems Atlanta Must Solve

THROUGHOUT this book we have reviewed the features of cities and of Atlanta in particular. We have been pleased with some of the features but consider others to be unhealthy in terms of city life. In a sense, our city is "sick" in some of its parts. Just as disease or wounds keep the human body from working to its best advantage, so these problems affect the health of Atlanta. If we are to improve our city, we must hunt down the unhealthy, or problem, features and cure them. This will mean that we study the most unattractive features of Atlanta.

While we look at these undesirable things, however, we must not forget that we have a good city in other respects. You may sometimes have personal problems of your own which you would like to solve. But you are not entirely unhappy all the time because of them. You may have a headache or a cold, or you may want a new coat or a motor scooter. No doubt you will be happier when such problems are solved. But you must make the best of things until the solution can be worked out. You cannot stop living and wait for the solution.

The Problems Atlanta Must Solve

In the same way, we must not lose sight of the whole picture of Atlanta. Our problems are not only troublesome, they are also points at which we can start making improvements. We must see them as undesirable. But we must also see how solving them will improve the entire city.

We have seen how cities serve a great purpose in the work of the world. We have also learned how they at the same time create conditions which make people unhappy. Cities all over the world face similar problems. How do they apply to Atlanta? What are the greatest problems Atlanta people face? The kind of city you will live in depends on how well these problems can be solved.

WHAT ARE OUR PROBLEMS?

Perhaps the best way to see the problems of Atlanta is to list the features we have taken up and find the problems which are connected with each.

1. *The problem of our dependence on others:* One important fact we must keep in mind is that city and country depend on each other. The problems within Atlanta are often tied up with the problems and prosperity of the State of Georgia, the southeastern region, and the United States. We cannot separate all our problems from these larger regional ones because our local problems are part of regional, national, and world problems.

For example, we have no farm lands, forests, nor coal and oil deposits in Atlanta. Yet we must have food, lumber for houses, and fuel for our furnaces and engines. These must come from the country and often from distant parts of our state and nation. The laws and customs regulating their use are made by state governments or the federal government.

If Atlanta people want to assure themselves of wise use and a continued supply of natural resources, they must join with all the other people in working to see that such regulations are made. The last century or so has seen the results of great waste of forest and farming

This soil is washing away in Texas. We should take interest in it because all the people in the United States share all the food the soil produces.

lands. The same is true of coal and oil deposits. People all over the nation are now realizing that this waste must stop. We cannot afford it any longer. Atlanta people will suffer as much as anyone if our natural resources are depleted.

A citizen of Atlanta must remember that he is a citizen of Georgia, of the Southeast, and of the United States. He must be interested in the general welfare of the larger areas. It is only through serving these areas that Atlanta can solve her local problems. Atlanta people are just as responsible for voting and taking interest in state and national affairs as are people anywhere else. A great many of them seem to take little interest in this responsibility of being citizens.

Therefore, our first problem in Atlanta is to get people to use their privileges and responsibilities as citizens to better advantage. By this means we can work to solve a great many of our problems.

2. *The problems of our economy:* The economic status of Atlanta is good only when compared with other *southern* cities. The average amount of money paid Atlanta workers is low compared to most of the

The Problems Atlanta Must Solve

cities in the United States. This low income level is caused in part by the fact that Atlanta has a large number of unskilled, very poorly-paid workers. A great many Negroes are in this low-income group. This group pulls down our average income. In many cases they have had little opportunity to learn skills which would make them more productive, better-paid workers. Income depends greatly on skill and productivity of workers.

We have seen that, except in times of inflation, high income means high purchasing power. The more money people have, the more goods and services they can buy. The more they buy, the more business they create to keep wealth flowing in our economic system. Thus a higher income level may support a higher level of living for everyone. The problem of a large low-income group also affects our ability to pay for civic improvements through tax collections.

Therefore, the problem of a better economy in Atlanta is a problem of higher skills and better jobs for more of our people. Our low-income white and Negro groups need jobs which pay higher wages and salaries. Perhaps this can be solved by new kinds of industries—further "diversification" of industry. In this way we may create new kinds of better paying jobs for people. They will have opportunities to learn new skills. If this is done, we may be able to do away with many of the prejudices and undemocratic attitudes that have come down from the past. It would seem a poor economy that did not permit all the people to use their talents and resources to best advantage.

Some features of Atlanta's economy are not always what they appear to be. Our city ranks high among cities of its size in the amount of money cleared through our banks and the volume of goods bought and sold. However, we must remember that as a regional center we have many "branch offices" and headquarters for agencies and firms. Some of the profits and benefits from such businesses go to owners and stockholders in other parts of the country. This money and goods are exchanged among people all over the region. Therefore, the benefit to local people is not as great as may at first appear. Our real income

Building Atlanta's Future

and benefit might be greater if this business were purely local in nature. However, many of our industries could not exist without the support of industries and markets in distant places.

Atlanta's economic problems, then, are grouped around the need for better job opportunities for many of our people. To be able to furnish more and better jobs is a complicated problem with many sides. It includes better distribution of wealth among income groups. Unemployment, inflation, and depression, and their effects on democratic ideals are also part of this great problem. Social and physical improvements in our city will move slowly if not built on economic improvements.

3. *The problem of our common wealth:* Land and the buildings thereon are the physical "body" of a city. If they are not used to best advantage, we cannot have a healthy city. Just as you must develop all the different muscles in your body if you are to be in the best possible health, so it is with Atlanta. The parts must develop together. We have seen how the uses made of land in a city affects the lives of many people. The social

Guiding the location and arrangement of new subdivisions will help assure a healthy city of the future.

Blighted areas show up dramatically beside good housing. We have much more yet to do.

results make it impossible to allow people to do just as they please with land and buildings.

There are many cases of poor use of land in Atlanta. Some of the city area is being wasted because of irresponsible use of near-by land. We have seen how slum areas may be created when industries are put up near residential areas. Property in business sections may lose value if other kinds of activities crowd in. A city cannot develop a "healthy body" unless individuals are sometimes made to conform to the needs of the group.

The problems of land use are easily seen in the most unattractive parts of Atlanta. The need for land-use controls is well recognized. Changes have been, and are being, made in the land-use controls such as zoning and subdivision development. We need many other changes before we can cure the problem of wasting our common wealth.

4. *The problem of housing:* Slums and blight are perhaps Atlanta's most obvious problem. Their effect on the health, happiness, and efficiency of our people is immense. Housing is so important in the lives

Many people would rather avoid our city than brave the traffic tangles. Merely adding more facilities will not correct this. It will take long-range community planning.

of individuals, families, and in the welfare of our entire city, that the need for action is immediate.

Housing problems touch not only the lives of the people who live in the houses, they also affect the property owner and the general public through the tax collections—the government's income and the cost of public services in blighted areas. Solving housing problems, as we have seen, is a step toward solving many other civic problems. The house one lives in is very much a part of his everyday life. It can hardly be separated from all the problems of living.

5. *The problem of our streets and services:* Atlanta is a regional center. As such, it demands the fast and easy flow of people, ideas, goods, and

services within the city. Hence, our economy and well-being depend greatly on transportation, communication, and related public services.

Yet it has often been said, as the *Reed Report* puts it, that "Atlanta is strangling in its traffic tangles." Despite efforts in recent years to improve the traffic situation, it is quite evident that much is still to be done. If such a troublesome problem is allowed to hang on, serious results will increase.

Traffic problems are symptoms of inefficient land uses, and related, therefore, to Section 3 above. Our street and traffic control systems need to be revised. If this problem is not corrected, people may soon avoid our city rather than brave the traffic tangles. In the same way, our utility services should be so good as to attract people and to serve well the needs of home and business. Dependable, cheap utilities are essential to modern city living. Whether municipally or privately owned, they should be the best and cheapest possible. Utility services are primarily public services, not profit-making enterprises. They must be available to the poorest as well as the richest of us.

6. *The problem of community and neighborhood:* The communities in and around Atlanta do not afford the best of local neighborly living. The people in them do not cooperate to make full use of all our social resources and to develop new ones as they are needed. Perhaps this is due to "city" attitudes in part, but the physical layout of the communities also hinders group cooperation.

However great our entire city may appear, most of our personal satisfaction comes from social relations with people we know and live near. The success of most city programs depends on whether people in community groups like and support them. To be able to use our social resources to best advantage, physical layout should foster community spirit and cooperation. Community centers, parks, greenbelts, and street-pattern design help create strong group cooperation. We can meet our group needs only through democratic group efforts.

Making our physical city serve better our social relations is one of the primary purposes of guided development. It increases our chances

Building Atlanta's Future

of finding new social inventions which may help us to better meet our wants and needs.

Under these six headings many of the problems of Atlanta fall. Under each of the headings we could list several sub-problems. We might also classify them differently—list them as problems of government, health, general welfare, education, crime, or other similar headings of a social nature. But the problems remain the same. In the long run, they reflect poor use of our natural, social, and human resources. We, as human resources, have not developed our abilities and ideals to their highest levels. We have not learned to use and control our natural and social resources to serve our needs as well as they might.

PLANNING TO SOLVE OUR PROBLEMS

Here, then, are our problems. What will be done about them? What *can* be done? For one thing, we can let them alone. Then they will continue to get worse. The bad features of a city tend to grow worse.

We have seen how slums spread to sound districts. Traffic problems lessen our efficiency as a city. Poor land use in new developments causes the same problems to be repeated unless we guide the develop-

Guided development through long-range planning means building anew.

ment to prevent them. All our problems and the evils that go with them multiply if they are left to themselves.

Or we can have guided development. This is not a panacea, a fast cure-all, for all our problems. There is no quick and easy solution for such far-reaching problems. We must attack them through long-range planning in the public interest. Only in this manner can we get our "house" in order and provide better living for our people.

The experts who made the *Reed Report* conclude: "There is . . . the gravest need in Atlanta and the surrounding territory for planning of the most fundamental kind. The bald fact is that the city of Atlanta presents, in the most aggravated form, the consequences of unregulated growth, and the metropolitan region surrounding the city is rapidly building up in the same unguided manner."

The route toward solution of many of our problems thus lies in the direction of *planning*. As in Chapter 12, planning is used here in its broadest sense. It means guiding the development of our physical and social environment to give the greatest public benefit. The term "city planning" has recently received much publicity. Some people have made exorbitant claims about the results gained from planning. As in all fields, we must be wary of such claims. The merits of intelligent planning are great enough, however, to warrant our special study.

means tearing out the old and rebuilding in the public interests.

WHAT IS GOOD PLANNING?

Good planning in Atlanta means several things. It means planning and building new residential neighborhoods, new parks and playgrounds, hospitals and schools, streets and factories. It means replanning and rebuilding old parts of the city for better residences or for other uses. Good planning also means conservation of sound areas threatened by age and deterioration.

We cannot tear out the old and rebuild all at once. The cost would be too great. We must have long-range planning through a master plan which will gradually replace the old with desirable new. Old buildings, streets, and service fixtures are continually being revised and rebuilt in Atlanta as they become obsolete. Why not rebuild them within a plan which will eventually guide into a city plan that we want?

Atlanta is also expanding. New developments around the outskirts and in the suburbs need to be planned, too. Otherwise they will grow up to have the bad features which we are trying to get away from. Planning must be for the entire metropolitan community, not just within the city limits. In the long run, anything less than over-all community planning is not satisfactory. For instance, suppose we plan traffic arteries in Atlanta to direct all northbound traffic through Decatur and Buckhead. We must also include in the master plan a way to get the heavy traffic through or around these suburbs. Otherwise we will create new traffic bottlenecks as bad as the ones we have corrected. The city limits do not mark the end of our real community.

Making a blueprint of streets, buildings, schools, and playgrounds is not over-all community planning. Over-all planning, or "master planning," includes long-range policies and goals. We must decide what kind of city we want, how we are going to get it, and which parts we should get first. After these decisions are made, then come the blueprints by which the actual construction is to be done. A good master plan, then, is not only a blueprint, but also directions for carrying out

Strategy and tactics change. These fortifications built for the Battle of Atlanta would be poor defense against bombers and guided missiles. The physical structure of a city must also meet the needs of today.

the entire plan. It includes the reasons for doing things and the purposes for which they are done.

In Chapter 12 we have discussed the machinery of planning, the Metropolitan Planning Commission. After the machinery is set up, what are the steps in actually making a master plan? What is a good master plan like?

MAKING A MASTER PLAN

A master plan for a city community may be compared to a plan for a campaign in a war. Before a battle or campaign, the generals plan their *strategy*. The strategy has to do with the purposes of the campaign. Just what do the generals want to accomplish? Strategy also has to do with the *ways* these purposes can be achieved and in what *order* they shall be done. Thus the strategy, or master plan, for a campaign to capture a town in warfare might be: "We must capture the town. First, the Air Force will bomb the military centers. Then the Artillery Corps will shell the town from a distance. Third, the Airborne Infantry will land by parachute and seize the military headquarters. Fourth, the Infantry will move in and capture the remaining troops. Civilians will be allowed to stay in their homes so long as they do not attempt violence."

After these decisions are made come the *tactics*. The over-all plan is the strategy. The detailed plans for bombing, shelling, and capturing are the tactics. The operations named are known as *tactical operations* in military terms. They can be compared to the blueprints for streets and buildings in a city plan. Before they can be carried out effectively, there must be a master plan into which they can fit in the proper order. It would be disastrous if the bombing and shelling did not start until the infantry had already reached the town. All the plans must be made in relation to one another if the master plan is to be truly effective. The tactics must follow the order set forth in the strategy. In the same way we must plan the strategy in our master plan for Atlanta and follow it in the actual construction.

The first step in making the strategy of a master plan is for the planning group—made up of both citizens and professional planners—to make a complete study of the community. They must know what we have to start with and what we may reasonably expect in the future. They should survey and analyze the community as a whole—the kind of a place it is and the trends which seem to show its future relation to the state, region, nation, and world. They should study the people. Is our population growing? What are our population's characteristics as families, age groups, races, and skills? What are the advantages and disadvantages of our present industries—raw materials, labor supply, markets?

They should also study where people live, work, and play. Is our land used efficiently for housing and business needs? Is sufficient area used for each need? Do all people have suitable houses to live in? Does our transportation system serve our needs well? Are there trends which are shifting the location of residence, business, or industrial areas? What is causing these trends? Are there special problems such as blight and slum areas which need immediate attention? These are among the features that must be studied before the plan is made.

In the light of these studies, the citizen groups with the help of staff planners can decide how much space is likely to be needed for expansion of industrial, business, residential, and other areas. They can decide which land can best be used for each purpose. Transportation

The Problems Atlanta Must Solve

lanes of greatest traffic can then be laid out among the areas. Provision can be made for moving people and industry from overcrowded sections to suburbs or open spaces. In short, we will know what we have now, what we would like to have, and how we can go about getting it.

PLANNING THE OUTSKIRTS

Atlanta is spreading out. We can guide the new suburbs and residential sections toward becoming the attractive garden city type. A master plan should contain zoning controls and proposed ways to make each new section beautiful and useful. The location of such suburban centers may be guided in the plan so that they grow up in the most advantageous places. Otherwise they may grow up in spots which will later interfere with the best land-use developments of the metropolitan district.

Each new subdivision or suburban town should be located for the best possible living conditions, transportation facilities, raw materials, labor supply, markets, and so forth. This requires skillful master planning. The blueprints can then be made to keep the growth of residential neighborhoods in balance with the number of jobs. The transportation system must afford means for excess workers to get to jobs outside the neighborhood.

REPLANNING THE CENTRAL CITY

Within Atlanta our problems are more numerous and complex than in the suburbs. If the present trend of moving out of the central

Modern transportation allows cities to spread out. People can live farther away and still travel into the central city in a short time.

Building Atlanta's Future

city continues, the time may possibly come when parts of the city will be abandoned. Property values would then fall to the point that the taxes would not support our city government. The goals for replanning the interior of a city were well stated in an article in *Fortune* magazine, January 1944. The article, entitled "So You're Going to Plan a City," gives the goals as:

1. Good dwelling accommodations for all who wish to live in the city proper, with apartments, detached, double, row, or group houses to meet the various kinds of family requirements.
2. Location of residential neighborhoods in relation to business and industry so as to provide easy access to places of employment.
3. A coordinated transportation system, including all forms of public facilities and the terminals for them, to make travel and transport as pleasant and efficient as possible.
4. The arrangement of roads and streets and parking space in such a way that all private automobiles (or helicopters or hitherto undiscovered gadgets) can be used with pleasure and safety.
5. Ample cultural and recreational facilities within easy reach of all who want to use them.

Highways, crossings, and streets will be planned with new transportation needs in mind.

The Problems Atlanta Must Solve

6. Property values that will remain reasonably stable—to provide valid incentives for home ownership and other investment in real estate and to permit the municipal government to organize its fiscal affairs on a sound basis.

With these goals in the master plan, the possible location of residential areas—perhaps like the neighborhoods mentioned in Chapter 8—can be laid out. Within this plan of strategy, the "tactics" of making blueprints for each neighborhood can be brought up-to-date as we get to rebuilding them. We can plan the rebuilding so that slums and blighted areas give way first to the new neighborhood developments. The use of expressways and green parkways can be planned in the correct relation to homes and jobs and transportation needs.

Along with residence areas, the master plan will set forth the most likely areas for business and industrial use. Changes in land use will be planned to fit into our city's function as a regional center of commerce and distribution. This will mean shifting some land-use districts. Business or industrial districts may be replaced by parks or by residential districts. This shifting must be shown in the master plan. Then the rebuilding can be done as occasion permits and in the order which will be most beneficial. Only through such a long-range plan can we achieve the metropolitan community made of smaller garden city type neighborhoods which we desire.

However, when this shifting of land use is done, land values will also shift. The total land value will possibly go up. But there will be some land which will be less valuable. For instance, a property owner will not get as much rent from his land if it is made into a park or spacious residential area as he would if it were a crowded slum area. That is where the rub comes. People must be willing to accept the changes if our planning is to be carried out to its best advantage.

THE CITIZEN'S PLACE IN PLANNING

Changing land values is a complicated problem. Ways to take care of it must be included in the master plan. But the large property owners are not the only people who are affected. The "average citizen" is affected, too. Over-all community planning cannot be achieved by a few citizens. Making regulations as to what *cannot* be done is not good planning. There must be some way to get the actual, positive, everyday participation of our citizens.

The people of Atlanta must help develop and must like a plan if it is to work. We must not only stop the bad practices, but we must also put our efforts to doing the desirable everyday things which are in the spirit of making a better city. People themselves make a plan succeed or fail.

Suppose we had the best planning machinery it is possible to devise. We may then make a master plan which is second to none. We may make blueprints of each neighborhood and district. We may plan an almost ideal city. But what about the people? Will they work to carry out the plans? Or will they do just as much as they are required by law and "get by" with all the violations they can?

Suppose the replanning of your neighborhood is in progress. You and your family own your home and are fairly well pleased with it. But you see that the neighborhood in other places needs changing. The new plan is drawn up. It calls for changing the street system. The street by your home is to be moved. The new street will cut across the corner of your lot and some of your shrubbery will have to be cut away. Your driveway must be moved. These are troublesome and somewhat expensive changes to you. They are more important to you at the moment than the thought of the future beauty and utility of the neighborhood.

Some of your neighbors are also irked at having to move the stores, filling stations, and other property from a section which is to become residential. These changes are necessary if we are to replan. If people are to receive the benefits, they must share in the inconveniences also. Yet, if most of the citizens are going to fight the plan because it inconveniences them, the plan can never succeed. How can we get people interested in working for a better city? How can we get

The Problems Atlanta Must Solve

them to look toward the future instead of thinking only about today?

For one thing, we can help to show them how much better our city can be. Through our schools, newspapers, radio programs, books, clubs, everyday chats, and other means we can learn the benefits of community planning. Then we can put all our knowledge together and work for the planning we want. Since it is for the benefit of the people, they must take part in the planning. We must decide for ourselves that we need some changes. Then we must decide together what kind of changes we want as a group—whether it is as a metropolitan community group or as a local neighborhood group. If we do the deciding and planning to some extent ourselves, we will be interested in seeing that it is well carried out.

This does not mean that we can learn to be accomplished city planners in a short while. But it does mean that we can learn that well-planned places are desirable. We can learn the kind of surroundings that will fit our needs. Then we can get experts to do the actual plans and blueprints to give us the kind of surroundings we want. They cannot do that until the citizens see the need and provide the oppor-

The attitudes and interests of the "people on the street" as they go about their daily routines are the real powers that can bring about civic improvements. The people make the city.

tunity. Planning imposed upon people by government or small groups smacks of totalitarianism. In a democracy, action must be asked for and carried out by the people.

Enough citizens in Metropolitan Atlanta have been concerned about their city to cause a Metropolitan Planning Commission to be set up. How well the commission will succeed, only time can tell. But it is certain that if it is to have any measure of success, it must have the support and assistance of the people.

If planning is to succeed in the metropolitan district, it must succeed in each of its smaller communities and neighborhoods. The citizens in each neighborhood must take part in the planning of their surroundings. They must stand behind the planning commission even when it causes inconveniences and sacrifices. You can have a part in spreading the knowledge of the benefits to come from guided development. Such knowledge is the spark from which the flame of progress starts.

DISCUSSION QUESTIONS

1. What kinds of problems in Atlanta are receiving most attention in newspapers at present? What solutions are being proposed? Do they have to do with planning?
2. What is the difference between the master plan, or "strategy," and the blueprinting, or "tactics," of city planning?
3. What is the main purpose in replanning our city?
4. Why are streets and services so important to Atlanta as a regional center?
5. Why are health and welfare authorities interested in better housing and street systems in Atlanta? Does our economy enter into this?
6. Why should the average citizen take part in the planning of his neighborhood? What can he do?

HAVE YOU READ?

1. Greer, Guy. "After the Plans, What?" Reprinted from *Fortune* Magazine, July, 1944.
2. "So You're Going to Plan a City." Reprinted from *Fortune* Magazine, January, 1944.
3. *The Atlanta Letter*. Atlanta, Georgia: Community Planning Council.

14. How to Meet Our Challenge

WE have reviewed some of the problems facing us in Atlanta. These problems are a challenge to our effort and our abilities. The more of them we can solve, the better our city will be as a place to live. As we think back over the kinds of problems we have studied, we see that most of them are "community wide." They affect most of the people in our communities and the entire metropolitan district. Solving them will require the cooperation of large groups of people.

Thus the problems of Atlanta stand before us, in a sense, and seem to dare all of us to "Come on out and fight." They are between us and the kind of city we would like to have. If we accept the challenge and defeat them, we can move faster in making progress. In the Bible story of David and Goliath, David did not attack the giant until he was prepared. It would have been useless to attack empty-handed. But with his slingshot and stones ready, he accepted the challenge and won the victory.

Building Atlanta's Future

We can prepare ourselves to meet the challenge of Atlanta's problems. Since they are group problems, the challenge is for the entire group—all the people in Atlanta. But a "group" cannot think. It cannot make decisions as a unit. Each person in the group must think for himself. Learning to do things in groups is based on the knowledge and skills of the individual members. In the end we see that the challenge is for each person to prepare himself to make the greatest contribution to the work of the group.

How can we prepare ourselves to meet this challenge? What are the steps in learning to be efficient citizens and in developing a finer city? There are three great steps.

1. Developing ourselves as persons.
2. Learning to work together as a group.
3. Learning to work together as groups within the community.

Each of these "levels" of activity are important to getting things done. On the first, or personal level, are things which you can and must do for yourself. Then on the second, or group level, are things in which you cooperate with others. These cover a larger scope and cannot be done by individuals working alone. The third level includes those things which affect the entire community. Groups must work together to achieve action on matters of this scope. Perhaps it would help if we illustrate each of these points.

OUR CHALLENGE AS INDIVIDUALS

You probably have some very definite ideas about the kind of life you want to live. You know some of the types of jobs you might like. You may know what kind of house you want to live in. Of course these

Some things one person can do alone. They can be done faster and easier with cooperative help. Larger jobs require larger groups.

We are forever seeking information that will help us meet our needs.

ideas may change as you grow older. But until they do, they are the *goals* for your future. They are the targets at which you are aiming your efforts.

How do you go about reaching these goals? First, you probably think of the steps you must go through in arriving at each of them. You plan for some of the experiences which will help you. You continually strive to build up the fund of information which you will need. This information comes from your study, reading, listening to the radio, seeing movies, talking with well-informed people, and many sources. You can hardly learn too much. The search for new information can become a valuable habit. We must continually add to our knowledge if we are to grow to our fullest capacity and reach the goals we set for ourselves.

Knowledge is one essential to reaching your life goals. But you must also have *skills*. Nearly everything we do requires a set of skills. You must have skills in order to be able to tie your shoes. Many more are needed to operate a complicated machine, paint a great picture, handle legal problems in a court of law, or perform a delicate operation in surgery. Just as we search for information, we must continually try to improve our skills to do better work.

As we gain in knowledge and skills, we move toward our goals. Our capacity to reach those goals depends upon the information we have gained and the skills we have for putting that information to work. Every day each of your activities gives you a chance to add to your knowledge and skills. If you set up your goals and guide your study and work toward them, you are beginning a systematic approach. It should point you toward becoming a useful citizen of Atlanta or any community.

Let us consider the type of person who does not plan his life. He drifts from day to day letting events shape his life for him. We know that "events" will always happen. But they may not be the kind he wants. He will not become a productive citizen unless by great chance everyday happenings push him toward some type of useful work. His mind will not be sharpened by the drive to learn information leading to a goal. His ability will not broaden as he learns the skills necessary for using his talents.

It is likely that such a "drifter" in the whirlpool of community life may become embittered. He may feel that the world is against him. He may find no spot into which he can fit in a useful way. These conditions may affect him to the extent that he becomes mentally or physically ill. He has a much greater chance of ending up as a criminal. Even though he may "get along fairly well," he is wasting his talents. If he does not manage to get along, he may waste public funds

Your friends all have about the same opportunity. Some of them will "succeed" better in life than others. Why?

which must be used to take care of him. He has not tried to order his life in such a way as to become a responsible citizen, contributing to the welfare of his community.

Each of us is born with a certain capacity. We differ in some respects. But it is very important that we develop ourselves to contribute to our highest possible capacity. The information and skills that we learn are for our own personal welfare. Each of us will use them in his own everyday work. But they will also be used in working with others.

If everyone worked by himself and for himself, we would be no better off than savages or cave men. But there is more to working together than merely assisting each other with our jobs. We must learn to get along with people, to stimulate one another to higher effort, and to plan and cooperate as groups. Several persons in a working group can bring their knowledge and skills together to add up to a capacity they could never achieve as individuals.

OUR CHALLENGE AS GROUPS

Have you ever thought about the skills you need in order to be a really good member of a group? What do you need to know and do to get people to work well together? How do you get them interested in doing a good job, and how do you keep them interested? Of course in all our dealings with other people we must observe the basic rules of courtesy. Politeness and kindness are the first principles of social relations. We must also have rules which members of groups follow in conducting their meetings.

There are other skills, however, which we use in working in groups. They help us in reaching better decisions in meetings and in doing something about the decisions after they are made. Not all the work of groups is done in their meetings. Skills of working with people outside the groups are often of great importance. They include all the ways of getting along with and understanding people, as well as getting them to think about and act upon group problems. An example may help illustrate these skills.

Skill in understanding and guiding other people is one of the most valuable things we can learn.

A drugstore is a good place to get a soda but it is not designed as a recreation center.

Suppose your class is studying your community. You are considering the problems which bother most of the people in the community. You are, of course, most concerned with those problems which affect you personally. So are your classmates. The problems of young people are best known to you. What kind of problems do you have? What are the things that make you unhappy most often?

Perhaps you find that you are all frequently unhappy because outside of school you lack companionship. When you meet with your friends at home or at the corner drugstore, there is little to do and you disturb others. Your parents object to your going to some places. You feel that you are unjustly prohibited from doing many things you would like to do. Perhaps some of you have been in trouble—reprimanded or punished because you have violated the customs of the community and your families. The problem of expending energy in acceptable ways is a common problem for boys and girls.

Why do these problems exist in your community? There may be several reasons suggested. In discussing them your class may decide

Building Atlanta's Future

that many of their troubles arise because they have "nowhere to go." Adults seem to have priority on all spots. They do not like the same things you like. There are very few places in the community that you can call your own and where you can do as you like.

What can we do to remove the reasons for the unhappiness of young people in your community? The members of your class would no doubt suggest several solutions. Some of them will possibly be good, some not so good. One possibility is that of a meeting place and recreation center for high school boys and girls only. Most of your classmates will probably agree that a "Youth Center," or teen-age "Canteen," or "Nite Club" would be a good idea. It would help solve their problems of a place to get together for parties, after-movie snacks, dancing, and other recreation. As you discuss it, a great many ideas about the kind of center you would like and the possibilities of getting it are suggested. Let us follow through on what some of them might be.

PLANNING A COMMUNITY PROGRAM

In your class discussion there may, of course, appear some very wishful suggestions. We would like a palatial center with expensive furnishings, a huge swimming pool, acres of play space and dance

The contributions of each member of a group add up to give more information and skills than any one member could contribute alone.

floor, free sandwiches, and the like. But such things are beyond reason. What do we want the center for? To give us a place for recreation and social gatherings. What features are necessary to give us this? Can we hope to get all of them? If not, which are most important, and which could we do without if necessary? You want to set your goals as high as is practical, but not so high you will never reach them.

The class may agree on such things as: coke bar, juke box, dance floor, table tennis, lounge with comfortable chairs, large and small rooms, and so on. One person's suggestion calls forth an idea in someone else. Together you can probably make a long list and perhaps reason why some items are not practical. That is a great strength of working in groups. But do the members of your class know enough about youth centers to plan a good one? Perhaps they do not. It would be a good idea to call in someone who does know about them.

What groups in your community and city are interested in, and responsible for, recreation for young people? Your first thoughts may be the City Department of Recreation, health and welfare agencies, and physical education teachers. Members of these groups have made special studies of recreational needs and will probably be glad to come and talk to you about youth centers. With them you may discuss the kinds of youth centers that have been tried in other communities. They can tell you some things which have been found to turn out well and others which have failed.

From talking with specialists and reading the books and other materials they suggest, your class may decide in general the kind of center you need. It may be different from any you have heard of because your community is different and your needs may be different. This preliminary planning is important in making sure that your problems are to be taken care of. Through talking with you the specialists learn more about your problems. Through talking with them you learn what others have tried and how well they have succeeded. Together you can work out a plan which has a better chance of succeeding than either of you could have made alone.

Building Atlanta's Future

Now that you have in mind the kind of center you want, where is it to be located? Your class group can make suggestions as to likely places, but here again you need advice. The City or Metropolitan Planning Commission can best help you. They have information about zoning regulations, population density, and predicted shifts in population. They may know of new residential subdivisions being planned and changes in street plans. You must know these things in order to place it in a permanent location where it will best serve the most young people. They may suggest several possible locations which fit these purposes and will be in the proper environment.

Gathering together the facts about your community, you will need to study and decide such things as:

a. Shall the center be for your neighborhood only or for a larger area?
b. How many young people must it serve?
c. What size building will be needed?
d. What equipment will be needed?
e. How many people will be required to run it?
f. Where will it be located and why?
g. How much will it cost, and how will it be financed?
h. Will it grow or shrink in the future?

Perhaps committees or small groups will be assigned to study and report on each of these questions. They will of course need to go to other people, organizations, books, and many community sources to get information and advice on them. Then they can bring their findings back and report to the class so that all of you can help make final decisions in the light of all you have learned. If everyone has done his job well, you now have a wealth of information on which to reach a group decision. Even then you may have to discuss and weigh some points carefully before you can get a majority vote of agreement.

Whether or not you realize it, you go through a definite process

By dividing the work and study, each can do a special job and report to all the others. Everyone shares in the knowledge gained.

in such a study and planning project. Let us analyze the steps in this process.

a. Identify your problems
b. Explore the reasons these problems exist
c. Decide on a way to meet the problems
d. Decide what other groups have a stake in the project
e. With them, explore how other communities have handled the same problem
f. Decide exact requirements of planned changes
g. Appoint committees to work out details
h. Combine all their work into a complete report

Your report contains a great deal of information about the need for a youth center in your community and the details of such a center. The

Building Atlanta's Future

entire class has learned even more than is in the report. They are much concerned about the problems because each has had a part in studying and deciding about them. The same steps which you have used can be applied to other groups and other problems. Knowing these steps is part of the skill of working in groups. If you use a system, you are likely to get more done in group work.

But your job is not finished. Just having knowledge about how to solve your problems will not solve them. You know about the need for a youth center and what kind of center would meet these needs. How can this information be put to work to get the center built and put in operation?

PUTTING IDEAS INTO ACTION

The second part of your project has to do with transforming the ideas which you have in your minds and on paper into an actual building and equipment. How can we get them into action? Can one class or one school build a youth center? You are not carpenters and brickmasons. You do not have the skills nor the money to build it yourselves. You must again look for assistance. Perhaps you can get others to help you solve this part of your problem.

Many of the organized groups as well as individuals in your community are interested in the welfare of young people. Teachers, ministers, civic-minded people, and leaders of community affairs are all very much interested in the improvement of the entire community. You may want to call on them to help you make your plans for action.

A community program will succeed only if it is supported and wanted by most of the people in the community. If you can get most of the people interested in your program—and get them to work together, your youth center will soon be built. How can we get a large number of people interested in the same thing at the same time? One way is to go to the organized groups who are already interested in community affairs and get them to help promote interest and work

How to Meet Our Challenge

with you. Some of these groups may be: Parent-Teacher Association, the churches, Community Council, labor unions, Rotary Club, Civitan Club, Lions Club, Kiwanis, YMCA, YWCA, City Department of Recreation, Welfare Associations, Community Chest, Chamber of Commerce, garden clubs, and perhaps others.

These groups represent some of the *social resources* of the community. Many of them are members of the Community Planning Council of Metropolitan Atlanta. Through this organization they work together on many problems. The Community Planning Council may be able to give you assistance in your program. Its staff members are experts in the skills of group work. Even if the groups we have mentioned do not have funds and do not actually take part in working for the center, the people who belong to them may also belong to other groups that will help you. These people can help greatly by enlisting others and by spreading the news and creating interest.

Many community groups set up goals—community improvements —toward which they are to work for the year. If you can manage to get several of them to set up a youth center as one of their goals, you will be making progress in your program. If they are to do this, you must get the members interested in the need for a youth center. To interest

In many cities "Teen-age Centers" are provided for young people's recreation. They afford wholesome recreation of the kind you like.

them you should present your project to them in the most attractive ways. How can you do this?

There are several ways to get information to people. Newspaper articles, radio programs, community rallies, distributing pamphlets and leaflets are all ways to spread information. You may use them to inform the public of the need and possibilities of a youth center. One of the most effective ways, however, is to send speakers to talk to small groups of people in their meetings. This personal approach gives the listeners a chance to talk to the speaker and to discuss the matter among themselves. Talking and arguing about problems often help people become interested enough to work toward correcting them. If they only read about them while they are alone, they may not take them so seriously.

Good youth centers include a variety of facilities for quiet and active games and for social gatherings.

How to Meet Our Challenge

Suppose you are a member of a committee appointed to talk to the Rotary Club about getting a youth center. You must do a good "selling" job if you are to convince them that it is needed and that it is possible. Together, the committee prepares a talk. Good speakers present the facts. There is no youth center in the community. Young people have few places to go for recreation. It has been proven in many communities that these centers are worth much more than they cost. They help prevent delinquency, improve health, and promote social education. Young people have great times and learn many things in a good youth center. You may quote figures showing improvements in communities which have them.

Then you may tell how much it is estimated that a center will cost if built in any one of several places. How much expense it will be to run. How much will be earned through admissions, entertainments, sale of sandwiches, cokes, and ice cream. Perhaps you will end by asking the members to suggest ways to improve your plans, ways money could be raised, and the like. Getting people to talk about it is part of your plan. The more interest you can arouse, the more cooperation you can expect. Some of the Rotary Club members may disagree with you at first. Even if they never agree, they may spread the news to others who will become interested—even disagreement sometimes brings things to mind more clearly.

Now the Rotary Club does not have as it major purpose the building of youth centers. Why did you go to their meeting? You went because you knew most of the members are civic-minded people. They are interested in all kinds of community improvements. They will tell other people about your project. Some of them belong to other organizations. They may spread the news and good will in these groups. By the time your committee gets to a meeting of the Parent-Teacher Association or the Chamber of Commerce, they may find several people who have already heard of the youth center in other groups. As more people become interested, the news spreads more rapidly.

As various interested people mention the youth center in group discussions all over the community, your plan takes hold. Some of the groups decide to make the setting up of a youth center one of their objectives for the year. You are not surprised when several adult organizations soon start working for a youth center. That is what your work has been aimed at. If enough people work at it, the interest spreads very rapidly. One person passes it on to several more. When enough groups set a youth center as a goal, it becomes a community project. When most of the people in the community become interested, the final details are easy to arrange. Money may be raised by many organizations, donated by individuals and foundations.

When the new youth center is finished, you can be justly proud. You did not build it. You may have had little to do with the actual arrangements at the last moment. It may be a somewhat different place than your class planned—maybe more money or less money could be raised than you had thought. Many things may have happened that you did not foresee. Your class may get little or no credit for their work. But you have the center. The drive which you started has done the job. Credit is less important than results.

Perhaps this example will not apply to your community. You may already have a community center or recreation places which fill the need. But the principles for group effort are the same in most communities and in most civic efforts. The same skills and techniques can get many jobs done.

THE SKILLS OF GROUP WORK

Perhaps you have seen community programs start and grow in a similar fashion. Most communities have had successful drives to accomplish goals ranging from voting in a new parking ordinance to building new school buildings. If enough people become interested and work through organized groups, they can create almost any civic improvement they desire. We see that they usually work by our formula given at the first of this chapter. Individuals set up goals and work

This student council meeting is a good example of cooperative planning. The way it reaches decisions and the quality of its plans will depend on the members' store of skills and information.

toward them; they lead to the setting up of group goals; then the groups in the community agree to work toward the same goals. The final action is done by the community as a whole—by the groups working as a team.

All this work is done by individuals. Their effort is made more effective because they work as groups instead of alone. The individuals, however, are the users of information and skills which bring about the group cooperation. We have seen how in our example these skills were used to show the people the need and get them interested in a youth center. They were not rushed along or made angry. Some people no doubt got impatient waiting for others to make up their minds. But it does not always pay to rush. It is better to wait until people are ready to join together by their own decision. Then they work harder because they have helped select the goals and ways of achieving them. Knowing when to go slowly and when to prod people along is an important skill of working with groups.

But, you say, these skills are only common sense! That is perhaps true in part. But too few people ever think of them as skills. They are so busy thinking their own thoughts and doing things the way they like best that they pay no attention to the effects they have on other people. One of the skills you may need is that of spotting such individuals and keeping them from making others angry and doing more harm than good in group meetings.

A watchmaker would probably tell you that the workings of a fine watch are based on common sense also. But if you want to take it apart and put it back you will probably need to study it for a while to gain information and skills before you feel that you are competent. Have you ever studied that closely your skills of getting people to cooperate? Try setting up simple projects in your own mind and see what methods work best in getting your friends to cooperate. Don't be discouraged too easily and expect results too fast, but keep trying and looking back from time to time to see if you can tell what would have been a better approach. The chances are that the most popular and successful people you know use this system in getting along with others. It can be a valuable addition to your store of information and skills.

The skills of working with other people cannot be set up as a simple formula. You cannot always predict what a person will do. Each individual is different from all others; no one person is the same at all times. Perhaps that is one reason life is so interesting, but it also creates many problems. Understanding people and the way they act is a field of which we know very little. It is one of the greatest challenges that faces us today. Why is it so difficult to get the people of a community to work together for their common good? If we could find the answer to that and the solution for it, we could solve many of our problems much more easily.

OUR FUTURE TOGETHER

Atlanta can be in the future what the people in its communities make it. We have seen how people can get together and solve problems like the need for a youth center. Other problems can be solved the same way. We do not lack resources—materials, knowledge, and scientific skills—so much as we lack social skills of putting them to the best use. If the need is great enough, such as in time of war, fire, flood, or hurricane, we can work together with a will. Then people lapse back into their routines. If the school were to burn in most communities, it would soon be rebuilt by cooperative effort. But the same effort is seldom applied to clearing slums and building decent houses for all the people. Neither is it applied to guiding the growth of the community so that it becomes a better place to live and work.

Perhaps some of this lack of interest is due to ignorance. Some people do not know how much these things affect living. Others are too interested in their own business of making a living to see how a better community could help them live better. Whatever the cause, your challenge is to overcome it.

Through study and research we have learned much about our physical and chemical worlds. We have not applied so precise a method to the study of human problems.

Building Atlanta's Future

All Atlanta people have, or can develop, the knowledge and the skills to make our city a vastly better place. If they work together in a manner similar to that we have just described, our problems will begin to disappear. We have learned to use scientific knowledge and inventions in industry to produce goods in unlimited quantities. But we have not learned to use our social skills in nearly so precise a way. The vast resources of our soil, minerals, forests, and power, and the knowledge we have gained through science are being wasted. They could be used for improving living conditions for all our people.

We have learned much about human behavior since the time of the ancient philosophers. But we have much more to learn. Our social skills are centuries behind scientific knowledge. We can solve industrial problems, invent new machines, develop plastic materials, harness the power of waterfalls—and even of the atom. But people still have personal and social problems which we do not seem to know how to solve. Many people do not have proper food, nor good clothing, nor decent houses. They cannot get along with each other peacefully. Why do these conditions exist in Atlanta and in the world when we have such vast resources and knowledge? The answer seems to be that we have not learned to apply our resources in the best way. We have them but don't know how to use them.

We have not attacked our social problems in the same way that scientific problems are approached. We seldom study people with the viewpoint that we use in studying a new chemical or a way to speed up production in a factory. Perhaps if we begin to think of the problems and opportunities of people in the same way, we can make discoveries to equal the importance of the splitting of the atom. This is one of the greatest challenges we face in the future.

City planning as we have discussed it is one method of applying science to the study of our city problems. Through long-range planning we may guide our city's development to steer away from conditions which cause many problems. But as we have seen, the success of guided development depends on the cooperation of the people in our

Perhaps we will some day learn to harness human energy as efficiently as we harness the energy of falling water. Social invention is as necessary as is mechanical invention.

communities. No matter how good the machinery of planning may be, the people themselves must make it operate.

The Metropolitan Planning Commission will get a competent staff of specialists. They will have information and skills with which to make great improvements in our communities and in the Metropolitan district as a whole. But in a democracy they can do little alone. They are there to serve when the people call on them. They can give expert advice and assistance to programs like the example of the teen-age

Building Atlanta's Future

center. However, unless the people see their problems and work together to solve them, the planning commission is powerless.

YOUR PERSONAL CHALLENGE

What is your part in the future of your community? How can you help make Atlanta a better city? One challenge is to keep a broad vision of the kind of city it is possible to make. Do not set your goals too low. Then strive always to find better ways to reach these goals. Our city can be no better than the imagination and effort of its citizens make it.

The challenge for you at the present is to develop yourself to your highest capacity. Prepare yourself by gaining information and skills which you can use in reaching your life goals. Keep in mind that conscious study of the effect you can have on other people is a valuable set of skills. They can make your contribution to your own welfare and that of your community much more effective. Your influence in getting people to work together in groups—and in getting groups to work together as one great community team—can be a great force for improvement. Until we learn to work together as community teams, we are wasting many of our human and natural resources.

DISCUSSION QUESTIONS

1. Why are the knowledge and skills of individuals so important to group effort?
2. How many organized groups can you name that are found in your community? Do you know their major purposes for being organized?
3. Give some examples in which you have used good social skills to get a group to work toward a common purpose. Had you ever thought of them as "skills" before?
4. Give some examples of successful community projects you know about. Did they follow a plan similar to that of the youth center example? What are some reasons that many community projects fail?
5. Give some reasons why groups can solve problems better than individuals. How can you apply this to your challenge of building a better Atlanta?

How to Meet Our Challenge

HAVE YOU READ?

1. Adams, A. Elwood, and Walker, Edward E. *Democratic Citizenship in Today's World.* Part I. "Social Living." New York: Charles Scribner Sons, 1944.
2. Blaich, Theodore P. and others. *The Challenge of Democracy.* Unit VII. "Every Individual, as a Citizen, Has a Vital Interest in His Local Community." New York: Harper and Brothers, 1942.
3. Capen, Louise I., and Melchior, D. Montfort. *My Worth to the World.* Unit I. "Yourself and Others." New York: American Book Company, 1942.
4. Johnson, Stanley, and Alexander, William M. *Citizenship.* Part I. "How Can We Plan for Citizenship in American Democracy?" Part II. "What Are the Goals and Plans of American Democracy?" Boston: Ginn and Company, 1944.

Acknowledgments

GRATEFUL acknowledgment is made to the following persons and organizations for permission to adapt background material and random data: Atlanta Chamber of Commerce, *The Atlanta Constitution*, Atlanta Housing Authority, Board of Education of the City of Atlanta, Community Planning Council of Metropolitan Atlanta, Georgia State Board of Education, and the State Highway Department of Georgia. Their publications are listed in the suggested supplementary reading lists, as are other parallel readings. The material on pages 9 through 11 is adapted from the preface of "What's Ahead for Cleveland," by courtesy of the Regional Association of Cleveland, Ohio, and the excerpt from "So You're Going to Plan a City" from *Fortune* magazine, January, 1944, on pages 274 and 275 is reprinted by special permission of the Editors of *Fortune*. The population pyramids on pages 84 and 85 are reproduced from Social Planning Council, *Report on Health and Welfare in Fulton and DeKalb Counties*, Chapter III. The source of data for the Indian trails map on page 7 is *Official History of Fulton County* by Walter G. Cooper, page 17. The map on page 44 is adapted by the Institute for Research in Social Science from Goode's Base Map Series by permission of the University of Chicago Press. Other maps are adapted from the above named general sources and city maps by Atlanta City Planning Commission. "The Food Cycle in Nature" on page 59 is reproduced from Erich W. Zimmermann, *World Resources and Industries*, by permission of Harper and Brothers.

The photographs used in the book by specified pages are by courtesy of: Adams-Cates Co. 115; Allis Chalmers Mfg. Co. 42; American Forest Products Industries 61 photo by George Lohr, 63; American Transit Association and Committee on Urban Transportation of American Institute of Planners 152, 274; Atlanta Boy Scout Council 218 (top); *The Atlanta Con-*

Building Atlanta's Future

stitution 27 (left), 171 photo by Kenneth Rogers; Atlanta Health Department 211; Atlanta Historical Society 6, 9, 11, 160, 182, 192, 237, 238, 239, 241, 249, 252, 271 photo U. S. Army; Atlanta Housing Authority 17, 20, 25, 90, 137, 156, 157, 168, 169 photo by Kenneth Rogers, 163, 166, 175, 216 photo by Kenneth Rogers, 235; *The Atlanta Journal* 24, 119, 260; Atlanta Park Department 247; Atlanta Police Department 193, 243; Atlanta University 206; Atlanta Water Department 198, 199; Atlanta YMCA 218 (center); Atlanta YWCA 218 (bottom); Atlantic Steel Co. 96, 107; Beck and Gregg Co. 101; Chief of Construction, City of Atlanta 200; Clemson College Extension Service 51; Communication Center, University of North Carolina 31; Davison-Paxon Co. 71; Department of Audio-Visual Education, Atlanta Board of Education 3, 4, 5, 16, 18, 37 (bottom), 47, 54, 56, 65, 67, 80, 88, 93, 111, 113, 120, 121, 124, 127, 129, 131, 139, 141, 143, 144, 145, 147, 148, 153, 161, 172, 183, 184, 186, 194, 195, 197, 201, 202, 207, 213, 220, 221, 222, 223, 225, 229, 251, 264, 265, 268, 269, 277, 279, 281, 283, 284, 286, 289, 295; Eastern Air Lines 37 (top); Farm Security Administration 27 (right), 35 photo by Lange; Federal Reserve Bank, Atlanta 49 photo by F. & L. Photo Service; First National Bank of Atlanta 28 photo by Lane Bros.; General Motors Corp. 103; Georgia Power Co. 180 photo by Lane Bros., 190, 191 photo by Taylor, 245, 266 photo by Lane Bros.; Georgia State Employment Service 209; Georgia State Library 15; Grady Memorial Hospital 76; Hilda Kuper 181; Lane Drugstores 285; Look, Inc. and Tietgens-Monkmeyer Agency, New York City 41; C. F. Palmer 170, 174 photo by Taylor, 176, 177; Peachtree Christian Church 30 photo by Reeves studios; Retail Credit Co. 75; Rich's, Inc. 55 photo by C. E. Layton, Jr., 187; Royal Crown Teen-Age Headquarters, Columbus, Ga. 291, 292; Shreveport, Louisiana, Chamber of Commerce 57 (center) photo by Langston McEachern, Shreveport Times; Smith-Hughes Vocational School 226, 227; Soil Conservation Service 29 photo by Gordon Webb, 57 (top) photo by E. W. Jenkins, 60, 125, 262; Southeastern Greyhound Co. 37 (center), 273; Standard Oil Co. (N. J.) 62 photo by Libsohn, 63; Tennessee Valley Authority 299; U. S. Dept. of Agriculture 57 (bottom) photo by Forsythe; United States Homes, Inc. 178; Joe Veal's Restaurant 109; John J. Woodside

Acknowledgments

Storage 78 photo by Lane Bros.; Western Union 204; Judge Jessie Wood 214; Judge W. W. Woolfolk 215; Zep Manufacturing Co. 297.

The excerpts from pictures used in combinations on the title pages for the four parts are by courtesy of: Atlanta Health Department, Atlanta Housing Authority, Atlanta Police Department, Department of Audio-Visual Education, and United States Bureau of Reclamation.

Source of data for pictographs: Bureau of the Census *Current Population Reports*, 1947, 81, 95, 97; Bureau of the Census *16th Census of the U. S.*, "Population" 82, 99; Bureau of the Census, *Vital Statistics*, Special Reports: "Georgia Summary of Vital Statistics, 1940" 86, 87; Atlanta Housing Authority, *Eighth Annual Report* 1945–46, 159, 164.

www.ingramcontent.com/pod-product-compliance
Lightning Source LLC
Chambersburg PA
CBHW081150290426
44108CB00018B/2498